When Push Comes to Shove

When Push Comes to Shove

A Practical Guide to Mediating Disputes

Karl A. Slaikeu

Jossey-Bass Publishers • San Francisco

"Ruler's Wife Called Key in Agreement" by David LaGesse is reprinted with the permission of the *Dallas Morning News*.

Substantial discounts on bulk quantities of Jossey-Bass books are available to corporations, professional associations, and other organizations. For details and discount information, contact the special sales department at Jossey-Bass Inc., Publishers (415) 433-1740; Fax (800) 605-2665.

For sales outside the United States, please contact your local Simon & Schuster International Office.

Jossey-Bass Web address: http://www.josseybass.com

Manufactured in the United States of America on Lyons Falls Turin Book. This paper is acid-free and 100 percent totally chlorine-free.

Library of Congress Cataloging-in-Publication Data

Slaikeu, Karl A., date.
When push comes to shove : a practical guide to mediating disputes / Karl A. Slaikeu. — 1st ed.
    p.   cm. — (Jossey-Bass conflict resolution series)
    Includes bibliographical references and index.
    ISBN 0-7879-0161-X (alk. paper)
    1. Mediation. 2. Conflict management. I. Title. II. Series.
HM136.S644   1996
303.6'9—dc20

95-22873

FIRST EDITION
HB Printing   10 9 8 7 6 5 4 3 2

The Jossey-Bass Conflict Resolution Series

The Jossey-Bass Conflict Resolution Series addresses the growing need for guidelines in the field of conflict resolution, as broadly defined to include negotiation, mediation, alternative dispute resolution, and other forms of third-party intervention. Our books bridge theory and practice, ranging from descriptive analysis to prescriptive advice. Our goal is to provide those engaged in understanding and finding new and more effective ways to approach conflict—practitioners, researchers, teachers, and those in other professional and volunteer pursuits—with the resources to further their work and better the world in which we live.

This series is dedicated to
the life and work of
Jeffrey Z. Rubin
1941–1995

Contents

Preface

Are you a "new" mediator? Or are you a seasoned veteran, instructor, or trainer of other mediators? Regardless, I wrote this book for you. Perhaps a bit of my own story can explain why.

I am a psychologist turned mediator. I got started in this field fifteen years ago by developing research instruments to evaluate the process of divorce mediation. I soon came to believe that the process was too good to save for divorce, and began looking at the use of mediation earlier in the life of any conflict, not only for couples and families but also in the workplace and for corporate, community, and international disputes. I took every forty-hour course (the entry-level event for new mediators) I could find, and it did not take long for me to become a "true believer" in the idea that mediation at its heart was not only a humane way for human beings to resolve differences but also held the promise of numerous other benefits for individuals and organizations: reduced emotional wear and tear, savings in money (litigation expenses), and preservation of business relationships, to say nothing of saved lives. Building on my background as a professor and clinical psychology practitioner, I took notes over the years as I began to offer mediation for a wide range of disputes: family, personal injury, and organizational, sometimes involving only two parties but often involving very large numbers of individuals and groups. I also began offering mediation training to a new breed of practitioners, those who were offering in-house mediation in corporations, schools, government agencies, and religious institutions. It is these "new" mediators who are my primary audience for this book, though I believe the model presented will meet a need for seasoned veterans and trainers as well.

Here are the questions I have tried to address in this mediation primer:

1. *What are the essential steps that any new practitioner must learn in order to guide two or more parties through the mediation process?* For example, what can you expect to do in your first phone contact with one of the parties, and in the opening meeting, caucuses, joint/shuttle meetings, and closing? The book takes you through each of these five key steps, one at a time.

2. *How can you build on strengths from your "other life" as you develop mediation skills?* This book assumes that you already have a lot going for you as a human being or you would not be this far along in exploring mediation. Appendix A summarizes critical communication skills for conflict situations. In all the chapters, you will find suggestions that will complement your other skills learned in life at home, at work, and in your community.

3. *How can you reconcile the methodological differences between various mediation models, for example, the role of caucuses as opposed to joint meetings?* For new and seasoned mediators, this book presents an *integrative* model of mediation. The five-step model uses a combination of caucuses and joint meetings for every mediation event and draws from three important foci during each phase:

- *Awareness/empowerment:* The mediator assists each party in becoming aware of the underlying interests and emotional hot buttons that created the conflict or now drive the dispute. Through coaching and other forms of support, the mediator offers a structure that can empower the party to deal with the problem and the other side.
- *Understanding/recognition:* The mediator encourages accurate understanding by each party of the other side's interests, facts, and proposed solutions, with the additional option of each party's eventually offering stated recognition to the other side regarding that party's rights and interests (even though they may not yet have reached an agreement of any kind).
- *Agreement/reconciliation:* The mediator offers a process that may result in either agreement or no agreement (impasse). The agreement may take the form of a commitment not to take up arms (physical and verbal) for a short period of time, or it may involve acknowledgment of past wrong, apologies, new plans for the future, restitution, and forgiveness.

While mediation is typically understood to aim for an agreement of some sort, the integrative model, by identifying these three foci, allows for the fact that some mediations will result in awareness/empowerment, and perhaps also understanding/recognition, without achieving agreement/reconciliation.

4.   *For all of us—new mediators, veterans, trainers—what exercises can we use to hone our skills?* Without intending this book to serve as a formal training manual, I have included brief exercises at the end of each chapter that will enhance the practice focus of the book. Also, through liberal use of "coaching tips" (presented as boxed text), I have tried to address a range of discrete yet very significant issues that can make the difference between a successful or unsatisfactory mediation process.

Background

In its simplest form, mediation is a process through which a third party assists two or more others in working out their own solution to a conflict. The power of the process lies in the opportunity for two or more adversaries to examine a problem in both private and joint meetings with a goal of creating a win/win solution, one that honors enough of their individual (and common) interests to allow them to willingly turn away from other approaches such as lawsuits or power plays, instead agreeing to willingly carry out the agreed-upon plan. As distinguished from an attorney in court proceedings, the mediator does not make decisions for the parties, but instead uses listening, questioning, probing, brainstorming, and at times cajoling, challenging, and confronting to help the parties fashion an integrative plan to which all can say *yes*. In this sense mediation is an *assisted* negotiation. Its power lies in the fact that the parties will often reveal underlying interests and worries to a mediator that they would not dream of revealing to an adversary, for fear of having this information used against them. The mediator is more than a buffer between the parties. Through confidential caucuses and careful questioning of each party, the mediator gains more information than either of the parties has alone, and can often use this information to assist them in fashioning a solution that would have been unachievable had they relied solely on their own efforts.

While mediation is neither new nor uniquely Western (it was a part of primitive cultures and has a long tradition in China), the late twentieth-century interest in mediation has been nothing short of phenomenal. Widespread discontent with the financial cost and emotional wear and tear of adversarial court proceedings such as litigation has made mediation the cornerstone of the alternative dispute resolution (ADR) movement in the United States. Among the marker events in the growth of mediation:

- Companies such as Motorola have reported up to 75 percent savings in defense costs by using mediation to resolve disputes without litigation.[1]
- Mediation is increasingly used as the critical second step—after negotiation, and before arbitration or litigation—to resolve consumer complaints or other commercial and insurance disputes.
- Many judges now order mediation before they will hear a case in court.
- Membership in professional organizations such as the Society of Professionals in Dispute Resolution (SPIDR), the Academy of Family Mediators, the Association of Family and Conciliation Courts, and the ADR sections of county and state bar associations increased dramatically in the 1980s and 1990s.
- With the blessing of both human resources and legal departments, corporations are increasingly using in-house mediation teams to resolve a wide range of employment disputes well before they reach the lawsuit stage.

Key Premise

This book is based on the premise that mediation is both a social skill and an emerging professional discipline. The best examples of the former come from training programs to equip schoolchildren to mediate playground disputes and from the increasing recognition that interests-based problem solving is an entry-level skill for both personal and work relationships. Side-by-side with the emphasis on mediation as a social skill is mediation as an emerging professional discipline. Special capabilities are required to mediate hospital turf battles, cross-cultural international disputes, multimillion-dollar commercial disputes, and business partnership dissolutions, where combinations of economic, social, religious, and psychological dynamics can lead not only to intransigence by the parties but all too frequently to the threat of physical violence.

The Five-Step Model

What is required to bring disputing parties to the point where they willingly stop the fight and work together to implement a common solution? More to the point, how do you get parties "to the table," and, once there, how can you discover the heart of the matter for each party to see whether integrative solutions will be possible—solutions that will allow the parties to drop lawsuits, lay down arms, or even go forward with former adversaries as new partners?

This book is written around five key events in any mediation: (1) first contact, (2) opening meeting, (3) caucuses, (4) joint/shuttle meetings, and (5) closing. To be effective when "push has come to shove," the mediator brings calm control to an intense situation and guides the parties through creative problem solving, all the while paying careful attention to the interests of a wide range of players.

I wrote this book as if I were coaching you the week before you were to begin a new mediation. We will look at what you might expect as you take telephone inquiries, prepare for the opening meeting, and then talk with the parties in confidential caucuses. At times, it may feel as if I am looking over your shoulder, helping you interpret what you hear as the parties tell their stories and as you review your notes to determine if there is any hope of a solution. Since the five-step model is generic and can be applied to a wide range of situations, we will use case material along the way for illustrative purposes, with a goal of assisting you in applying the principles to your own particular situation, whether your special interest is commercial, family, corporate, employment, or any other area of dispute resolution.

If you are new to mediation and dispute resolution, then Chapters One through Three, grouped under the heading "Introduction," will provide you with critical building blocks for everything that follows. For example, Chapter Two provides a necessary frame of reference for conducting effective caucuses. The three chapters included under the heading "Variations" (Chapters Sixteen through

Eighteen) are especially important for in-house mediators and managers since they offer ways to use the essential heart of mediation while adjusting the steps to fit with other organizational realities.

In order to stay true to the task of providing a brief description of the mediation process, I have deliberately excluded several important topics from this volume. Licensure, certification, and marketing and practice development, as well as guidelines for setting up in-house mediation programs, are all related topics that fall outside the scope of this primer on steps in the mediation process. Each is also a subject of considerable debate in professional mediation associations, with articles frequently appearing in professional journals.

Acknowledgments

I am indebted to numerous individuals who helped shape the model presented in this book. I owe a particular debt to William Ury and Richard A. Salem, whose work inspired me over the years as I made the transition from psychologist to mediator. Ralph Hasson, with whom I have had the pleasure of serving as a co-mediator and trainer, certainly had an influence on the practical aspects of the model presented in this volume, including assistance in drafting role-plays to isolate skills and methodological choice points (Appendix F). More than anyone else, Diane Weimer Slaikeu, as an attorney-mediator and trainer, served as a reality check for the overall conceptual framework and its application in the widest range of settings, including business, governmental, nonprofit, and community. Special thanks also to Ingrid Ramsey for able assistance in typing more drafts of this book than any of us would care to count. Finally, I am grateful to the numerous managers, community volunteers, and the "new" mediators from such fields as law, mental health, business, and education who attended seminars and, through questions and challenges, brought a clarity to the model that would not have been possible otherwise. It goes without saying that any success this book achieves is as much a reflection of the influence of these people as it is of my own organization of the ideas and principles we all hold in common.

Austin, Texas   Karl A. Slaikeu
August 1995

The Author

Karl A. Slaikeu is president of Chorda Conflict Management, Inc., in Austin, Texas. He has taught in the departments of psychology at the University of South Carolina and the University of Texas, Austin, and has published two books and over thirty articles on crisis and conflict management. He is a graduate of the University of Nebraska, Lincoln (B.A. degree, 1967), Princeton Theological Seminary (M.Div. degree, 1969), and the State University of New York, Buffalo (M.A. degree and Ph.D. degree, 1973). He frequently leads seminars on conflict resolution for corporate leaders, attorneys, health professionals, educators, counselors, and managers, and he is a specialist in the design of comprehensive dispute resolution systems aimed at controlling the costs of conflict.

To Diane,
whose intellectual insight, spiritual depth,
and interpersonal strength inspire me as a mediator
and give me hope as a human being.

A Brief Introduction to Mediation

It can be unnerving to be in the middle of any fight, even if you have been invited to be there by the disputants themselves. At times, you will feel like the referee who catches a punch meant for one of the players, or the messenger who says, "Don't shoot me!" At the psychological level you may feel like a living ink blot on whom angry and hurt individuals project their own feelings. In order to use the five-step model presented in this book, you will need a clear picture of what mediation is and what it is not. You will also need a model for analyzing problems and a clear sense of your own boundaries for influence. The three chapters in this section are intended to help in each of these areas. Chapter One will be especially useful when parties question or challenge the process as well as your role in working with them. Chapter Two offers a cognitive map—the Conflict Grid—for analyzing disputes and any problem or issue that the parties may present for exploration. And finally, Chapter Three offers motivational grist for the mill, all aimed at helping you to frame the limits of your own control and influence with warring factions.

Chapter One

Starting Out: The Key Concepts of Mediation

While mediation is increasingly understood and appreciated in business and community settings, every new mediator soon learns that someone is sure to confuse the process with medi*t*ation (a confusion that is more than semantic, since mediation is often wrongly perceived by some to be a relatively soft process of conciliation that is inappropriate when parties are truly angry with one another). At the other end of the scale, it also tends to be confused with arbitration (a process that has more in common with litigation than it does with mediation). This chapter will offer definitions and a conceptual framework for the mediation process. Think of what follows as material you will draw from in responding to initial requests for mediation and in helping the parties to make decisions about whether or not mediation is the treatment of choice, given their particular situation.

Definition

Mediation is a process through which a third party helps two or more other parties achieve their own resolution on one or more issues. Mediation can be used when there is no dispute, as when a consultant helps an executive committee negotiate agreement on a strategic plan. At the other extreme, mediation can be used as an alternative to litigation or bloodshed to help parties resolve disputes. Mediators do not make decisions for parties (as arbitrators and judges might); instead, they assist the parties by structuring a process for communication and negotiation that allows them to analyze problems, generate solutions, and eventually agree on a series of steps to be taken to solve a problem.

Alternatives to Mediation

You can expect that parties will frequently confuse mediation with its alternatives. Table 1.1 presents mediation in the context of four options for resolving any conflict involving individuals or groups (whether two people or two or more countries).

Avoidance involves a "wait and see" approach; you take no action, in the hope that the problem will solve itself or go away. For example, your antagonist might move or be transferred.

At the other extreme is the *unilateral power play,* which may involve physical violence, strikes, or behind-the-scenes maneuvers to solve a problem. Dietrich Bonhoffer, a Lutheran pastor who was a part of a plot to assassinate Hitler in the 1930s, chose this route because other options had not worked. Civil rights demonstrations in the United States in the 1950s and 1960s offer another example of unilateral power plays intended to break laws, fill jails, and thereby expose inequities in the system and lead to legislation to protect the rights of African-Americans.

Higher authority options involve "chain of command" resolutions, through which employees can refer matters up the line for resolution (going either to the boss or through a grievance panel). Litigation through the courts is a chief example of higher authority resolution in the United States. Arbitration, through which an individual or panel renders an award, is also a form of higher authority resolution.

Table 1.1. Four Options.

Avoidance	Collaboration		Higher Authority		Unilateral Power Play
Wait and see	Negotiation by the parties	Mediation by third party	Referral up chain of command	Litigation through the courts	Physical violence, strikes, behind-the-scenes maneuvering

Finally, *collaboration* is an option through which the parties themselves make the decision, one form of collaboration being negotiation and the other mediation. In negotiation, the parties talk directly with one another (or through attorney advocates) in an attempt to achieve a resolution. In mediation, a mutually agreeable third party convenes the disputants, takes opening statements, meets privately in confidential caucuses, and then conducts either joint meetings or shuttle diplomacy to assist them in reaching a resolution. The hallmark of mediation is that the parties retain control of the outcome. Mediation is simply an assisted negotiation.

You can use the four-option model in several ways:

• At some point, you might want to simply identify the four options for the parties, to help them look at mediation in the context of other alternatives.

• Parties who have been discouraged by their own direct negotiations often will wrongly conclude that mediation will not work. As we shall see later in this chapter, mediation, through its private caucuses, generates information that the parties may not have revealed to one another, and hence, it may get a more satisfactory result than direct negotiations.

• The choice of options will always depend upon social, political, cultural, and religious considerations. Encourage parties to consider all options and not to confuse mediation with one of the alternatives.

• It is possible for parties to take a stepwise approach: negotiating first, then trying mediation, with the litigation or power play options as a backup.

Table 1.2 sketches the main elements of all four options, to make them easier to understand and to describe to parties considering mediation.

Outcomes

Mediation is frequently identified with win/win outcomes, while higher authority, avoidance, and power plays are identified with win/lose or lose/lose outcomes. At the heart of win/win outcomes are *integrative solutions* to problems, which means that the final action plan includes elements that honor the interests of each side. The action plan has something for everyone, or more precisely,

Table 1.2. Conflict Management Options.

Options	Avoidance	Collaboration	Higher Authority	Unilateral Power Play
Activities	Wait and see.	Negotiation (via direct talks).	Internal (chain of command).	Political action.
	Avoid person.	Mediation (formal and informal).	External (courts, litigation).	Strikes, civil disobedience.
	Change own behavior.			Physical force.
Decision making	By chance.	By the parties.	By third party.	By force.
Primary focus	Isolation from the problem.	Integrative solution based on interests and other facts.	Right and wrong according to objective criteria.	Power contest.
Primary outcome	Unpredictable.	Win/win.	Win/lose (lose/lose).	Win/lose (lose/lose).

Constructive form	For both negotiation and mediation:		
• Wait to see if passage of time will bring change.	• Individual rights are protected.	• Due process observed.	• Political and nonviolent strategies are used as first choice, with violence as last resort.
• Change own behavior to solve problems without expecting other side to change.	• Alternatives (best alternatives to a negotiated settlement) are considered.	• Individual legal rights of parties are protected.	• Loopbacks to mediation are available as under higher authority.
	• Both/all parties are willing to talk with one another either in direct discussions or with assistance of a mediator.	• Balance of public and individual interests recognized.	
	• Power imbalances are identified and adjustments are made in order to protect individuals.	• Mediation loopback to control costs and/or to allow another opportunity for consensual decision.	

Table 1.2. Conflict Management Options, cont'd.

Options	Avoidance	Collaboration	Higher Authority	Unilateral Power Play
Destructive form	• Denying that the problem exists. • Avoiding confrontation based on lack of skill in negotiation.	For both negotiation and mediation: • Individual legal rights are not protected. • Other options not considered or offered. • One or more parties coerced into using this process. • Power imbalances operate unchecked.	• No due process ("railroad model"). • Individual legal rights are not protected. • No balance of public and private "good." • No loopbacks.	• Move to violence without exhausting other means.

When to use	• No opportunity to talk to the other party.	• Compliance of each party is important to eventual success of settlement.	• Need to establish legal or administrative precedent.	• Activities required in all other options have failed.
	• Passage of time might help.	• Desire to preserve relationship after dispute is resolved.	• Policy ruling is needed.	• When perceived "unjust" laws or policies cannot be changed by other means.
	• Delay will not hurt.	• Interest in protecting against emotional fallout and other side effects of higher authority resolutions.	• Collaboration has been rejected.	• Dealing with evil.
	• Other avenues temporarily blocked.			

includes actions to honor the interests of each side. You will find that it will be difficult if not impossible to create integrative solutions unless you use an analysis similar to the one in Chapter Two (separating interests from other facts and positions). However, as a result of such analysis, mediation has the potential for creating outcomes that to a lay observer at times look like magic, since they are often unavailable to parties who engage in positional bargaining. While mediation is typically thought of as an interests-based approach, we will define integrative solutions in Chapter Two as those that pass a three-part test: (1) honoring (or at least not violating) key interests of the parties; (2) squaring with a range of other facts (for example, relevant law or organizational policy); and (3) being better than each party's Best Alternative to a Negotiated Agreement (BATNA), a concept defined by Fisher and Ury[1].

The typical outcome of any mediation is either agreement or no agreement (impasse). While most mediations will begin with a definable issue (for example, steps the parties might take to settle an insurance claim, or to resolve a termination dispute between an employer and an employee), it is not uncommon for new issues to emerge along the way. This means the eventual outcome of mediation on any particular issue may be very different from what the parties envisioned when they began. The parties may reach agreement on one or more topics, and still face an impasse on others. In this case, they can either live with the remaining issues as they are or refer them to other avenues, such as higher authority resolution through grievance panels or the courts.

Caucuses

Caucuses are what allow a mediator to help parties reach an outcome that they would not reach on their own. By holding private meetings with each side, the mediator will hear interests and other matters of the heart that the parties are often reluctant to reveal to their adversaries. The mediator is then in a position, having more information on the matter than the parties themselves, to help them fashion solutions that they might not have achieved otherwise.

Caucuses are important for another reason. When there are threats of physical violence, whether between family members, neighbors, employees, or armed nations, the mediator must explore interests and concerns in a private setting. In some cases, the mediator would not hear about such threats if he or she relied exclusively on face-to-face meetings. Consider the wife whose husband has beaten her and continues to exercise threats of violence during the divorce negotiation process. She will be very unlikely to raise this issue in its clearest form in joint meetings but may well disclose it to the mediator in a private setting where confidentiality is guaranteed. A mediator proceeding without such information would court disaster—hence the requirement that at least one round of caucuses occur in the very beginning of mediation.

Integrative Model

The integrative model for mediation can be distinguished along three dimensions.

Outcomes

As described above, mediation aims for integrative solutions with actions that honor (or at least do not violate) the interests of the parties, while they also square with a range of available facts and, at the same time, provide benefits that are better than the individual BATNAs (discussed in Chapter Two). Throughout this volume, the outcome of mediation will be evaluated in terms of its ability to integrate actions that meet these criteria into one unified text.

Process Focus

Is agreement the ultimate and only goal? How about the equally worthy goal of the personal growth and understanding of the parties, which may occur without their ever reaching an agreement? An integrative model offers three mediation foci for the mediator, as follows:

- *Awareness/empowerment.* Through individual interviews (caucuses) and through the facilitative comments that the mediator makes in all sessions, the focus is for each party to become increasingly aware of his or her own interests, feelings, views, needs, desires, and hot buttons, and to appreciate how and why some remedies that have been chosen up to that time may well have failed to satisfy individual needs or to achieve agreement with an adversary. In this sense, the mediator, through the structure of the process and through the use of solid communication skills, serves the same function that a good counselor or therapist does in enhancing individual awareness. The assumption is that absent some level of awareness, the parties are less free to create solutions they will be able to honor and are less likely to make constructive overtures to each other. Furthermore, by coaching each party on how to analyze the problem (see Chapter Two) and how to communicate and negotiate with the other side, the mediator can be viewed as empowering the parties to deal with the situation.

• *Understanding/recognition.* It is not enough for a party to be aware of his or her own situation. Understanding of the other side is a second focus of each step in the mediation process. This occurs when the mediator assists the parties by asking for restatement of what they have heard from the other side, engaging in reality testing (in private caucuses) to see if each party is truly appreciating the other side's interests, needs, and proposals. Whether encouraging direct communication or helping interpret data, the mediator has a second focus throughout the process of promoting understanding by Party A of Parties B, C, and others as well as their constituencies. A more advanced form of this focus is stated recognition by Party A of Party B's rights, interests, and needs, recognition that can occur in joint meetings. As with awareness, recognition has a value in and of itself, separate from whether or not the parties eventually agree or not to take certain steps to solve a problem.

• *Agreement/reconciliation.* A third focus of mediation is for the parties to reach an agreement of some sort to solve the problem, to take steps to implement a plan, or to resolve a dispute. As we shall see, this may involve something as discrete as a monetary figure to settle a medical malpractice claim or something as complex as interpersonal soul-searching leading to acknowledgment of harm done, apologies, new plans for the future, and even forgiveness.

By focusing on three aspects of the process at every point, the mediator creates conditions for possible agreement, in part by facilitating each party's self-awareness and understanding of the other side.[2] The first two foci can be viewed as secondary benefits of mediation, albeit benefits that may turn out to have significant meaning to the parties, separate from whether or not they reach agreement. The strength of the integrative model is that the mediator focuses on all three foci at the same time, at every point, and allows the parties to eventually determine which focus (individual awareness, understanding of the other side, or agreement and reconciliation) is most important. Sometimes, it will be all three. Figure 1.1 diagrams the role of the mediator at each of the process foci.

Methods

The integrative model makes use of both joint meetings and individual caucuses. After a joint opening meeting, the mediator holds a round of caucuses to generate confidential information and also to hear about potential threats of violence that might not be disclosed absent private talks. The process then continues with either joint or shuttle meetings, as the situation requires. The model therefore draws from the best of both worlds and escapes the controversy of some models that rely exclusively on either shuttle diplomacy or joint meetings.

The mediator maintains the three-way focus through all five steps in the mediation process. While the three foci become especially important during caucuses and joint meetings, the mediator considers them from the very beginning, under first contact and on through to the closing. Each of the five steps in the mediation process provides an opportunity for the mediator to assist the parties in one or more of these three areas of awareness/empowerment, understanding/recognition, and agreement/reconciliation.

The communication skills identified in Resource A (active listening, self-disclosing, questioning, reframing, brainstorming, and confronting) are all intended to encourage progress in the three focus areas. For example, active listening by the mediator is one way to assist the parties in becoming aware of key interests (as distinguished from positions). The mediator also encourages progress along these three dimensions by encouraging the parties to use these skills with one another. For example, self-disclosing on the part of one party can enhance understanding/recognition on the part of the other, and active listening and questioning can be used to refine these understandings.

Figure 1.1. Process Focus.

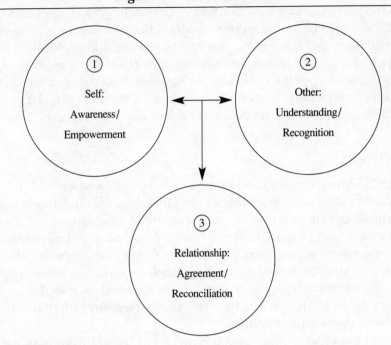

Definitions:

① Mediator assists each party in developing an awareness of interests, facts, and other Conflict Grid data (see Chapter Two) important to this party. In caucus, this includes exploration of hot buttons or strong emotions to better understand key interests. Also, by offering respect to the party, and at times coaching on how to use the mediation process, the mediator empowers the party for problem solving.

② Mediator assists each party in understanding the other side's point of view, interests, needs, and feelings, and possibly in offering recognition or acknowledgment of the validity of the other side's interests, or at least the right of the other side to have certain needs met.

③ The mediator assists the parties in creating mutually agreeable solutions, steps that could be put into a one-text agreement. The most elementary form under this focus may be a partial agreement to collect new data and to continue talks, and the most advanced form may be true reconciliation through which the parties acknowledge past wrongs, make apologies, restitution, and plans for the future, and forgive one another as they go forward to implement a mutually agreeable plan.

When to Mediate

The topic of what cases are appropriate for mediation and what cases are not frequently appears in mediation literature and seminars. Standard answers are that mediation must be voluntary; there must be an openness on the part of each side to look at creative solutions, as well as a willingness to give and take (or compromise); and the parties must be capable of negotiating with one another (or at least doing so through attorneys).

Taking the Long View

It is possible, however, to take a broader look at this question. As a general rule, the only cases that might be totally inappropriate for mediation are cases where parties need a legal precedent established, since mediation is uniformly inadequate as a method for creating case law. Therefore, if your parties need a court ruling, advise them to pursue litigation.

In cases where there are threats of violence or intimidation (in the family, community, or workplace), the main adjustment will be reliance on separate meetings instead of face-to-face sessions (which might further intimidate one or more parties).

In all other cases, you can consider mediation as the next logical step if negotiations themselves have failed to achieve resolution. Mediation then becomes a second collaborative method (the first being negotiation, see Table 1.1). Even if the parties hate each other or have already engaged in behavior that has led to bloodshed, mediation can be a forum for achieving resolution. The standard solutions required for resolution are often more available through mediation than they are through the courts. It is even possible to mediate punishment, and the process is ideally suited to assisting parties in making apologies and in offering forgiveness.

One Necessary Condition

For mediation to get off to an appropriate start, the parties must trust the mediator and the mediation process. It is far less important that the parties trust one another. Do not be surprised if one side or the other says, "Well, trust is important here, isn't it? I don't trust him." Your response can be: "You need not trust the other side—as a matter of fact, people typically don't trust each other when they begin mediation. However, it is important that you understand and trust the mediation process, and trust the mediator to serve both sides well according to rules of mediation."

Cultural Influences

Some aspects of conflict are assumed to be universal. For example, the fact that there are four ways for human beings to resolve conflict (avoidance, collaboration, higher authority, and power plays) applies across cultures. Similarly, the five-step structure for mediation offered in this volume can serve as a general framework for parties who have very different values and cultural roots. Other aspects of the mediation process, however, are very different from culture to culture. In order to successfully assist parties, mediators must pay attention to cultural mores and folkways regarding communication, expressions of discontent, confrontation, religious practices, and the values associated with various forms of resolution. For example, under what conditions will the parties choose power play resolutions (by personal force or acts of war) instead of peaceful paths to resolution? The main requirement is that the mediator pay close attention to cultural influences both on the current conflict and on the form that an acceptable resolution might take.

STANDARD CULTURAL VARIABLES

Moore[3] offers eight dimensions along which cultural differences may evidence themselves in mediation. They provide a framework for gathering information and building rapport.

1. *Relationships.* To what extent is disclosure of feelings and views encouraged or discouraged? How do roles of hierarchy and power influence the ability of parties to talk directly with one another?

2. *Views of cooperation and competition.* What form would win/win, win/lose, and lose/lose take in this culture?

3. *Problem solving.* What are the main dimensions for problem analysis—feelings, interests, or outcomes?

4. *Time.* What constitutes "too long" a time for working on a problem, as opposed to deferring to higher authority such as the courts?

5. *Language and communication.* How are variations in nonverbal communication apparent within the cultural framework of this dispute? If the party says yes, does that mean the party agrees with the proposal, or does it mean, "Yes, I want to keep talking, though I don't agree with what you've said; I just don't want to offend you by saying no."

6. *Impact of larger social structures.* What are the roles of religious and legal structures in understanding disputes?

7. *The role of third parties.* On what basis can third parties be involved, and how will they be viewed—as higher authority, facilitative mediator, or intruder?

8. *Physical space.* What does it mean to talk across the table or without the table as a barrier or protector between the parties?

Note that prior to first contact (and through all phases of mediation), the mediator pays attention to the particular form these cultural questions take with the parties to the mediation. If you are mediating with parties from a culture different from your own, ask questions of the referring agent regarding particular dimensions of the culture, using the preceding list as a guide. The five mediation steps described in this book are generic and can be adjusted to fit with the cultural dimensions identified here.

Mediators and Mediation

Mediators are a special breed of problem solvers. While there is no tried-and-true formula for selecting good mediators, the literature and feedback from disputing parties point to certain characteristics that will engender trust and rapport with the parties, and also lead to mutually agreeable solutions.

• *Mediators are good listeners.* They know how to put aside their own views and pay attention to interests, feelings, thoughts, and reports of events from disputants.

- *Mediators are able to take a stance of objectivity (some call it neutrality).* This allows them to listen for interests on all sides of the issue.
- *Mediators are aware of their own biases.* They are ready to declare conflicts of interest that might interfere with objectivity.
- *Mediators are familiar with strong feelings in disputants.* Therefore, they are not uncomfortable in structuring a process for parties to express feelings of anger and fear in private and joint meetings.
- *Mediators have a realistic assessment of their own abilities as well as their own limitations in helping parties reach agreement.* They know that the parties themselves must take responsibility for the outcome, though the mediator takes responsibility for structuring a fair and equitable process.
- *Mediators are good communicators.* They know how to state their own thoughts, feelings, and concerns and how to assist parties in expressing themselves to one another.
- *Mediators are assertive.* Instead of passively sitting by as parties fight in the presence of the mediator, mediators structure a process for constructive talk and analysis of problems that leads to the creation of solutions. This includes enforcing ground rules that protect parties from one another during the mediation process.

Procedural Versus Substantive Experience

Mediators need to be experts on the process of conflict resolution, and "quick studies" on the substantive issues that the parties will be discussing. This requirement for mediation is, of course, different from arbitration, where the neutral third party often may be required to possess special knowledge about the subject of the dispute, whether a medical malpractice, construction, or employment matter. Since mediators will not be rendering a decision for the parties, their primary qualification must be an ability to convene the parties under specific rules for communication and conflict resolution, and so structure and monitor the process that the parties can unbundle the problem, back off from entrenched positions, and break new ground with one another. Mediators will also be required to develop clear understandings of new subjects by reading documents and especially by listening carefully to presentations by the parties in order to understand the finer points of the dispute. It can be helpful if a mediator has prior substantive knowledge about a dispute (for example, an engineer who serves as mediator for a construction dispute), but many mediators take on new cases and learn about the substantive issues prior to the mediation and along the way.

Social Skill, Emerging Professional Discipline

Mediation is both a social skill that can be learned by elementary school children (starting at the fourth or fifth grade levels, according to models developed in the public schools) and a professional discipline for which disputing parties may pay several hundred dollars an hour. Since, in its simplest form, mediation is a process whereby a third party helps two or more individuals work out a problem, it is a sort of skill that we would hope children would learn early and apply later in family situations, with friends, at school, and at work. At the same time, many large multiparty disputes, those with complex legal components, and those involving parties and constituencies at the international level, will require a level of professional expertise that depends on academic and other experience, as well as on high-level skills for which the parties will pay a professional fee. The assumption of the present volume is that the mediation model applies across the board to children on the playground, to volunteers in community dispute resolution centers, to human resources managers providing third-party mediation within organizations, and to professional mediators who charge for their services. In each of these cases, the parties will need to adjust the model and create a contractual relationship with the disputants that is appropriate to the training of the mediator and to the requirements of the situation.

Mediator Ethics

With the growth of mediation in community settings, and as a professional service offered to parties who pay top dollar for the mediator's time, there is the additional requirement that mediators examine the process, assess their own values, and formulate ethical standards for practice. The Society of Professionals in Dispute

Resolution has taken the lead in formulating such standards (see Resource C). At the heart of these ethical standards is the notion that the mediator is retained (or employed) to serve all parties to the dispute, not just one, to behave in such a way that the parties maintain responsibility for the outcome of the process, and to structure the process in such a way as to protect the integrity and safety of disputants throughout. Unless mediators are clear about such standards, they run the risk of participating in a process that not only leads to weak outcomes, but even more importantly, threatens the parties along the way.

Learning Mediation

It is standard practice worldwide for people to learn the mediation process after they have spent years working in some other capacity. This means that mediators will find much in their individual backgrounds that they can transfer to the mediation process— things like interviewing and listening skills and substantive knowledge of individual personality dynamics or of the legal parameters of a dispute. At the same time, they will also need to acquire other knowledge and develop other skills as they learn mediation. The premise of this volume is that mediation requires, first of all, knowledge about the nature of conflict and, next, communication skills that can then be integrated into the five-step mediation model.

Credentialing

As this book is being written, there is no governmental license for mediators, though many organizations certify participants who have attended mediation training seminars. Similarly, in the international arena, mediators are selected more often for their trust or acceptability to the parties and their perceived past experience than for any professional credential or academic training. If the growth of mediation as a professional discipline follows that of fields such as medicine, law, and psychology, then we can expect that mediators will soon be licensed and regulated by various state boards. The present volume is written to assist mediators and disputants in a world where licensure and certification are still in the very beginning stages of development. Until such time as they may be regulated by state boards, our counsel to beginning mediators is to (1) affiliate widely with local and national professional organizations in order to profit from the reality check of colleagues in the development of models and standards of practice; (2) follow the ethical guidelines of organizations such as the Society of Professionals in Dispute Resolution, or create alternatives (and publish them for the benefit of colleagues) where disagreement may occur; and (3) follow a truth-in-advertising model with all clients, disclosing credentials, training, and other relevant information to those who may use their services.

EXERCISE

1.   You may do this exercise with a partner or as a group task. Imagine that Party A has suggested to Party B that they take their dispute to mediation, and they have selected you as a candidate. Party B is skeptical about mediation, believing that there is no need for outsiders on this matter. However, Party B has agreed to talk to you on the telephone to ask a few questions. Ask your partner or a member of the group to play the role of Party B while you play the role of mediator.

Note to Party B: Scan the main headings in Chapter One (for example, definitions, alternatives, outcomes), and create your own trick questions for the mediator. For example, "Why should we use you as an arbitrator when you don't even have a medical background?" Discuss the strengths and weaknesses of the mediator's responses. Switch roles and repeat the process, debriefing after each round.

Chapter Two

Using the Conflict Grid to Analyze Disputes and Generate Solutions

A famous woodcarver was once asked how to fashion a horse out of a block of wood. The master's reply was simple and to the point: "Take the block of wood and cut away everything that doesn't look like a horse."

Like wood carvers, good mediators learn to visualize possibilities and outcomes that others do not see. You can begin learning to analyze cases by referring to the Conflict Grid (Figure 2.1), a tool I created to summarize the key diagnostic variables in any mediation. Think of the Conflict Grid as your cognitive map for collecting information and breaking a problem into its component parts. The middle phase of mediation (Step 3: caucuses) is devoted primarily to collecting data based on Conflict Grid categories, but you will begin to gather information with your very first conversation about the case.

You will collect Conflict Grid data primarily through conversations with the parties: first contact, opening meeting, and caucuses. You will use the standard communication skills of questioning, active listening, and self-disclosing (described in Resource A) to invite information, clarify its meaning, and organize it for subsequent negotiations. You can also use written reports, newspaper accounts, and any other information source that identifies parties, interests, relevant facts, and possible solutions. The Conflict Grid can also serve as a guide for other activities, such as strategic planning, with the various components providing a way to identify both interested parties and the data that will be important in order for each party to sign off on the eventual plan. With every single contact you have with the parties, beginning with the first telephone call and on through joint meetings and caucuses, and with every piece of paper you read regarding the dispute, whether a newspaper article, letter, memorandum, or deposition, use the information to sharpen your analysis of the situation according to the categories on the Conflict Grid.

Parties

The first thing you want to know in any dispute is, who are the *parties*—the direct players—and who are their constituents? In the version of the Conflict Grid given in Figure 2.1, there is room for five parties to be listed across the top, but there may be more or fewer, depending upon the situation.

There will always be at least two parties. An employee and a supervisor may be the two primary parties in an employment dispute. If two team leaders are talking with one another about a project that involves themselves and two suppliers, then there are at least four parties involved in the negotiations.

Each party also reports to other people. Some mediators refer to these others as the party's *constituency*. A team leader may have to go back to a group of five coordinators to get their approval on whatever the team leader has negotiated. A negotiator from one country may return to seek approval of a treaty from the parliament of that country. Spouses and family members should also be considered as members of any party's constituency. A shrewd mediator always thinks of the individuals and groups to whom the negotiating parties must ultimately report or with whom they will talk before making an agreement. If the interests of these others are not considered in the process, the final deal may be rejected or sabotaged.

There is a rule of thumb for identifying parties. You obviously begin with individuals who are identified as a part of the dispute in the beginning, for example, a supervisor and her subordinate. However, include also in the analysis those people or groups who, if their interests are honored, could help the two original parties in reaching an agreement. For example, in caucus, you will ask the parties about others who have an interest in this matter, such as team members whose performance rating might be affected positively or neg-

Figure 2.1. Conflict Grid.

Variables	Parties				
	1.	2.	3.	4.	5.
• Interests (Hot Buttons)					
• Other Facts					
• BATNAs					
• Possible Solutions					

→   "One-Text" Integrative Solutions.

atively depending upon whether a particular supervisee's permanent record is changed as a result of mediation. A second question to ask in identifying parties is, Are there any parties who, if we ignore their interests, might derail the process? For example, in an organizational mediation, are there individuals or groups who may think their "turf" and influence is jeopardized if they are not given opportunities for input into the mediation process?

If you approach the conflict or problem in this way, then you might have two parties with whom you are working directly, though you may identify other individuals or groups that you will need to think about throughout the process. You may not include them in the face-to-face negotiations, but you will elicit Conflict Grid information on each of these parties along the way.

After identifying the parties, a mediator will want to know four things about each party involved in the dispute:

- What are the *interests* of the party?
- What are *other facts* related to this dispute that are important to this party?
- What is the party's *BATNA*, or Best Alternative to a Negotiated Agreement?
- What are *possible solutions* for the party in question?

BRINGING IN OTHER INTERESTED PARTIES

Suppose a case involves a legally protected right, such as freedom from sexual harassment or racial discrimination? What role should a government agency charged with protecting civil rights, such as the Equal Employment Opportunity Commission (EEOC), play in the mediation? A prudent mediator will include an agency representative either as a part of the mediation or as a secondary party to whom any potential agreement will be brought for input and review prior to implementation. In the opening meeting, the mediator can ask the parties to discuss how to include the other interested parties in the process. The mediator's options will include conducting a caucus with these parties at some appropriate time or convening a meeting involving everyone to review a potential agreement at a point later in the process. The important thing to remember is to use the two-part rule of thumb: identify parties who could help, and those who might derail in the early going and then assist the primary parties in finding some appropriate way to include these other individuals in the process.

Interests

Interests are the heart of the matter in any dispute. To illustrate the concept of interests, consider the possible reasons for a manager to ask for a promotion: Better compensation? Prestige? Power? Influence? An office with a window? More freedom?

Each answer refers to an underlying interest that someone might have as he or she negotiates for a promotion. Think of interests as the underlying needs that a person has as he or she takes a particular position in a negotiation or as a demand is made. If the position is, "Promote me, or else (or else I leave; I protest; I make trouble for you)," the underlying interests may be, "I want more influence, prestige, better compensation so I can buy a new house," and so on.

Another way to understand interests is to consider the classic story of the orange, which is told in most negotiation seminars. As the story goes, two children are fighting over the last orange in the house and take their dispute to a parent. The parent, instead of cutting the orange in half and giving each child half, asks the first child what she wants to do with the orange. She says she is hungry and wants to eat the orange. The same inquiry to the other child gets the response that she is making a cake and needs the peel. Soon the integrative solution emerges of peeling the orange, giving the meat to the one who is hungry and the peel to the one who wants to bake a cake.

Another classic illustration of interests is attributed to Mary Parker Follet, an early twentieth-century advocate of creative conflict resolution. The story is of the two graduate students in a dispute over whether or not to have the window open or closed in a library room. It appears to be a win/lose situation. However, an astute librarian inquires of the interests and hears from the first student, "I've got to have the window open. It's so stuffy in here I can't breathe." The other student responds, "The draft is blowing my notes all over the place. The window has got to be shut." The librarian stands back and notices the solution. By raising all the windows wide in an adjoining room, the students are able to receive fresh air, without a draft.

An employee may demand an annual raise of 10 percent. Upon inquiry, we learn his underlying interests when he says: "I need the cash to qualify for a loan on a home. Besides, Harry got an annual raise of 8 percent. I'm better than Harry, and I want that recognized." An employer who can't give the 10 percent raise but who knows the underlying interests may find another way to help with the home loan issue and also to address the comparison concern.

Underlying interests drive conflicts and disputes. As internal data, motives, wants, and desires are also included in this category. This is information you will know only if it is disclosed by the party or if you infer it from behavior. Disputants often do not talk about their interests with one another. Instead, they hide them and make demands or declare positions. Often, they do not trust the other side enough to declare these matters, preferring instead to conceal them for fear that if they reveal their true, heartfelt interests, the other side will use this information against them. The opportunity provided by mediation, of course, is for the parties to be able to discuss these interests with a trusted third party, who then can facilitate a communication process about interests and options that the parties had been unable to achieve up to that point.

This category of internal data (as opposed to external, observable facts discussed below) includes a full range of psychological hot buttons that may lead to emotional reactions during caucuses and joint meetings. For example, any abusive childhood experience (sexual, physical, or psychological damage by an authoritarian caregiver) can make for adult vulnerability that can be touched off by a conflict involving relationships, work assignments, or any other life event. Parties themselves may be quite unaware of the underlying fear, anxiety, anger, or other feelings that bring tremendous energy and power to a current conflict. Based on childhood experiences, one employee may interpret a negative personnel evaluation as a personal assault, while another may take it in stride as a problem to be solved. A mediator may be faced with two sets of concerns: the immediate precipitating event (for example, sexual harassment in the workplace, wrongful termination, or failure to promote an employee) as well as unfinished business from the past that has been triggered by the recent event. While the aim for the mediator is not to offer psychotherapy in these situations, it is desirable to listen carefully, and to reflect back (especially in caucuses) the data presented by the party. The importance of this dimension of the Conflict Grid is to prepare the mediator to listen not only for standard interests such as a desire to save face, to protect long-term relationships, and the like, but also to listen for psychological hot buttons as well.[1]

Standard Interests[2]

- To be "made whole"
- To put the matter to rest
- To avoid costs (time and money) of litigation
- To avoid stress and protect health
- To have harm acknowledged (apology)
- To protect and preserve reputation
- To establish precedent
- To punish
- To be vindicated (proven right!)
- To save face
- To save time
- To honor values of fairness and justice

Other Facts

A focus on interests is clearly not the whole story in any dispute. There is a range of other facts that bear on the conflict. Questions such as the following may need to be answered: How much money is there in the account? What does the law require? What is the relevant organizational policy? How many members are there on the team? How long has each of them been with the company? What did the police report say? What does the contract say about this issue?

These other facts can be grouped under several headings, as follows.

History of the Dispute

What were the first signs, symptoms, or indications that there was a conflict or dispute? Who hit whom, and when? When did the person first start showing up late for work? Have there been charges filed against anyone? How about the written record? What notes are there in the personnel file?

The focus here will typically be on observable events, written records, and the narratives each person gives on the history of the dispute.

Costs/Losses

How much time did an injured employee miss from work? What did it cost to repair damage to the house after the fire? How about future medical expenses? All of these are examples of costs and losses that fall under general heading of other facts.

Previous Attempts at Resolution

Did anyone try to solve the problem? How? Why didn't it work? Were there any attempts at mediation? Were lawsuits, grievances, or other formal proceedings initiated? When, by whom, and with what result? Have there been any unilateral power plays? Were there fights, physical violence, or anything else as a part of the attempt to resolve the situation?

As an example, in a conflict involving the marketing and production departments of a high-tech organization, the marketing team leader stated that all attempts at reasoning with the production people about a particular problem had failed. She reported raising the problem on two occasions during staff meetings, and sending one memorandum (with copies to three other interested parties). In terms of Conflict Grid data, these attempts at resolution represented other facts for the mediator and parties to consider.

STANDARD OTHER FACTS

- History of the dispute
- Costs/losses associated with the dispute
- Previous attempts at resolution
- Characteristics of the parties
- Organizational context
- Relevant objective standards
- Applicable law

Characteristics of the Parties

Is one party a recovering alcoholic? Has he undergone treatment? Has another been diagnosed with clinical depression? Is she tak-

ing medication? These are other facts that you will consider in analyzing the conflict. Depending upon your own professional training, you may have greater or lesser skill in evaluating these and
other conditions. Later you may, with the cooperation of the party
(or parties), elicit more data from a mental health professional on
the exact nature of a disorder. For now, however, treat the information as a set of other facts to consider, to be distinguished from
the interests of the party.

Organizational Context

What are the formal rules and policy guidelines of the organization within which the dispute is occurring? If the dispute exists in
a hospital, for example, there will be grievance procedures, medical bylaws, employee rules and regulations, and other guidelines
that provide a context for the dispute. Any possible solutions will
have to be measured against these standards, and in particular, cannot violate them if the solutions are to last.

Relevant Objective Standards

Fisher and Ury[3] remind negotiators to insist on objective standards
in resolving differences with adversaries. In the context of the Conflict Grid, ask about outside criteria that the parties might use to
evaluate proposals under consideration. For example, what is the
appraised value of a piece of a property, the blue-book value of an
automobile, the entry-level wage (and standard benefits) for a particular job classification?

Applicable Law

How about municipal and county ordinances or state and federal
laws that might apply to this dispute? In many cases, the parties will
require consultation with attorneys to identify legal rights and create mechanisms for protecting these rights.

In summary, think of interests as internal data and think of
other facts as observable, external data. In mediation, you will need
information from both areas in order to assist the parties in generating options for resolution.

BATNAs

The third piece of information that a mediator wants to know about every disputing party is that party's "Best Alternative to a Negotiated Agreement" (BATNA).[4] This is what the person will do if he or she does not strike a deal with the opposing side. For example: if I can't get you to agree to what I propose, what will I do? Will I leave the company? File a lawsuit? Will I go above your head and talk to the boss and try to have someone else make a decision in my favor? What will I do?

Good mediators want to know what it is that people are likely to do if they do not reach a collaborative resolution. Think of the conflict options presented earlier: avoidance, power play, higher authority, and collaboration. These all present standard BATNAs, for example, (1) living with the pain (avoidance); (2) filing a lawsuit (higher authority); (3) filing a grievance or going to a state agency or up the chain of command (another form of higher authority); (4) engaging in behind-the-scenes political maneuvers (power plays).

The importance of the BATNA is that it gives a standard against which to measure any proposed solution. A party will never make a deal that is not better than his or her BATNA. However, parties are often ignorant of their BATNAs (or have unrealistic BATNAs) when they enter negotiation or mediation. For example, the person in our previous example requesting a 10 percent pay raise may assume that it will be easy to get another job paying that kind of money. If that employee does not have a job lined up, he is relying on a BATNA that does not exist. A BATNA should be so concrete and well defined that you could walk out of a negotiation and exercise it immediately.

A second common problem with BATNAs is that a party who has not done the necessary homework may overestimate the strength of a BATNA. The employee in the pay dispute, for example, may not realize the downside to leaving the company suddenly over that dispute. Exercising the BATNA described may have very heavy and negative consequences for one's career.

STANDARD BATNAS

- Live with the situation as is (avoidance).
- Refer to higher authority (lawsuit).
- Take unilateral action (power plays).

Possible Solutions

The last quadrant of the Conflict Grid asks for possible *solutions* for the party in question. Define solutions this way: any actions that will resolve a given piece of the problem or the whole problem. You can generate solutions as we have defined them through the skill of brainstorming (see Resource A). To continue with the example of the employee whose interests include sufficient compensation to qualify for home ownership and recognition for superior performance, possible solutions might include: a raise, some increase in compensation now plus a review later to consider additional increases, a plan to decrease benefits so as to increase salary, early payment of a bonus, a promotion to a job with more responsibilities, a recognition ceremony of some sort, an article about the employee's achievements in a company newsletter, and so on.

Solutions are steps that might resolve any one issue or the whole problem or conflict. The goal in this portion of the Conflict Grid is to generate as many solutions as possible.

As you follow the Conflict Grid, you will do the same analysis for each party. This means that if you have two parties, you will look for information for each party along these four variables: interests, other facts, BATNAs, and possible solutions. If you have five parties, the same analysis applies for all five. In addition, think of how each party's constituents might view interests differently from the negotiating representative.

One-Text Integrative Solutions

Once you have conducted an analysis such as this for each of the parties, you are in a position to refine the possible solutions you have identified and create a one-text integrative solution that can bring the parties together. The phrase *one-text,* or *single text,* is borrowed from literature first presented through the Harvard Program on Negotiation and made popular through Fisher and Ury's book *Getting To Yes.* The one-text idea is that there should be a single list of behaviors that the parties agree to take that will honor (or at least not violate) the interests that have been identified and that will square with available facts and, at the same time, be better than each party's BATNA. The term *integrative* refers to steps that include, or integrate, the three tests from the Conflict Grid: (1) Does the agreement honor the key interests of the parties? (2) Does it square with the other facts? and (3) Is it better than the respective BATNAs?[5]

Continuing with the example regarding an employee's request for a promotion, a solution would need to meet the employee's interests in cash for a home mortgage and in a demonstration that the employee is at least as good as and appropriately appreciated in comparison with Harry. From the company's vantage point, if the money is not available or a promotion violates organizational policy, there are additional constraints on the deal. Finally, any proposal must be better than the parties' respective BATNAs. So what might work? What solutions might honor the interests of each party, square with the facts, and still be better than the respective BATNA of each? Maybe the solution would be to provide a certain raise now, along with some other assignment of responsibility that gives recognition (not cash, which the company may not have), thereby honoring the employee's interest in recognition over Harry? Perhaps some part of the promotion could be given now, with some increase in salary occurring this year and the promise of a review for more compensation next year. Perhaps the company could send a letter to this effect to the employee's mortgage company.

A one-text solution summarizes the entire agreement. Consider the Camp David accords. An American mediating team under President Jimmy Carter worked with Israeli and Egyptian representatives in achieving an agreement that allowed for peace between Israel and Egypt. After shuttling back and forth between two cabins at Camp David, one for Israel and one for Egypt, the American mediators formulated a list of steps that might bring the two sides together. The mediators then carried the one-text solution—the list of steps—back and forth, negotiating refinements in it.

Notice how different this is from allowing the negotiation to deal primarily with the parties' own position papers. Mediators might allow this in the beginning but will quickly help the parties move behind the position papers to see what the Conflict Grid information might be: the interests, other facts, BATNAs, and possible solutions. There is nothing more difficult than trying to reconcile positions that come through several sets of written documents. Two parties, two position papers. Five parties, five position papers, and so on. A careful negotiator or mediator will thank those involved for the effort that went into presenting the documents and then begin an inquiry to unbundle the documents to go after interests, other facts, BATNAs, and possible solutions. The end result will be the mediator's own one-text listing of agreed-upon steps that work for all parties.

Think of the one-text statement as the deal, the covenant, the agreement. It is typically written, but it need not be. It can be a verbal statement between the parties. As it is formulated, it will grow from the solutions identified by the parties.

Figure 2.2 offers a visual image of the one-text path involving four parties. Building on information gained in caucuses and joint meetings, the mediator encourages the parties to look beyond their own "boxes" and, instead, to fashion steps for a one-text box that will pass the three-part test of honoring (or, at least, not violating) individual and common interests, squaring with the facts introduced by the parties, and being better than the parties' individual BATNAs. In some cases, it might be useful for the mediator to draw a version of this figure to help parties visualize a path that allows each to maintain his or her individual integrity while at the same time recognizing the values and interests of the other side(s).

Standard Solutions

As an assist, consider four standard solutions that mediators frequently find helpful in generating one-text integrative solutions: (1) apologies or acknowledgment of wrong done, (2) restitution, (3) new plan for the future, and (4) forgiveness.

Figure 2.2. The One-Text Path for Four Parties.

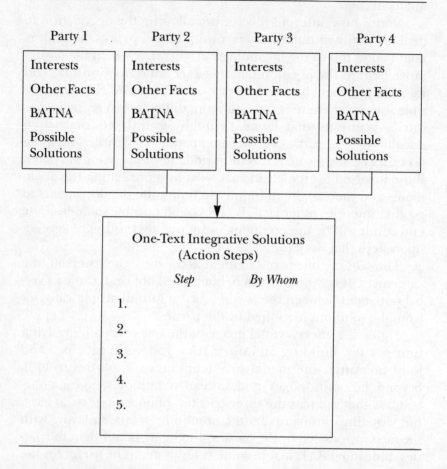

Apologies may involve expressions of regret or remorse for something done in the past, and must begin with an acknowledgment of a problem and of a party's culpability. Some parties balk at apologies or acknowledgment for fear of opening the door to payment of damages and/or to losing face. Mediators frequently need to coach parties in understanding the role of acknowledgment and apology in resolving a problem, whether it involves an interpersonal conflict between family members or damages done to one or more individuals by a large organization. As we shall see in later chapters, mediation is uniquely suited as a forum for exploring acknowledgment and apologies in private and confidential caucuses on the way toward joint meetings and eventual fashioning of an integrative solution.

Restitution involves payment for some wrong or harm done in the past. In legal circles, this can involve helping a party to be "made whole" by the payment of money, and it may also include punitive damages, money changing hands to, in some sense, teach a lesson for a wrong done in the hope that it will not happen again. For example, suppose the city is repairing the street in front of your house and knocks over two cherished trees. The public works department clearly can't replace trees that took twenty years to grow, but the payment of money may somewhat ease your emotional pain and compensate for the increase in your electric bill due to lack of shade previously afforded by the trees. Restitution can also take other forms, such as community service. This is an area where creative thinking can be a key to fashioning a solution that meets both monetary and emotional interests. One should always look to other forms of compensation, such as goods or services, as ways to make people whole.

A third standard solution involves creating new plans for the future. This is especially important in the workplace, where an employee may not be performing up to par, or when there has been some problem that can be corrected if the parties behave differently in the future. Suppose you are my supervisor and determine that my performance suffers due to my poor organization and weak interpersonal skills. If I agree to take a course in time management and planning, and perhaps take other concrete steps to improve my relationships with co-workers, then this plan for the future may be a critical part of our resolution of a conflict. We will also need to include follow-up procedures so that you can determine whether or not these plans have been carried out and have been effective.

Fourth and finally, forgiveness is a standard solution in conflict situations. While there is a rich theological tradition for this word in many religious contexts, the collaborative version goes like this: if I forgive you, I agree to stop holding this conflict over our heads as we work together in the future.

This is true in business as well as in family disputes. To be sure, forgiveness is often easier to come by after apology, restitution, and agreement to change behavior in the future than if one or more of these is absent. By the same token, many times an agreement never feels quite right to one or more of the parties; even if there has been an apology, a restitution, and a plan for the future, one party may not let the problem go. So, always consider forgiveness as one of the standard solutions you may need to check in helping parties reach an agreement.

To summarize, you can use the Conflict Grid to analyze any conflict situation, even a brief segment of a conversation involving two people. As we shall see, you can get information about the situation from conversations and also from written reports, newspaper articles, and other sources. The Conflict Grid will give you a framework for collecting this information from the parties and for working with them in creating integrative solutions to disputes.

EXERCISES

1. Choose one of the two newspaper articles quoted at the end of this chapter (or use another of your choosing) and write out the following:
    a. The parties identified in this article and their constituencies.
    b. For each party: possible interests (from the article), facts the party would bring to the table, BATNA (if available from the article), and solutions the party might propose.
    c. Finally, based on the article alone, sketch a preliminary one-text agreement that might emerge from a mediation involving these parties, their interests, and the facts that they bring.
2. Selecting one party from the article, imagine that you are a mediator preparing to meet with that person in a private caucus. List the key questions you would ask to clarify or expand the data available from the article in terms of Conflict Grid categories (for example, interests).

Suits Accuse Dioceses of Hiding Sex Abuse
Lawyer Says Boys Were "Sacrificial Lambs"
by Mark Neuzil (Associated Press)
Austin American-Statesman
Wednesday, July 15, 1992, p. A-6

ST. PAUL, Minn.—Lawsuits filed Tuesday accuse Catholic Church officials of covering up reports of sexual abuse by a former priest who has admitted molesting dozens of children.

The lawsuits were filed by seven Minnesota men who say they were abused as children by the former priest, James Porter, while he served at a parish in Bemidji in northern Minnesota.

Porter, 57, already has admitted sexually abusing dozens of children while serving at three Catholic parishes in Massachusetts in the 1960s. One Boston attorney says he represents 59 people who say they were molested by Porter.

Scores of cases have been reported in recent years in which priests allegedly abused youngsters sexually. U.S. bishops, meeting in June, vowed to deal more vigorously with such priests.

Attorney Jeffrey Anderson, who filed the lawsuits, said the church knew of Porter's behavior. "It is their problem and it is their practice, and it has caused these children to be sacrificial lambs," Anderson said.

"I was a sick man when I was a Roman Catholic priest in the 1960s," Porter said in a statement released by his attorney. "As a result of my illness, I sexually abused a number of children. I sought help for my illness on several occasions, and, when I finally realized that I could not control my behavior while remaining a priest, I left the priesthood."

Porter—who lives with his wife and four children in Oakdale, Minn., a St. Paul suburb—hasn't been charged with any crime.

Named as defendants in the lawsuits are Porter, the dioceses of Crookston, Minn., and Fall River, Mass., and The Servants of the Paraclete Inc., a treatment center run by the Catholic Church in Jemez Springs, N.M.

The Fall River Diocese released a statement expressing "profound sadness" at the accusation. The Crookston Diocese and the New Mexico treatment center wouldn't comment on the lawsuits.

Church officials earlier had asked members of the Bemidji parish to come forward if they had been sexually abused by Porter.

"If there are any victims, the church wants to respond pastorally in terms of emotional and spiritual well-being," said the Rev. Rick Lambert, pastor of St. Philip Church in Bemidji.

Two of the seven plaintiffs, Dan Dow, 34, and Jim Grimm, 34, attended a news conference Tuesday and said they were both altar boys when Porter was in Bemidji.

"I was repeatedly abused by Father Porter in any way you can imagine," Grimm said.

After one incident, Dow told his mother, who told her husband. Dow's father called Grimm's parents and they went to the church pastor. Not getting any satisfaction, the parents contacted a Bemidji lawyer and went to the bishop, threatening to call the police, Grimm said.

"He (Porter) was gone the next day," Grimm recalled.

Porter came to Bemidji from the New Mexico treatment center, where he had been sent in 1967 after sexual abuse allegations against him in Massachusetts.

The Crookston Diocese acknowledged that Porter was made an assistant priest at St. Philip Parish in August 1969, after being treated for child molestation. He served in Bemidji until September 1970.

Because the alleged abuse in Minnesota took place more than seven years ago, the state's statute of limitations prevents criminal prosecution.

Ruler's Wife Called Key in Agreement
Team from U.S. Describes Twists During Weekend Talks
by David LaGesse
Washington Bureau of *The Dallas Morning News*
Tuesday, September 20, 1994, p. 1-A

WASHINGTON—A personality little known in the United States emerged Monday as a key to U.S. agreement with Haiti—the wife of Haiti's military leader.

Yanick Prosper, wife of Lt. Gen. Raoul Cedras, merited a personal visit at home Sunday from former President Jimmy Carter and President Clinton's other emissaries trying to avert an invasion.

"His wife is one of the strongest and most powerful women I've ever met, and she was adamantly against any sort of an agreement," Mr. Carter said.

Ms. Prosper's surprising role was among the intriguing turns in the weekend's talks as described by the U.S. team, led by Mr. Carter and including Senate Armed Services Committee chairman Sam Nunn of Georgia and retired Gen. Colin Powell, former chairman of the Joint Chiefs of Staff. They recalled their hectic 30 hours in Haiti in interviews broadcast by CNN and at a White House news conference Monday.

They described a peace process nearly torpedoed by the launching of warplanes from a U.S. base, having to wrestle with Mr. Clinton for more time, and unexpected authority exerted by the military-installed Haitian president.

"We had long and painful conversations, and there was a lot of emotion in the room," Mr. Powell said.

The U.S. negotiators traveled to Haiti on Saturday at the invitation of Gen. Cedras and with the blessing of Mr. Clinton. They met with members of Haiti's de facto government, or the "de factos" in the language of Secretary of State Warren Christopher.

The important de factos, it seemed, included Ms. Prosper. The importance of the 38-year-old wife of Gen. Cedras arose at dinner with Haitian businessmen on Saturday night, Mr. Nunn said.

One of the dinner hosts suggested the Americans meet Ms. Prosper.

"About the time we were requesting it, General Cedras himself decided it would be a good thing," Mr. Nunn said.

Gen. Cedras was coming off an anxious day, having slept little for several days and having missed his 10-year-old son's birthday Saturday, Mr. Carter said. "So they were in an emotional state," he said of the Cedras family.

The profile of Ms. Prosper, the daughter of a prominent Haitian family, rose alongside her husband's this summer.

One of the papers published by expatriate Haitians called her "la Generale" after aides to Jean-Bertrand Aristide sought her help on behalf of the exiled president.

Haitian press reports say she portrayed Mr. Aristide as a leftist firebrand who threatened the country's business elite. She also reportedly profited from the sale of import licenses after her husband's rise to power following the September 1991 coup that dislodged Mr. Aristide.

The U.S. negotiators said Ms. Prosper spoke passionately Sunday of patriotism and sovereignty.

"She had a deep sense of honor. Her family was military," Mr. Nunn said. "Frankly, I think that family had taken the decision the evening before to die together."

The Sunday morning family visit apparently demanded the best of Mr. Carter's negotiating skills.

"President Carter made wonderful statements showing sensitivity," Mr. Nunn said.

Mr. Carter, however, threw most of the credit to Mr. Powell, whose leadership during the Persian Gulf War drew respect from the Haitians. The former general argued Gen. Cedras' highest calling was to protect the lives of Haitians, not to give his life or the lives of his wife and children, Mr. Carter recalled.

"General Powell was extremely effective in saying, "This is what military honor is, this is what courage is,'" Mr. Carter said.

"I don't know what went on after we left the house."

Ms. Prosper later appeared frequently on the balcony of the military headquarters, smiling and chatting with staff members as her husband negotiated the accord.

In the end, Gen. Cedras said he could not sign the pact. His ultimate authority would come from Emil Jonassaint, the 81-year-old former chief justice installed by the military as their president.

That raised a sensitive point since the United States and United Nations do not recognize the authority and power of Mr. Jonassaint. But after the final round of talks Sunday evening had moved to the presidential palace, Mr. Clinton agreed to accept the de facto president's signature.

The U.S. team said it expected a figurehead in Mr. Jonassaint, who gained recent notoriety in the United States by promising voodoo gods would protect Haiti from U.S. aggression.

Instead, the U.S. mediators say they found a statesman in command of those around him—including, apparently, Gen. Cedras.

Mr. Jonassaint listened to the contrary opinions from his Cabinet members, particularly his defense minister, Mr. Carter said. Mr. Jonassaint responded in a strong and emotional manner, citing his age, experience as chief justice of Haiti's supreme court, and authorship of the 1987 constitution under which Mr. Aristide was elected.

"I say to you that we'll have peace, not war," Mr. Carter recalls him saying.

That stunned Mr. Jonassaint's subordinates into silence for several moments, until the defense minister said he would resign, Mr. Carter said.

Mr. Nunn agreed that it was a turning point.

"He was a very strong person," he said of Mr. Jonassaint. In the final analysis, he pointed his finger around the room . . . and he said, 'We're going to do this.'"

It was also Mr. Jonassaint who went on Haitian television, Sunday night to explain the agreement. His personality again emerged after he finished a staid, prewritten speech in French and spoke to his countrymen in their native Creole.

U.S. forces were on the way "to wipe us out," he said. "We couldn't let the annihilation of Haiti happen without any reason. Hence we signed an accord."

In fact, U.S. forces had been launched while the talks were under way. Gen. Philippe Biamby, the army chief of staff, delivered the news he'd apparently received from Haitian Americans in the United States, Mr. Carter said.

The news startled both sides, and Gen. Biamby threatened to break off the talks so the military leaders could lead their troops.

"We saw the entire agreement coming apart," Mr. Carter said.

The U.S. negotiators instead convinced Gen. Cedras to

leave alone, and the talks continued to a successful end with Mr. Jonassaint.

Originally scheduled to leave at noon Sunday, the U.S. mediators had found themselves too close to an agreement to leave, and told Mr. Clinton by phone, putting him in the nervous position of granting more time knowing the invasion was about to begin.

"The thing kept getting put back. They were very dogged," Mr. Clinton told reporters at the White House. "They were just determined to stay until the last minute."

The president finally told Mr. Carter their long friendship made it awkward, but that he would order them out in another 30 minutes.

"They had to get out before dark," Mr. Clinton said. "So they worked it out."

Chapter Three

Preparing to Be a Mediator

Good mediation is hard work. Often, you will feel as though you are functioning in an interpersonal war zone, and you may lose your bearings. This chapter offers a summary of reminders to help keep you on track.

• *Make no mistake, you are going to have a chance to do some good.* I once overheard two young attorneys talking about their first jobs, and one said she liked the work she was doing because she got to be "on the right side of the issues!" In her case she saw herself as a protector and advocate for disenfranchised clients, and her work had a good fit with her own personal values.

Mediation is, in its own way, on the "right side" of issues involving stress, hardship, economic waste, and loss of life. As a mediator, you will have a chance to help people save money, preserve relationships, create a new future, and, in some cases, keep from killing one another. Even if the parties fail to reach a settlement, you will have provided them the opportunity to examine the issues in a safe setting. That in and of itself is worth a great deal.

• *As a mediator you will typically be neutral on the content, though an advocate for the process.* The issue of mediator neutrality is a common and recurring theme, not only in the literature, but also in mediation conferences and training programs. Can a mediator truly be neutral? Should a mediator offer his or her own ideas or solutions to the conflict? How far should a mediator go in pushing the parties toward settlement?

In answering these questions, remember to distinguish between content and process. On the content, or substantive, issues, mediators are typically neutral. For example, a mediator does not begin a mediation with a bias about who is right or wrong, whose interests should take precedence, or what solutions might best fit the circumstances. However, a mediator definitely does bring very specific views on the steps that must be taken in order to honor standards of fairness and to preserve the integrity and well-being of the parties throughout the negotiations. Think of yourself as an advocate for a process that goes through certain steps (the ones identified in this book) and think of yourself as one who will use his or her energies to coach, encourage, and sometimes reprimand the parties, all in the service of following the process. For example, as a mediator, you will not allow interruptions, verbal threats, or intimidation of one party by another.

•   *Think of yourself as an agent of problem solving and assisted negotiation.* As we have already discussed, mediation is simply an assisted negotiation. As a mediator, therefore, you are an agent, a catalyst, an instrument that allows negotiations to proceed. This means that if the parties are negotiating well on their own, you will probably back off and let them proceed. However, if their negotiations derail, you may intervene more aggressively to get things back on track.

In mediation, problem solving is the art of translating any dispute, conflict, or attack into a new form that is more manageable for the parties than the original dispute was. For example, picture two persons negotiating with one another. Left to his or her own devices, each perceives the other to be the problem. The mediator as problem solver, however, encourages the parties to focus on a third entity, not one person or the other person but something outside the two of them, called the problem. As a mediator, you will encourage them to be gentle with one another while being ruthless in dealing with the problem. This may at times be easier said than done, though the concept can be a lifesaver. Model it for the parties: be gentle with the parties and hard on the problem.

In many disputes, one side is in fact (or feels himself or herself to be) ill-equipped to deal with the other side. One person might have less information, less negotiating skill, less money, or fewer friends in high places and therefore feel at a disadvantage in dealing with an adversary. The mediator clearly cannot change many of the power dimensions in a negotiation. For example, the mediator cannot give the person more money or more friends. On the other hand, by virtue of the way the process is structured, the mediator can ensure that both sides have access to the same information on parameters that are critical to the negotiation. Similarly, the mediator can allow each side to talk without interruption and can privately coach each side on successful steps for negotiating the matter at hand.

Believe going in that each of the parties is a human being with interests, needs, values, desires, and feelings and that these feelings are to be respected in the mediation process. Let everything you do be in the service of honoring these values for each side as you coach the parties toward focusing on interests and creating solutions.

• *Allow yourself to be active and assertive throughout the process.* In my first research on the process of divorce mediation, begun in the late 1970s, I interviewed master mediators around the country, and I will never forget what one seasoned labor/management mediator said to me: "Do not be deceived, mediation is not a soft, easygoing process. Mediators need to be aggressive and work hard with the parties to achieve solutions." The key question, of course, is active and aggressive in what way, and toward what end? As we will see when we define the process in the next several chapters, the answer lies in actively assisting the parties in identifying interests and other facts, and creating integrative solutions.

Be prepared to be tested. Some parties will wonder: "Can this mediator protect me here?" Needless to say, you cannot offer total protection to anyone, though it will be your responsibility to monitor what happens in the mediation sessions and enforce ground rules. To be actively engaged as a mediator means to serve as a convener and referee for joint meetings (coaching, reinforcing, encouraging, and at times reprimanding) and as a skilled interviewer and counselor in private caucuses (actively channeling each party's energy toward analyzing problems according to the Conflict Grid).

Remember that the focus of analysis at each step in the process will be to encourage (1) awareness/insight of the parties about their own situation, (2) understanding/recognition of the interests and needs of the other side, and (3) areas of possible agreement or areas that may lead to reconciliation.

• *If in doubt, listen, and then listen again.* A colleague once told me of his search of the mediation literature and his dismay at finding so few references to the importance of mediators being good listeners. Active listening is one of the mediator's required communication skills (see Resource A). Incorporate listening into your self-concept as a chief feature of what you have to offer people. Disputants by and large will not have been listened to very well up until the time they reach you. They may be, as a computer buff once said to me, in a "data dumping" mode. You can advance the cause tremendously through listening.

• *Be ready to teach and coach.* Since many of the disputants you will deal with have poor negotiation skills, at times you will most help the cause by offering a brief tutorial on how to negotiate. Usually carried out in private caucuses, these teaching and coaching sessions can often be critical factors in turning a dispute around. Perhaps the parties have not learned to think about interests. Or perhaps they have not let each other know that they even care about anyone's interests but their own. Your contribution may be to teach this principle, and coach in its implementation.

• *Know your limits.* Even though as mediator you adopt all of the preceding attitudes, it is equally important to know that you do not possess the power to make settlements, but only to help arrange circumstances so that they can occur. Remember that it takes only one of the parties (or the mediator) to declare an impasse. Remember also that the parties have options; as we discussed earlier, they can avoid the problem (living with the situation as it is), give it to higher authorities, or take it over in a power play. Later we will discuss when and how to declare impasses. For now, remember that, right alongside the rather lofty goals of doing good, being active in the process, and teaching and coaching the parties is the concept of *limits*. Never forget that in many circumstances there will be no mediated solution, the parties simply will not be able to agree, and they will need to resolve the matter later on through one of the remaining three methods on the conflict continuum: avoidance, higher authorities, or power plays.

I WILL REMEMBER . . .

1. The parties do not have to mediate; direct negotiations, avoidance, higher authority, and power plays are other options.
2. Assisted negotiation is what I have to offer; if they can negotiate well unassisted, then they do not need me.

3. I must aim to be objective, balanced, fair, facilitative, and if needed, assertive in structuring the process.

4. At times, I may need to translate, redirect communication, reinforce, encourage, or confront (to stop negative behavior).

5. A win/win outcome is possible, though not promised.

6. I must aim for integrative solutions that (1) honor (or do not violate) key interests of each side, (2) square with the facts presented, and (3) are better than the parties' respective BATNAs.

7. The parties probably will not trust each other at the start, but it is my job to help them trust me and the process I offer.

8. Good communication is necessary but not sufficient for getting the job done; at times, I may have to help create alternatives that the parties do not see.

9. We will need at least one round of caucuses at the start to hear key interests (or dangers) that frightened or threatened parties will not reveal in a joint meeting.

10. I need to be an expert on the *process* of conflict resolution and a quick study on all *substantive issues*.

11. While mediation is also a social skill, when I offer it to disputants I am providing a professional service that is bound by ethical guidelines that I will attempt to follow at each point in the process (see Resource C); for example, I will reveal to the parties at the outset any biases that may affect the process.

12. There are distinguishing cultural differences in the way individuals and groups perceive conflict and the resolution options available to them; I must listen and learn what these are in each case where I serve as mediator.

13. While the mediation process covers certain formal steps, there are many variations on the theme, and I may adjust the process to fit the situation and the needs of the parties.

• *Cultivate your sense of humor.* The oft-repeated saying that pain and humor are actually two sides of the same coin applies also to conflict. It is no accident that television situation comedies, great theater, and stand-up comedy often have to do with conflict involving individuals and groups. Comedy and humor offer constructive ways to cope with these trying circumstances. And the same will be true for you as mediator, both in caucuses and in joint meetings.

Chances are that if you are reading this book, you already have a fairly well-developed sense of humor, or else you would not have been able to walk this far into the world of conflict without retreating. It is still a maxim more true than not that it is better to laugh with people than at them (though, at times that line may be a fine one indeed). Laugh at yourself, and it may keep you from taking yourself too seriously. In private caucuses, allow the humorous side of the conflict to emerge along with the dark side. You will find that it may be a key to your own survival and sanity.

• *Think of the mediation process as a series of steps or phases.* Mediation, like chess, has an opening, middle, and end phase. Certain moves must occur at the beginning, and others must wait until the middle part of the game, and others can succeed only in the latter stages. Disputing parties, of course, will not think of it this way. By the time you meet them, they will often have tried to impose solutions (end game demands!) on one another and may have exacerbated the problem through positional bargaining. Your goal as mediator will be to use your very first words to the first party who contacts you to begin reframing the dispute toward a path that has specific checkpoints for problem solving.

In the chapters that follow, we will go through the mediation process from beginning to end, beginning with first contact and moving on through to closing. It is entirely possible that all five steps could be covered in one session, or they may be spread out over a period of months. Here is a quick summary of the process:

- *Step one: first contact.* Someone contacts you, or you make the first move yourself; what will you say to help this party and the others get to the table? If mediation is to replace a battlefield or a courtroom, how should you arrange the environment to increase the chance of successful negotiations?
- *Step two: opening meeting.* What should the agenda be? What essential points must be covered in order for the parties to go forward within the ground rules for mediation?
- *Step three: caucuses.* How can you get to the heart of the matter,

the key interests that drive the dispute for each party? Individual meetings, under an umbrella of confidentiality, are your primary tool.

- *Step four: joint/shuttle meetings.* Building on what you have learned in caucuses, what form might an agreement take? What has to happen to get the parties on a common path? Should you bring the parties together to work jointly or should you shuttle back and forth to help fashion the agreement?
- *Step five: closing.* How can you test an emerging agreement to see that it will last? What can you do about follow-up and preparation for possible future disputes?

EXERCISES

1.   Before you developed an interest in the formal mediation process, under what other conditions had you performed the function of mediator; for example, mediating children's disputes at home or offering informal mediation as a manager of a work team? List as many situations as you can think of, creating your own personal history of mediation experiences.

2.   Analyze these experiences. What are your strengths as a mediator? What are your weaknesses, that is, areas needing improvement? Write down your answers and discuss them with a partner or with your training group.

First Contact

Imagine that your phone rings and, when you answer it, the caller says: "I think we may need a mediator for a dispute between two of our vice presidents. Tell me about your services."

Or imagine that a judge sends you a letter referring a case for divorce mediation and asks you to contact the parties' attorneys.

Or imagine that you are a patient representative at a hospital and a head nurse asks you to talk to the husband of a woman in intensive care: in violation of hospital policy, he refuses to leave her bedside, and the nurses and other patients are beginning to complain.

Picture yourself in one of these situations or any other that might be closer to your own current job responsibilities: What must you accomplish first, and how do you make it happen?

Think of everything you do in responding to the initial inquiry and securing a commitment to proceed with mediation as the *opening game.* Just as in chess or in most sports the objectives are limited. The objective is certainly not to solve the problem or anything close to it. Seasoned mediators consider the opening game a success if the parties are eventually seated (physically or metaphorically) at the table and ready to talk, all within certain ground rules.

We can break the opening game into two parts: orienting the parties (Chapter Four) and arranging the meeting space (Chapter Five).

| **Orienting the Parties**

Whether your first contact is over the telephone or face-to-face, the points in this chapter can guide you in listening to the problem as it is presented and in asking your own questions of the person who contacts you. In some cases, you may be asked to contact a disputant and present the mediation option. This might happen in an intraorganizational dispute, for example, when an ombudsman is told about a problem and asked to contact one of the parties directly. In any case, the same points need to be covered, and your objectives are

- To obtain a summary of the problem
- To define the process in enough detail that the parties can make an informed choice about whether to proceed
- To secure a preliminary agreement to start mediation (or at least to attend one meeting)

Do not worry much about the order of the steps described below. They may be collapsed together in some cases or rearranged in others. The important point is to cover them all in some way.

Summary

Ask for a summary of the problem and of events leading to this inquiry. In most cases, the person contacting you will begin with a summary of a problem that might have the same features as the problems described in the introduction to this section, such as the need to refer the spouse of the patient in intensive care to a mediator. Ask open-ended questions and listen in particular for dimensions such as the following:

• *Who is most bothered by the situation?* In the hospital case, we might learn in the very beginning that the other nurses are bothered and that other patients are as well. We may be able to assume that the head nurse who called us perceives the situation as a problem, but we do not know for sure. At some point, we want to ask the head nurse to clarify this. Listen especially for who will need to be satisfied for the problem to be resolved.

• *Who are the key parties, and who are their constituencies?* Define parties as anyone involved in the conflict or, more specifically, as anyone who if included could help achieve resolution and who if excluded could derail whatever solutions might be negotiated. If you have been asked by the CEO of a corporation to mediate a dispute involving two departments and if the CEO has identified two department heads as the key parties, then you will consider the members of these departments as the constituencies of the department heads, as the groups of people to whom they will report back with results or lack thereof.

Sometimes, key parties are behind the scenes and are not identified as part of the chain of command. This is particularly true in organizational disputes, where significant individuals might not be members of the governing body but might contribute heavily and be active behind the scenes in creating both problems and solutions.

• *What attempts at resolution have been tried so far?* In the case of a personal injury referral for mediation, have the parties filed a lawsuit yet or not? What negotiations have occurred? How far apart are the parties right now?

• *Are there time constraints?* Does one or more of the parties need to achieve a solution within the next several hours, days, or weeks? Are there court dates that need to be considered?

• *Has mediation been discussed?* To what extent are the parties knowledgeable about what mediation is, and have they said yes or no to the prospect?

A BALANCED START

As a way of setting a tone for balance and objectivity from the very start, tell the person who first contacts you (and the others when you speak with them later) that your policy is to answer questions and provide the same introductory information to each party before scheduling the opening meeting. You can do this by providing written materials (see Resource B) followed by very brief telephone conversations using the outline in this chapter. You might also consider a conference call so all parties can begin the process together, at the same time.

Expectations

Define the mediation process, your role, and how you would use the process for this case. Remember that most people will be unfamiliar with mediation and that even those with some experience may have gone through a process that is very different from the one you offer. Some people may be unfamiliar with the role of private caucuses with the parties or may have questions about confidentiality or about legal representation for the parties in the mediation meetings. Be prepared for one party or another to have already rejected mediation based on a misconception about the process. Though this happens less frequently now, I have had many conversations with attorneys who stated, even after receiving a letter in which I defined mediation, that they did not "want to do arbitration," assuming that the two processes were the same.

THE ROLE OF ATTORNEYS IN MEDIATION

In some disputes, the mediator will deal with attorney advocates as representatives of the parties through all phases of mediation. This is common in court-ordered mediation, when the parties will likely have engaged attorneys to file a lawsuit, and the matter has now been referred to mediation as an alternative to litigation. In these cases, the rule of thumb is for the mediator to treat the attorney advocates as representatives of the parties unless otherwise instructed. For example, you will ask the attorneys about the appropriateness of the parties speaking for themselves during the session (usually the attorneys will encourage the parties to do so), and also whether there will be meetings with the parties alone when the attorneys are not present (often a helpful shift in the negotiation mix, requested by the attorneys themselves).

In other situations, one party will have an attorney, and the other will not. A standard example is a personnel evaluation where the manager has already consulted with the corporation's legal department though the employee may or may not have talked to an attorney. This situation presents a special problem for mediators in the employment arena, and you will need to deal with it on a case-by-case basis. Guidelines for dealing with it include the following:

• *Discuss the issue of attorney consultation in the very beginning (first contact or opening meeting).* Offer a ground rule that insofar as the mediation involves (1) legally protected rights or (2) contracts that may be binding on either party, the parties should consult with attorneys regarding their rights and the eventual form of the contract.

• *Offer various avenues for securing attorney consultation.* Some progressive organizations have provided for legal consultation for employees involved in dispute resolution through mediation. For example, Brown & Root, Inc., pays legal fees for employees (up to a specified limit each year) to consult attorneys of their choosing when they are involved in mediation or other forms of alternative dispute resolution with the company.[1]

• *Be cautious about presenting your own list of attorneys to the parties.* This puts you in the lawyer referral business, which can create additional problems. Instead, direct parties to local bar associations or other groups that can provide consultation.

• *Be alert for conflict of interest on the part of attorney advocates as they participate in the mediation process.* The reality of the practice of law is that many attorneys will have more billable hours if the process goes to litigation than if it is resolved in mediation. Until this issue is addressed by the bar, parties may offer their own solutions to it. As an example, I once mediated a divorce case in which the couple declared that they had hired two prominent family law attorneys to consult with them throughout the mediation. The parties stipulated, however, that if they failed to reach agreement in mediation, they would fire both attorneys and hire new ones for any subsequent litigation. This effectively removed any financial conflict of interest from the process.

In Chapter Six, we will discuss the mediator's opening statement, and the points that it should cover. For now, expect to cover some of the same points in the initial phone call. Be prepared to give a short and simple description that includes the following:

- *What mediation is.* It is a process through which a neutral party works with two or more other parties to help them reach their own resolution of a conflict or dispute. (Possibly add that it is to be distinguished from arbitration and litigation, through which an outsider actually makes a decision for the parties.) (See Chapter One for a more detailed definition.)

- *Who you are.* You are a mediator (or patient representative, or ombudsman, or attorney/mediator), and your role is to meet with the parties together and then to conduct private caucuses, followed by shuttle diplomacy or joint meetings to help reach a resolution. You structure the process and serve as a facilitator, but do not make a decision for the parties.

- *Why mediation works.* Sometimes, the mediator serves as a buffer; at other times, helps keep negotiations on track; and at other times, carries messages back and forth. Often the mediator, through the caucuses, will hear information that the parties are unwilling to reveal to adversaries. By treating these revelations as confidential, the mediator may be able to help fashion solutions that the parties had not been able to create up to that point.

- *Confidentiality.* Under state guidelines governing mediation and alternative dispute resolution, communications to mediators are protected as confidential and cannot be subpoenaed into subsequent court proceedings. The mediator should say, "I will not reveal to the other side anything you say to me in private caucus unless you ask me specifically to do so."

- *Fees.* In private mediation, specify the fee, when it will be payable, and how it is to be shared by the parties. For intracorporate disputes, such as those mediated by ombudsmen and patient representatives, there will be no discussion of fees, though lines of authority and confidentiality may need to be discussed. (For example, someone may ask, "Will this go in my personnel file?" Answer: "No, unless you and the other side(s) agree to do so and specify what will be put in the file.")

FEES

Mediator fees should be discussed during the initial telephone conversation. Many organizations charge an administrative fee for opening a file and contacting the parties. Separate from the administrative fee is the charge most mediators make for their time, with the fee being shared equally by the parties. In most cases, fees are paid at the time of the mediation session, or the parties retain a block of hours and get a refund at the close of the mediation for any unused time.

Preliminary Correspondence

Arrange for delivery of information packets and other written materials. For formal mediations, ground rules that address the role of mediator, confidentiality, and other issues will be forwarded to the parties ahead of time. During the first inquiry, the mediator must secure identifying information for the parties and their attorneys, including phone numbers and also addresses for mailed materials. For some other mediations, such as those conducted by an ombudsman or in-house mediation teams, a small brochure that describes the process can be handed to the parties (see Resource B).

PRECONFERENCE WRITTEN MATERIALS

Use caution in asking the parties to create any new written materials prior to the mediation. If they are asked to write out anything at all, they will likely write position statements (instead of statements that focus on key interests), which might lead to more emotional investment in these positions, making your job more difficult later on. Instead, ask them to submit materials that have already been generated, such as depositions, pleadings for the court, or any other materials they wish to provide as background. These materials should be distributed to all parties before the opening meeting.

Commitment to Mediate

Secure a commitment to mediate. The objective in the early going is very simple and straightforward, namely, to agree to attend one meeting, the first mediation session. The parties will often be fearful that they are committing to too much, and it may be helpful to simplify this. For example, in a medical malpractice mediation, the parties will need to receive certain information beforehand (discussed below), in order to make a decision whether or not to proceed with mediation. They will need to have all of their questions answered through the written ground rules and materials sent by the mediator and through telephone conversations before they will be able to decide whether to attend the first meeting.

For mediations conducted on personnel matters, like those carried out by an ombudsman or an employee relations specialist, the mediator may actually begin the process immediately if the parties agree. In any case, bear in mind that the objective is to get a yes or no to proceeding.

IF THEY SAY NO TO THE PROCESS

It is not at all unusual to have one party want mediation and one or more other parties reject it outright. Sometimes the rejection grows from ignorance and other times from a strategy to delay or buy time or move the dispute to another playing field, such as the courts. Absent a mediation clause (discussed in Chapter Fourteen), there may be a great deal of jockeying back and forth in order to get the case to the table. If one party presents you with the problem of getting the other side to the table, consider the following:

- Make sure that you communicate to the party who contacts you that you want to spend equal time talking on the phone with all other sides, *before* they reach a decision to mediate.

- Aim for small behavioral steps: Will the other side agree to talking with you on the phone? Will the other side agree to having a packet of information sent to each party, so he or she can know what the mediation option would be?

- If you have been contacted by one party, state your objective as giving information to all parties at the same time, and ask that person to contact the others to see if they are willing to have information packets sent.
- If the contacting party fails to secure permission for you to send packets, then consider calling the parties yourself.
- In talking with an intransigent party, listen actively (Resource A) to objections and concerns, offer clarifying information if needed (for example, mediation is not arbitration), and always aim for limited steps, for example, attending one meeting.
- Bearing in mind that the objective is to get the parties to the table once and to allow for opening statements and at least one brief round of caucuses (which might be done in one hour), propose adjustments to the process in order to achieve that objective. For example, would the other parties attend if the referring party paid the fee for the first hour? If offers for one meeting are still rejected, make sure to leave the door open for a change in view at a later date. The passage of time, or the addition of parties and/or attorneys, might lead to the acceptance of mediation later on.

Initial Scheduling

Schedule the first meeting. Following the objective of getting the parties to the table, the immediate need is to identify a time and place that is agreeable to all parties. As veteran mediators know, this in itself can become an occasion for more conflict. One approach is to "unload" the time and place issue as much as possible; this is best accomplished by asking the parties directly to avoid investing too much meaning in the issue of time and place. Alternatively, mediate the selection process by exploring key interests (finding neutral ground, working around other work commitments) and helping the parties create a plan to at least start the process.

FIRST CONTACT DO'S AND DON'TS

DO	DON'T
Listen carefully to opening narrative and take notes (as a first run at filling in the Conflict Grid).	Ignore key interests and other facts that are offered at the very beginning.
Listen and talk with balance to each side. As a general rule, talk to each person on the phone in such a way that you would not mind if the opposing party were listening to the conversation. Consider using conference calls with all parties on the phone at the same time to explain the ground rules.	Allow yourself to be pulled in on one side or the other at the very beginning.
Be prepared to define the process clearly in simple language.	Allow the person who contacts you to proceed with distortions about the process (for example, suggesting that it lacks confidentiality or confusing it with procedures such as arbitration).
Secure a commitment to proceed from each party.	Ignore one party or allow the meeting to go forward without one party, running the risk of that person's feeling left out or questioning the neutrality of the mediator for having gone

	ahead with the process without including everyone at the start.
Make sure everyone has the same information, delivered at the same time.	Send information to one person before offering to send it to all other parties at the same time.
Schedule the first meeting at a time and place agreeable to all parties.	Allow one party to derail the process over scheduling issues.

Flexibility

The preceding steps will vary depending upon the circumstances. For international mediations, it is not uncommon for the process of covering each of these steps in the opening game to go on for many months and sometimes years. In getting cases to the table, there can be deadlocks, which may be broken through external events (the threat of armed conflict, sudden reversals for one party or the other) that lead to new motivation to mediate. Even if the parties do not agree to come to the table now, your thoroughness in covering the points above may lay the groundwork for a different decision months or even years later.

EXERCISES

1.   Do this exercise with a partner. In the first round, imagine one of you is a party calling to inquire about mediation. As the mediator, the second person will ask for background information, answer questions about the process, and describe what the next steps will be (using information from this chapter). Take turns in each role, challenging each other with questions about the process, and debriefing after each round on the strengths of this first contact as well as on the areas that need improvement.

2.   Using the information in this chapter and the material in Resource B, create your own set of written materials to be used for mediation in your setting.

Chapter Five

Arranging the Meeting Space

Just as courtrooms are set up to allow for orderly presentation of arguments to a judge or jury, including separate chambers for the different parties to go to in order to reflect on what they have heard before rendering a decision, so mediation rooms must be set up to allow the parties themselves to present their interests and points of view, hear the interests of the other side, and do so in such a way that the sides begin to work cooperatively with one another in creating mutually acceptable solutions. Seasoned mediators know that they can get the job done in any number of different circumstances: over the telephone, talking with one party in a corridor, taking a walk around the block, or meeting in a conference room or around a negotiation table.

Prepare Basic Elements

The one necessary environmental condition that must be met is that the caucuses be private, conducted in rooms or circumstances where outsiders cannot hear the conversations. Beyond this, all other considerations—room size, table shapes, and furniture and other supports—will likely vary according to what is available to you in the particular circumstance. That being said, in preparing the opening meeting, caucuses, and shuttle diplomacy to follow, you will find it useful to consider the following in setting up rooms and preparing for the parties to join you.

Neutral Ground

One side may feel uncomfortable going into the other side's territory. There can be a tremendous amount of one-upmanship that

occurs at one's home site. If you are a private mediator, you can
certainly invite the parties to your own office. If you are mediating
in a hospital or corporate setting, you could invite the parties to
meet at a conference room where each is out of his or her own
home territory.

Ideal Space

In most cases, you will need a conference room for an opening
meeting, and for all subsequent joint meetings, with sufficient seating for all parties around the table. You will also need at least one
or two private caucus rooms. In addition, you should take advantage of corridors for brief informal talks and consider walks outside the building as an additional option.

Think of yourself as playing host to all the parties, much as you
would if you were having people over for dinner. If the mediation
occurs in one party's home territory, do not be reluctant as mediator to take the lead in structuring the environment to suit the
mediation agenda.

Privacy

If you are in someone else's conference room, and you notice that
the door won't close firmly, or that there is a big gap under the
door, or that you yourself can hear voices coming through an air
conditioning duct, then you must take steps to correct for this. The
most obvious option is to ask for another meeting room. If this
does not work, then consider, for example, taking a walk with parties with whom you are conducting a caucus, or talking in the lobby
of the office building or outside the building. It is important to pay
attention to these conditions since you do not want them to have
an inhibiting influence on the party with whom you are talking.
Bear in mind that you will be asking people to disclose key interests, and to say things that they have not said to the other side and
may be reluctant to discuss with you. It is critical that the environment support this effort and not get in your way.

In setting up your own mediation offices, consider having
extra sound attenuation features built into your office suite. Engi-
neering specialists can make sure that the builders do everything

they can to enhance privacy in the rooms. While it is expensive and often out of reach to truly soundproof rooms, there are many things that can be done to make rooms more private, including caulking around electrical outlets, extending walls upward past ceilings to the deck above the ceiling, adding insulation to walls and above ceilings, and adding weather stripping to doors. You might also take a tip from psychotherapists, who have learned that an inexpensive white noise machine placed in a corridor interferes with sounds that drift from consultation rooms into the hall.[1]

Outside Communications

When you are meeting with one party in caucus, the other may need to make phone calls, possibly to talk to attorneys or constituents. Make sure that there are opportunities for those private communications in the space where you conduct the mediation.

Furniture and Seating

People were dismayed at the protracted negotiations concerning the shape of the table for the Paris Peace Talks during the Vietnam War. Mediators worldwide watched with trepidation as Gorbachev and Reagan conducted their negotiations directly across the table from one another, reinforcing an obviously "positional" and "adversarial" stance with one another.

What are the ideal room arrangements for a mediation? While mediators may differ in their responses to this question, the following guidelines would be supported by most:

• *If at all possible, seat parties so that they do not square off directly against, across from, or opposed to one another.* For example, if the parties can be seated at a round table, or even on the corners of a rectangular table, the physical setting may be more conducive to side-by-side problem solving than to looking at the other person as an adversary. Remember that the objective is to get the parties to move from their positions in such a way that they identify interests, create new options, and solve the problem together. Let their position at the table reflect this if at all possible (see Figure 5.1 for options).

Figure 5.1. Conference-Style Mediation Arrangements.

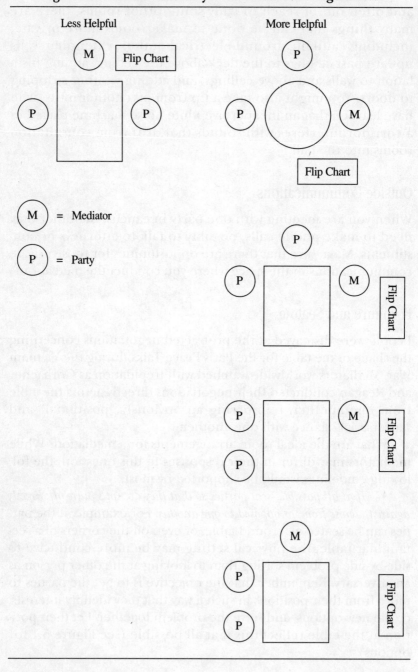

- *Have chairs for the parties that are equal in size and height.* It won't do to have one party sitting on an overstuffed low couch and another party sitting two inches higher in a Queen Anne or wing-back chair. The "power seat" gives an advantage to one party over the other.

- *Sitting around a table may help the parties get down to business, but parlor seating might be useful at times to give a more relaxed atmosphere.* Parlor seating is especially good for some caucuses (Figure 5.2). On the one hand, parlor seating can give parties the feeling of being in a living room and therefore bring more openness to the proceedings. On the other hand, at meetings other than caucuses, it exposes the parties to one another (there is no conference table to separate them), and if the parties are particularly adversarial, then the focus of a common table on which to rest elbows and lay materials will be important. Also, if there is a great deal of paperwork to be examined, then a table is required.

- *Sideboards and credenzas are useful for holding materials.* Remember that attorneys are used to walking into court with briefcases and files and will need a place to put their papers. Also,

Figure 5.2. Parlor-Style Mediation Arrangements.

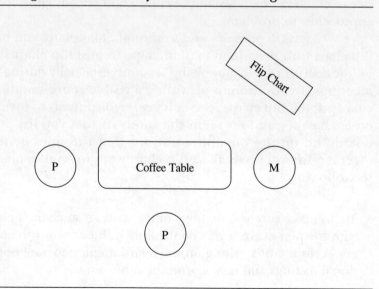

walking in and laying materials on the table can be a way of controlling the atmosphere. If you do not want someone to take over the table this way, then it is incumbent upon you to provide alternative space. Sideboards and credenzas are useful for this. The tops should be kept clear so that people can put things on them.

• *Flexibility and several options in furniture may give you an additional tool.* Moving around can encourage flexibility and the pursuit of various options in how the parties think about the problem. An ideal room arrangement might include both a conference table and space for parlor seating, with credenzas convenient to both. It can be useful in the mediation to be able to stand up from the table, walk over to a new place in the room, and sit down in another chair, as if to model or encourage trying another view of the problem. Any time you as mediator have environmental flexibility, you will be able to encourage the parties in more creative ways. For example, if a table is available, you can at some point say, "Let's go over and crank out these numbers and see what happens." Or you could walk in after a break and suggest, "Let's sit over here; these chairs are more comfortable," if you judge that move would be useful. Furthermore, if your room is set up with corridors and access to the outside, then you will be able to take a walk with people for a break, all in the service of creating flexibility and openness and encouraging creative approaches to problems.

• *Flip charts provide useful focal points.* Make sure you have a flip chart with pens (and masking tape to post flip chart sheets on the wall) for problem-solving sessions, especially during joint meetings. In addition to providing a visible representation of concepts, the flip chart helps you get the disputants to focus less on each other and more on the interests that you list on the board and on the possible solutions that the sides generate together. In order to make a flip chart work for you, remember the following:

• Try to make sure you do most of the writing, since the person with the pen exerts a very controlling influence over the others. A disputant's writing on the board might generate oppositional feelings and behavior in the other side.

- Beware of dignifying intransigent positions by listing them on the flip chart. Instead, list interests that the parties can explore and attempt to honor in negotiations, as well as relevant facts and options that grow from brainstorming.
- Let your trips to the flip chart be movements of hope. For example, as interests (the goal in any mediation) are identified, you might stand up, move to the flip chart, and say, "Let's write some of this down."
- Keep all flip charts generated throughout the mediation as confidential materials and keep track of them. Put dates on each sheet at the end of the session so you will know when that material was generated.

  - *Try a kitchen.* The Judicial Arbitration and Mediation Service (JAMS) in Houston set up a 1950s-style kitchen, complete with icebox, small-size Coke bottles, kitchen sink, tables, and chairs to give a feel of the family kitchen as a setting for talking over problems in caucus. Use your own creativity in setting up anything in your office environment that seems to encourage constructive problem solving for the parties.

Refreshments

As a mediator, you will want to have coffee and tea (decaf is recommended since tensions will be at their highest and caffeine can work against you), soft drinks, juice, and water available for the disputants. Some mediators set up the coffee, tea, and cookies in a part of the room where the parties are encouraged to serve one another. This is a variation on the hostage negotiation strategy in which individuals who have taken hostages are not simply given sandwiches but are instead sent food that needs to be assembled. The aim is to force people to work together, in the hope that they will build human bonds that may interfere with plans to hurt individuals should negotiations break down. Mediators differ on the extent to which they will mediate through mealtimes (for example, lunch and dinner). The main consideration is to provide for the physical needs of the parties and to make the social offer of something to drink and eat an overture that can create an atmosphere conducive to mutual respect and, one hopes, positive talk.

Make Adjustments

Honor as many of the preceding considerations as you can, though do not worry if the conditions aren't perfect. With the exception of privacy, everything else can be worked around. As a matter of fact, in some early research on differing environmental conditions for counseling, a colleague and I found that counselors who had the worst conditions actually performed the best on a number of counseling dimensions.[2] In speculating about our finding, we concluded that under more adverse circumstances, people actually worked harder to build rapport and bridges with counselees. Something similar may apply to mediation as well. The main point to remember is that you are a guardian of the process and that everything in the environment should be set up as best you can to encourage an atmosphere of fairness, respect for the parties, and problem solving (as opposed to adversarial positioning). Once you have set the table, you are ready for the opening meeting.

EXERCISES

1.   Having reviewed the material in this chapter, make a to-do list for improvements you need to make in your own office or conference room in order to equip it for mediation (for example, soundproofing caucus rooms).

2.   Describe features of the worst physical setting in which you have ever participated as a mediator or as a party in dispute resolution. What were the drawbacks of the physical setting? How would you improve them?

3.   Describe the best physical setting in which you ever participated as a mediator or as a party. What features made it an unusually positive setting for mediation?

The Opening Meeting

Once you have identified the parties and they have agreed to start mediation, and once the table has been set and preparations made, the process usually proceeds with an opening meeting where all parties are present. In some cases, this can be done over the telephone (for example, when the parties live in different cities and economic considerations argue for beginning the caucuses with each party before the parties are brought together in one room). Many things said in the opening meeting will have been covered on the telephone during first contact, though the credibility of the mediator and the process is enhanced when all parties hear the same guidelines and ground rules from the mediator at the same time. The next chapter outlines the main points to be covered in the opening meeting.

Chapter Six

Conducting the First Meeting

Imagine yourself as one of the disputants walking into the room for the first mediation session. Without a doubt, you will be experiencing one or more strong feelings, perhaps anxiety about what will happen or what you will be asked to say or do. Perhaps you will feel anger toward your opponent and a real pessimism whether anything good can happen here. Even if you have been a part of previous mediations, you may wonder if it will do any good this time. Even if the mediator has strong credentials, and even if you may have been impressed or reassured by the first phone conversation, you may be nervous as you anticipate what will happen next. You wonder how this mediator will handle the session. Where should you sit? When will you be asked to talk? What if the other side attacks you? What if you lose your temper?

It's Your Meeting: Take the Lead!

Now switch hats and picture yourself as the mediator, watching two or more anxious parties like the one just described walking into the room.

As a mediator, your best counter to the parties' worries is to lead the meeting in such a way that you reassure the parties about the process and educate them about how to make use of its possible benefits. The opening meeting is your second important opportunity (after the first contact) to begin educating the parties about how to approach the problem at hand and how to open their minds to a collaborative approach to resolution. Everything you say and do, coupled with the way you have the room set up, sets a tone for moving the disputants away from avoidance, higher authority posturing, and power plays and toward collaboration.

CONFIDENTIALITY

One of the hallmarks of mediation is the confidentiality given by the mediator to the material presented by the parties. Confidentiality is valuable because it allows the parties to talk openly about interests, feelings, worries, concerns, and fallback positions with a trusted outsider, the mediator. Even more, it lets the parties evaluate these issues critically in a private setting, without any danger of having the material used against the disclosing party. Your mediation ground rules should state clearly that the parties agree to this provision, which means that they will give up the right to pull you into a higher-authority proceeding such as litigation later. Let them know further that the notes you take are for your own purposes in tracking the volume of material that they arc giving you. As an additional protection, some mediators promise to destroy all notes following the completion of the mediation.

The second dimension of confidentiality, of course, is that promised to the parties by the mediator regarding information given in caucus during the mediation. The mediator here commits to using information for his or her own education and promises not to disclose the information to the other side without the permission or request of the original party.

The major exceptions to the confidentiality guidelines are those common to all professions in most states, namely, threats to life and limb, including abuse of children. Some mediators include a provision on their agreement to mediate that identifies this limitation on confidentiality.

Your objectives in the first meeting are quite straightforward:
- *To explain the mediation process,* saying enough about yourself so that the parties understand who you are, and to answer ques-

tions about mediation, so that the parties can say yes to mediation and sign the agreement to mediate.

- *To hear opening statements from each side,* and then to take questions of clarification (while allowing no bargaining, negotiation, arguing, or fighting) as a prelude to caucuses where you will hear much more about the problem.

- *To adjourn the meeting and begin caucuses* with one party, arranging for the other party or parties to either wait in another room, make phone calls, or leave with an agreement to be available at another specified time.

The Mediator's Opening Statement

You have invited the parties into the room, offered them chairs around the table (or in the parlor-style seating arrangement), and offered coffee, tea, or a glass of water to everyone. Introductions will have been made in the waiting room (introducing parties to one another, much as you would guests at a dinner party; in some cases, you will need to introduce yourself to new faces and then introduce the others to one another). Jokes about the weather, parking, office decor, and other expressions of nervousness will have been made. If the parties are totally at loggerheads, so angry with one another they will not speak or even look at one another, you will have noticed this already. Some people might position themselves as far away from the other disputant as possible. Others might search for ways to position themselves closer to or farther from the mediator, depending upon their own agenda or plan for seeking favor. Some may have their briefcases already open and may begin putting papers on the table, as if to pass them out in an attempt to control the situation by providing information (perhaps in neat folders), even though you have not asked for any such materials to be distributed in this manner.

As the parties sit down and settle themselves in chairs, eyes will soon turn toward you as mediator. What do you say?

Your opening statement must cover all of the essentials of mediation. It would be a mistake for you to assume that all the parties have read and fully understood your written materials even though they may say they have. This is your opportunity to highlight the chief features of mediation, to tell how you do mediation and what your background is, and to structure the ground rules, all on the way toward affirming an agreement to mediate.

"Here Is My Handout"

One of the last things you as a mediator want is for the parties to pass out statements of their positions or proposals. By committing their positions to writing, they may have become more firmly entrenched. Furthermore, they may put themselves in a situation where it is hard to move on from the written statement that they generated in the beginning. The tactic you may use is to simply "receive" the written materials, thank the party for generating them, and say something along the lines of, "We will talk about these in a while." The time you most want to talk about these materials, of course, will be in the private caucuses, when you can explore the interests that underlie the written words. Thereafter, your best approach is simply to soft-pedal these materials, using them primarily as a starting point for exploring interests—and *not* letting them take over the mediation. Instead of position papers from the parties, you will want to generate a discussion of interests, other facts, and proposals, on the way toward the written one-text statement that *you* will create (based on the parties' statements) and encourage the parties to test and refine.

Here is an opening statement used by one mediator:[1]

We're here today because your process improvement team ran into some problems. As you have described it to me, there was an open conflict at your last meeting, the meeting broke down and some of the team members then asked me to assist you in trying to reach a resolution.

As I have mentioned to each of you, mediation is a process through which a third party assists two or more other parties in finding their own solutions to problems. I'm not here as a judge, to tell anyone what to do, or as an advocate for any of you individually.

Mediation is confidential. Whatever you say to me, stays with me, unless you ask me to communicate a message to the other parties.

Here's how the process works:

After I finish my opening remarks, I'll ask each of you to tell us why you're here. I'll invite you to ask questions and clarify some issues.

We'll follow the opening meeting with a round of caucuses. Caucuses are private, confidential meetings with each party. I won't convey anything I learn in a caucus to another party without permission. The purpose of the caucuses is to help me understand more about what each of you wants or needs. I'll ask you not to attach any importance to the order or length of the caucuses—I'll conduct them in whatever way will best help us move forward.

After the caucuses, I'll either get us all back together or I'll continue to shuttle. I'll do whatever will work best to help you reach a solution.

We'll close with a joint meeting, either to confirm an agreement or to declare an impasse.

A few ground rules:

- I ask that you not interrupt one another.

- If you have questions or comments, please jot them down—I'll make sure you have a chance to raise them.

- I will assume that it's acceptable to use first names.

- If you reach an agreement, or if you don't, I'll help you decide what and how to report back to the team.

Any questions?

Okay. Normally I ask the party that requested mediation to start. Jack, can you tell us why you are here?

You may be interrupted during your opening statement, in which case respond to questions briefly, but then keep moving. Once you have finished, ask for questions of clarification, and answer each in a straightforward manner. Look at all nonverbal indications from the parties that might indicate confusion (quizzical looks, raised eyebrows, frowns) or outright disbelief about what they are hearing from you about the process. It is critical to the mediation process that there be a clear understanding up front about what mediation is, how the mediator will conduct the meetings, and what is expected of each person. Do not be surprised if you are asked questions about confidentiality and about your own bias or neutrality. ("How long have you been working for this insurance company?" a plaintiff's attorney might ask. Your response ought to be something like this: "I do not work for _____ insurance company. I have mediated cases where _____ has been one of the parties, but in each case, I am employed and paid by both sides. Perhaps you have a question, though, about my neutrality in this case. Do you?")

Most mediators develop an opening statement that can be adjusted to particular circumstances, though it will always include the essential elements to inform the parties about the process. Many find it useful to practice the opening statement with a colleague in order to identify areas that will need more explanation, or that raise additional questions.

EYE CONTACT AND BALANCE

Do not be surprised if one or more of the disputants tries to pull you in on his or her side of the issue through eye contact or perhaps even by saying positive things about you or the process. Your best protection against such maneuvers by disputants is to make sure your eye contact shifts naturally from one party to the other throughout your opening statement and that you do not allow yourself to give more nonverbal attention to one party than to the other. This is a simple skill that you can learn with practice.

In addition, make sure that you maintain your own physical position (chair and seating arrangement) of neutrality. I have seen situations where disputants will move a chair closer to the mediator as they address their opponent, thereby shifting the balance in the room arrangement. Do not be shy about making your own compensation by moving your own chair so that you maintain a position of balance with the parties.

The Parties' Opening Statements

The parties may well have already gone through depositions with one another, submitted preconference information to the mediator, and have been involved in verbal battles in parking lots, corporate suites, or bedrooms. Still, it is important for you as mediator to invite them now to make a simple, straightforward opening statement about what each one views as the issues to be mediated and each one's individual interests in being a part of the mediation process. In a very real sense, this is your opportunity to give them a new statement to put forward, one that has a chance to displace many of the other ineffective, dysfunctional, and perhaps ugly statements they have made to one another before the mediation began.

Invite opening statements as follows:

> Now I would like to hear from each of you as to how you view the issue that brought you to mediation. In particular, I would like to hear your own summary of the issues as you see them, and what you would like to accomplish in mediation. I am not asking at this time for you to negotiate or bargain with one another but rather simply to give your own summary of the issues as you see them. I will ask you to make these statements brief and without interruption from anyone else. After each of you has finished, I will invite questions of clarification only; there won't be any bargaining or negotiating right now but simply sharing information and clarifying anything that you did not understand in the opening statement from the other person. After these questions have been answered, then we will adjourn and proceed to caucuses.

Some parties will bring in written statements, others will pass out materials for people to read. (This can be a very controlling maneuver on their part. See the coaching tip "Here is My Handout" for ways to deal with it.) The main point is that you allow the opening statements to go on only for a matter of minutes or so, unless it seems to you that the time should be longer. This is not a time for lengthy arguments but rather for short summaries.

Reprimands and Reinforcements

If one party does interrupt another, as can certainly happen if someone is terribly angry or upset with another person, then you will have to stop the interruption firmly, though with respect offered to the person who is doing the interrupting: "I must ask that you not interrupt. You will have a chance to speak soon. Thank you."

A good tactic is to offer your thanks or encouragement immediately after you have made a reprimand or asked someone to do something, as if to imply: "I've now reprimanded you and asked you to stop doing something, and I know (or at least hope I know) that you will stop doing it; therefore, I will say 'thank you' to you right now." This gives you an opportunity to keep things on a positive footing throughout.

Questions of Clarification and Answers

I find it useful to invite questions of clarification only after everyone has had an opportunity to talk. In opening this phase of the first meeting, I will restate that we are looking here for questions of clarification only. This is my way of saying that the parties now have an opportunity to ask about something they have heard that they did not understand but not to spend a great deal of time elaborating on the disagreement. For example, in personal injury cases or medical malpractice cases, it is not at all uncommon for the parties to find out that they do not have the same copies of medical reports or other seemingly routine information. They can actually exchange this material at that moment, if that seems appropriate. Or someone may refer to calling an office on three occasions and getting no response, and someone else might say it is hard to understand why that happened because people were there. By allowing the parties to state such things, you are simply giving them an opportunity to highlight their differing views of past events.

Two good things come out of this approach. The first is that people are allowed to go on record with one another in the opening meeting as having different views, different perceptions, and different information. This might actually be a saving dimension for resolving conflict later: that is, it might suggest that if they have different information, no wonder they differed so much in the early going, and now that they have the same information, they may have a reason for agreeing.

In addition to clarifying past events, in some cases the new information itself may well lead to solutions that were not available before. Remember that as mediator, one of the most powerful things you are doing is getting the parties in the room together. The information sharing is the first opportunity these people may have for laying the groundwork for later agreement.

Co-Mediation

There are several circumstances in which it might be advantageous to have a co-mediator:

- *Multiple parties.* If you have multiple parties, each including many members of a negotiating team, then it helps to have more than one person listening, taking notes, and reflecting on the information generated in caucuses and joint meetings. In an organizational dispute, for example, a co-mediator and I held caucuses with some groups that numbered twenty-five or more people. It would have been almost impossible for one person to ask questions, take notes, and monitor the nonverbal communication of that group. For two people, the task was manageable.
- *Gender balance.* For some disputes, such as divorce mediation or team issues involving males and females in various levels of the organizational hierarchy, it can be useful to have a gender balance represented in the mediation team. The advantages of having a male and a female mediator, however, must be weighed alongside the expense of the parties paying for two mediators instead of one.
- *Training.* A co-mediator serving in a "second chair" position can learn a great deal about the mediation process as a trainee, and, at the same time, take an additional set of notes and serve as a reality check for the mediator in evaluating data. I have had uniformly positive experiences with co-mediation

and consider it to be one of the more enjoyable ways to do mediation. It alleviates the pressure of assimilating a mountain of data and always provides rich opportunities for discussion with my colleague regarding the process.

Signing Agreement to Mediate

Once the parties understand the nature of the mediation process and have had a chance to identify issues they wish to put on the table, including asking questions of clarification, the next step is for the parties and the mediator to confirm that they are willing to go forward under the mediation ground rules. This is typically accomplished through signing a written agreement to mediate (see sample in Resource B). For some disputes (for example, an intrateam dispute in an organization), the mediator may not have the parties sign a formal agreement to mediate. It will be important, however, to get the parties to state verbally their assent to proceeding with mediation according to the ground rules.

Adjournment

Once opening statements have been made, and questions of clarification asked and answered, you can adjourn the opening meeting and proceed to caucuses. In adjourning the meeting, review with the parties what you will be doing next (the confidential caucuses) and ask who might like to go first or second. Sometimes there may be a particular reason for one person to go first or second. In some mediations (such as those involving a number of parties in a large organizational or community dispute), the caucuses will be spread out over several days, and you will now schedule these meetings so that some people can leave and return at a later time. In all of your talks with the parties, just as in the opening statement, maintain your stance of neutrality and objectivity and let the parties know you will be talking with everyone, that the order makes no difference, and as discussed earlier, that even the amount of time you spend in caucus is not be "over-interpreted" by the parties. You may need to ask more questions of some people than you do of others, or they may have more to tell you.

Right through to adjournment, maintain a sense of control over the entire process, including the people who leave the meeting, where they go, and when they are to return. Do this with an approach of firmness and grace and let there be no doubt that this is your meeting and that you look forward to talking to each person in the individual meetings and then convening them at another time.

PROCESS DO'S AND DON'TS

DO	DON'T
Maintain eye contact in a balanced way with each party.	Allow yourself to get pulled into giving more nonverbal attention to one side than the other.
Explain the process in plain language, checking to make sure that everyone understands it.	Allow yourself to use jargon or leave terms vague.
Reinforce cooperative behavior whenever you can (for example, say, "It is good that you have taken this step to come together now").	Miss opportunities to offer verbal rewards for steps toward cooperation.

Telephone Mediation

In many cases, it is inefficient or too costly for the parties to meet face-to-face, and telephone mediation becomes the treatment of choice. Mediators can build on a long and strong tradition of the use of the telephone in counseling situations, dating back to hot lines during the 1960s, coupled with recent technological innovations such as easily scheduled conference calls, to turn this situation to the advantage of the parties. Since most business people spend a great deal of working time talking on the telephone anyway, the use of telephone mediation as a variation on the theme will in most cases be well received by the parties.

Research on telephone counseling yields the following peculiarities of telephone communication that you should be aware of in conducting telephone mediation:

- *Some people love the telephone and some people hate it* (often owing to childhood experiences where the telephone was a focus of conflict), so be guided by the parties in whether you use telephone contact frequently or at all during mediation.

- *The absence of nonverbal cues* (facial expressions, posture) to indicate acceptance or rejection of messages is the chief disadvantage of telephone communication.

- *Some parties will talk more candidly* with the mediator in a private phone conversation than they would face-to-face.

- *The major use of telephone mediation may be as a follow-up or adjunct to face-to-face meetings.* For example, in a large multiparty organizational dispute, once an opening round of caucuses has been completed, you may follow up with others on the telephone, often outside of work hours. The chief advantage is that there is no travel time involved, and it is often possible to schedule a very fruitful twenty- to thirty-minute talk around other activities.

- *It is possible to conduct the entire mediation by telephone when the parties live extreme distances from one another,* as long as ground rules are specified ahead of time. The most efficient approach is to send out information to all the parties at the beginning (after each has given permission to receive information), next to schedule individual calls with each party to explain the ground rules, and then to convene a larger conference call (after individual questions have been answered) to begin the mediation process in earnest. It is important for the mediator to take the initiative in guiding the process, asking each individual to speak in turn following formal opening statements, much as in the original face-to-face meeting described earlier.

- *You can take notes freely,* without worrying that your note-taking behavior will interfere with the parties.

- *Avoid cellular phones, as they do not ensure confidentiality.* It will be important to discuss this with the parties and to use phones that do honor confidentiality of communications.
- *Take advantage of speaker phones.* You can be in one office with a group of parties in another, and perhaps another group of parties elsewhere, and still hold a mutual discussion efficiently, without all the parties having to get together in a face-to-face meeting.

EXERCISES

1.   Using one of the cases in Resource F (or another of your choosing), pretend you are in the opening session of a mediation and assign roles to at least two other people. Make your opening statement about what mediation is and then answer questions from the parties. After completing one round, debrief regarding strengths and weaknesses of the opening statement and then exchange roles.

2.   Repeat the preceding, but in this case, have one of the parties interrupt the mediator to challenge the other party, with the second party responding in kind. In the debriefing, evaluate the mediator's ability to calmly yet firmly regain control of the process, coaching the parties to (1) allow the speaker to finish and (2) save their remarks for their own opening statements, which will also be completed without interruption.

The Caucus Process

You have identified the parties and convened them for an opening meeting. You have explained the rules of mediation, and the parties have agreed to abide by them. They have each given opening statements on the problem as they see it now and what they hope to accomplish in mediation. You have set the stage for private caucuses with each party and are now ready to walk into the room to meet with the first person (or group) for a private exploration of the conflict.

Chapter Seven

Conducting Separate Meetings

Think of the caucuses as your opportunity to get to the heart of the matter in the dispute. You are going to have a chance to talk to each person outside the hearing of the adversary, away from the public and the media, and ask questions to find out what he or she really wants and needs. What is really driving this dispute for this person? What will it take to get a yes from this person and to walk down a new path, or to put the matter to rest and go forward in the future? Your objective in each caucus meeting is to emerge smarter than when you went in about (1) this person's interests, (2) important facts as this person sees them, (3) what this person will do if the mediation fails to reach agreement, and (4) possible integrative solutions. Your approach will be to elicit enough solid information to begin completing the Conflict Grid (Figure 2.1) for this client.

You also have a second objective: to keep the parties on track and to maintain commitment and involvement in the process. It won't be easy, because the parties may still be demoralized about the dispute and discouraged about any possible outcome. After all, they have finished only one opening meeting at this point and likely still see no reason for hope. You will counter this in the caucus meetings by providing an atmosphere of trust and of acceptance of this person and the pain or worry as he or she sees it. If you are doing your job well, the party may feel that the "understanding" part of the caucus is like a counseling session. Your goal here is to give the person the opportunity to open up his or her heart about the dispute, with the confidence that feelings and views will be heard and respected and not carried to the other side or used against the person. Also, you will provide ample encouragement, positive reinforcement, and strokes for problem-solving behavior, that is, for talking about the problem and its parameters, interests, and other facts. You might say, "That's very helpful!" when a person describes the problem in detail. Or you might say, "I am impressed with how much energy you have put into this already," as a way of encouraging problem solving.

Caucus Steps

There is an identifiable flow to a well-conducted caucus. The party with whom you are about to speak may begin with more questions about the mediation process, a harangue about the other side, dire predictions about what will happen if mediation breaks down, or with a well thought out statement about interests and options for solutions. You will never know until you begin the conversation. It is a safe bet, however, that the party will begin with something far removed from what the five-step model views as the heart of the matter, namely, key interests and other facts that must be honored in order for integrative solutions to be created. While you cannot expect that every caucus will proceed in the same way, consider the following guideposts for leading the parties through the myriad of details, emotions, positions, and offers that are bound to emerge:

- Begin with a review of confidentiality and then ask an open-ended question to start the conversation.
- As the person begins to tell the story, use active listening and questions to clarify and summarize data for the Conflict Grid.
- Take notes.
- Test perceptions by asking questions about how this party views the other party's interests and positions.
- Use confrontation, evaluation of strengths and weaknesses of proposals, and focus on competing interests to loosen fixed positions and encourage movement.
- Summarize frequently and, if necessary, float test balloons for possible integrative solutions.
- Close with a reminder of confidentiality, an open-ended

inquiry about other topics, and a request for instructions on any messages to be communicated to the other side.

• Continue caucuses with the other party or parties.

Detailed Walk-Through

There are many things to think about in each of these steps.

• *Begin with a review of confidentiality and then ask an open-ended question to start the conversation.* Even though you will have already stated it in the opening meeting, every caucus should begin with a reminder about confidentiality. The statement can go something like this:

> I would like to remind you that everything you say to me in this caucus will be held in confidence by me, and I will not reveal it to anyone else unless you ask me to—and I agree to do so. My goal right now is to understand as best I can how you view the situation, and in particular to understand your interests, and what you will most need in order to achieve some settlement or solution. This being said, start wherever you like in telling me anything that you perhaps did not mention in the opening meeting, and would like to say now, or anything said in the opening session that you would like to underline or flag for my attention. Start wherever you like.

With an opening along these lines, your goal is to be both open-ended ("tell me anything you want") and, at the same time, to pave the way for a focus on key interests ("tell me what you need or most care about"). The confidentiality statement at the start will be repeated at the end of the caucus. Remember that mediation may well be an unfamiliar process to the parties, and you will need to continue to structure the process by reminding them of certain ground rules along the way. Emphasizing confidentiality is your way of inviting the parties to open up to you about key interests.

• *As the person begins to tell the story, use active listening and questions to clarify and summarize data for the Conflict Grid.* Active listening (see Resource A) is a basic communication skill that allows you to record vital information and, at the same time, let the speaker know that you are paying attention to what he or she is trying to say. Active listening is also a way to build and maintain rapport with the person who is talking. Whenever you make statements such as: "It sounds like what you care about most here is . . . ," or, "If I'm hearing you correctly, there are at least three parts of this that must be addressed in any solution that would emerge from mediation," or any similar statement, you are building a bridge of understanding between yourself and the party. While you may not agree with what is being said, you show respect by actively listening and demonstrating that you want to check the accuracy of what you are hearing. Done well, active listening communicates respect for the person and his or her right to have a view, feeling, or perspective on the matter at hand.

"I'LL BE TAKING NOTES . . ."

Let the parties know that you will be taking notes and that you encourage them to do the same. Provide them with pads of paper and pens, encouraging them to keep track of what they are hearing, all with a view to better understanding what the other person needs and clarifying points for discussion.

Note-taking behavior can also be an alternative to interrupting behavior for some parties, and you can encourage them to write down reactions they have to statements from the other side instead of interrupting at will.

Note taking can be a very useful tool for the mediator to use to encourage the parties in collaborative behavior. Later, you can model respectful listening by referring to your notes, and checking reality with the parties. For example, "As I look at my notes, I see at least two very clear interests that you both share, and I see a couple of others that are unique to each of you. Here's what I have so far . . ."

Beginning to work with the Conflict Grid. I recall an opening caucus with a wife in a divorce mediation several years ago. In the opening meeting, she had declared that there was no way she would say yes to joint conservatorship (whereby she would be involved in shared decision making with her soon-to-be ex-husband on matters involving the children) and that she would settle for nothing less than being named as sole managing conservator. Though her husband asked her in the opening meeting why she took this position, she avoided a direct answer, and instead gave a strong but general statement that her children "needed their mother," and she would be in a "better position" to take care of them. In the opening caucus, she began with the same statements. I asked her to say more about why she felt she would be in a better position to take care of the children and why they needed her. It was only at this point that she revealed her true interest, namely, protecting the children from their father's drinking. She reported that every night her husband would begin drinking as soon as he came home from work, continue through the dinner hour, and eventually pass out in the recliner. Her concern was that if there were a fire or emergency involving the children—aged two and four—he would be in no position to protect them, hence her stated position that the children should reside with her, and she be given sole conservatorship. The wife also freely admitted to me that the reason she did not raise the issue in the opening meeting was her fear of upsetting her husband and her concern that he might retaliate in some way for her having raised the issue in mediation. I have little doubt that had we not had private caucuses, the woman would not have been able to speak clearly about her concerns, and we never would have succeeded in truly addressing her underlying needs.

In the mediation caucus, sort everything you hear into one of the four main categories that constitute the Conflict Grid.

- Interests (also, wants, needs, desires, views, and other data internal to the party, that is, inside his or her head or heart)
- Other facts (such as statements about overt behavior and observable data such as the size of a piece of property, or the narrative on a police report, or the written organizational policy, or the stated law)
- BATNA (Best Alternative to a Negotiated Agreement) for this party—what he or she will do if the mediation does not achieve settlement
- Possible solutions (in particular, steps or actions that—if taken or agreed to by the parties—would both honor the interests identified above and square with the other facts)

The wife mentioned earlier identified one of her key interests in her first caucus statement: namely, her interest in protecting her children and her concern that her husband's alcoholism might put them in physical jeopardy. She also expressed fear of retaliation.

Notice that the position she took in the opening meeting, and the one with which she began the caucus, was clearly her own version of a possible solution. If she had spoken all of it out loud, she would have said, "If I am named as sole managing conservator, then I will have final decision on matters involving the children, including residence and other issues, and I can thereby protect my children from their father's alcoholism." Also, by implication, she was saying, "My silence on the matter is a way of protecting myself."

Filling in the blanks. In talking with this party, I now had discovered my first set of interests and was ready for further inquiry. I asked for more information about her husband's drinking patterns: how much he drank, and when? Had he ever been arrested for driving under the influence? Lost a job? Was there anything else about the drinking that she might wish to report?

I also asked about what steps had been taken to deal with the problem. Had there been any attempts at treatment?

I asked her to talk about solutions she had tried and what she might like to do now, inviting her to look at alternatives other than being named as sole managing conservator.

In asking these questions (some open-ended and some of the yes/no variety), I elicited information and mentally filled in the blanks of the Conflict Grid as she spoke. By the end of a brief interview, I had the following information for her column of the grid:

Interests

1. Interest in protecting the children and concern that her husband's alcoholism would pose a physical threat to the children since he might be too inebriated to assist them in an emergency.
2. Concern that he might retaliate and physically abuse her if she raised the issue of his drinking with an outside person, such as the mediator or a physician, and interest in protecting herself.
3. An interest in having the matter resolved as soon as possible

and in being free of the stress that the situation brought to her and her children.

Other Facts

1. Her husband had been unemployed for several months.
2. Alcoholism ran in the husband's family (father and two uncles diagnosed as alcoholic).
3. While the husband had not ever harmed her physically, he had made verbal threats to take the children and to hurt her in ways she "would never forget."
4. The husband had no history of treatment for alcoholism.

BATNA

1. If no agreement was reached in mediation, she planned on asking her attorney for a temporary restraining order to keep her husband away from her and the children. She was concerned that this would enflame the situation further but would do it if she had to.

Possible Solutions

1. Have the mediator talk to her husband to see if he would raise the issue of drinking himself (perhaps in response to a question such as, "What do you think your wife is concerned about?"), thereby giving the mediator an opportunity to talk with the husband about any concerns the husband might have, and to assess any flexibility or openness on his part to take steps that would reassure the wife.
2. Explore the possibility of treatment for the husband and postpone final decision on conservatorship until an evaluation of the situation with alcohol had been completed, and treatment had been begun, allowing for input from treatment personnel.
3. Fashion some temporary agreement about care of the children (especially during the evenings, when the drinking occurred) that could be supported by both husband and wife.
4. After eliciting more data on potential for physical violence (retaliation), secure a "no harm" commitment from the husband, with agreement to voluntarily stay away from the wife,

including a fallback plan (temporary restraining order) that the wife would trigger if necessary.

VIOLENCE

Violence is one form of unilateral power play (Table 1.1), whether it takes the form of a threat or an actual assault resulting in physical harm or death. Mediators need to take special note of the history of violent activity among the parties, as well as any current threats, since the presence of either will have a significant effect on the parties' ability to negotiate and their willingness to consider certain options presented for resolution. Also, there are differences in how mediators deal with the possibility of violent action in international dispute resolution as compared with workplace disputes or domestic situations such as divorce mediation. Throughout this volume, we will assume the following regarding the mediator's responsibilities in these situations:

• *The potential for violence is present in most disputes,* whether domestic, workplace, or international. The key diagnostic variables include the psychological state of the parties and the cultural variables that surround the conflict. And there are a host of other factors that can tilt the balance in one direction or another at any point.

• *The first contact and the first round of caucuses are the mediator's primary occasions for evaluating the history of violence* and the potential for future violence. For this reason, the model presented in this book will require at least one round of caucuses for every mediation. As a variation on this theme, some mediators use initial screening for domestic cases (see Resource D).

• *Once the mediator has determined that there has been a history of violence, or a current threat, it is important for the mediator to evaluate the potential danger with the party.* This should take place in the private, confidential caucus setting. As necessary, negotiate protections that may need to be built into the process in order for the mediation to go forward: for example, the use of separate meetings instead of joint meetings, or the making of formal commitments by the parties and their advocates to maintain physical separation of the parties outside the mediation sessions. In international disputes, the mediator will seek agreement to lay down arms for a specific period of time as negotiations continue.

- *When violence has been a part of the history, or there is a threat of future violence, the mediator must continually evaluate the situation with each of the parties,* and be prepared to make other adjustments in the process in order to allow the mediation to continue.

- *Mediators should seek training in the role of violence in the substantive areas in which they offer mediation.* For example, see Resource D for guidelines on mediation of disputes involving domestic violence.

- *Take notes.* You will hear so much information through the course of the mediation that it will be almost impossible to remember it all without keeping written notes. Tell the parties in the very beginning that the notes are for your benefit, to help you keep things straight, and will be seen by no one except you. With this background, the parties will view your note taking as a sign of your diligence and professionalism instead of something to fear. Remember that in most jurisdictions, neither the mediator's notes nor any other statements made in mediation may be subpoenaed into subsequent litigation.

Shorthand will certainly help in recording information when it is coming at you in the rapid pace that often characterizes caucuses and joint meetings, though even more important will be your own notations on the critical issues for use later. I use the following notations, presented here as an example of one approach only:

✓   I put a check mark by anything that is a key interest. To me, this is the most important information, and when I review all the check marks in the left-hand margins, I know where the interests are.

→   I put a little arrow whenever a possible solution is mentioned. This is an indication that in the future,

	down the line, in the direction of the arrow, this might be an action step that would help.
BATNA	I simply write the word "BATNA" whenever a party describes his or her contingency plans for a mediation impasse.
*	An asterisk reminds me of something that has special importance (alongside interests, it could apply to any piece of information).
t.a.	I write "t.a." for any temporary agreements. If I am in caucus with a party named Mary, and Mary has agreed to a solution, I put "t.a.(M)" in the left-hand margin by that solution. I add a question mark if this looks like a possible temporary agreement that Mary might go along with though we didn't finish it. The note would then read "t.a.(M)?" to remind me that at the next meeting I will need to go back to Mary to discuss this further.
f.a.	I save the "f.a." designation for final agreement. When I dictate the memorandum of agreement, the body includes all of the items coded "f.a." in my notes.

All these notations occur in the left-hand margin of a sheet of standard letter-size lined paper, and allow me to find key information readily. Anything that does not receive one of these notations will likely fall into the category of other facts—that is, narrative and background information.

Finally, at the end of each mediation caucus, I make a to-do list that summarizes who is going to do what before the next meeting. Later, as I review the notes from a caucus or joint meeting, I can see the most important information, and also see where we left the matter at our last talk.

• *Test perceptions by asking questions about how this party views the other party's interests and positions.* In the midst of a dispute, when the air is filled with accusation, defense, and verbal bobbing and weaving, it is the rare party who has a true appreciation of the underlying interests of the other side. There is a logic to this confusion, since the other side often obfuscates interests through positional bargaining.

You will learn a great deal about the party you are dealing with if you ask questions such as the following:

- What do you think the other side really needs or wants here?
- What are her interests, as you understand them?
- What do you suppose it really takes for her to reach an agreement with you on this matter?

Take careful notes on what you hear, and you will gain in several ways. For one, you may get some foreshadowing of what to expect when you meet with the other party. Having been forewarned, you may be able to conduct a better interview. Also, you will get a feel for how in or out of touch this person is with realities on the other side. If you discover that the person has missed key interests, this may shed light on why the two have failed to reach agreement up to this point, and you may be able to mention this to the party as a sign of hope ("You know, it seems that you have been in a rough spot, negotiating without knowing what the other side truly must have in order to settle. Perhaps if we can find out, we can get the negotiations unstuck.")

Or after talking to the other side and finding out what his or her interests are, and with the permission of the other side, you can compare the stated interests with what the perceived interests had been up to that point. This sort of reality testing is standard fare in mediation. Let's listen in on the way a mediator might put it to a client who has been out of touch with what the other side most wanted:

Mediator: Bob, you seem to be operating under the assumption that Joe wants your job and will do anything he can to get it. If you are correct, and this is all he wants and nothing else, then, I suppose, your battle stance with him (trying to stop him and subvert him at any cost) makes sense. It is a warfare approach that you have taken to counter what you consider to be an aggressive and hostile interest on his part.

But what if you are wrong? What if he's not simply out to get your job? What if something else is driving him? I can imagine he has other interests as well. I'll bet he wants job security. His children are at the age where a move may be disruptive to him. Maybe he has an interest in staying put. Maybe there are some aspects of your job that he wants, though he might be able to get them in some other ways. The fact of the matter is that, by your own admission, he has never told you in so many words what he really wants. All that you know about his interests now is by inference, extrapolating from his behavior—from things he has said, things he has done.

What if we found a way for you to better understand his interests? Perhaps we could structure a meeting where the two of you could talk more about what you most need here.

Bob: You can't expect me to believe that he will actually tell the truth on whether or not he wants my job!

Mediator: You're right; he may not tell the truth about that. But he may open up on other interests that he has, and if he does, that will give you more to go on than you have now. Besides, you must have some curiosity as to how he would respond when asked about this. Maybe I can structure it so the two of you can get together and talk about this, or with his permission, I could tell you what he says to me. What have you got to lose?

Bob: I think I know what he'll say; but go ahead if you want to.

Mediator: [*challenging*] What do you mean, "if *I* want to?" Don't you want to know as well?

Bob: Yeah, I suppose. Have at it. It should be interesting.

Mediator: I agree. I'll talk to him and get back to you.

• *Use confrontation, evaluation of strengths and weaknesses of proposals, and focus on competing interests to loosen fixed positions and encourage movement.* It is true that in the first caucus with each party the primary goal is understanding interests, facts, and the like. However, it is also true that you will be presented with opportunities to make brief interventions that can loosen the ground to prepare for examination of alternatives other than the fixed positions the parties may have brought to mediation in the first place. As the person talks, listen for opportunities to make interventions that will loosen a tight grip on a particular position, or open a door for moving to new and different ground.

Confrontation. Confrontation is an advanced communication skill whose primary purpose is to stop certain behavior, or to channel the discussion in a more constructive direction (see Resource A). If a person is abusing me verbally, then I might want to use confrontation to stop the abuse. If a person won't budge from a fixed position on demand, then confrontation can also be used to get the person to move.

I was well into the caucus with a husband in a divorce mediation, following an opening meeting where I had had to be very assertive in maintaining control of the parties (who had begun by attacking each other verbally), when it became absolutely clear to me that the husband's abrasive, attacking, overbearing way of talking must surely have been a key ingredient in his wife's resistance, not only in these negotiations but also throughout the history of their marriage, leading to her desire to leave him. Based on the strength of my perception of his behavior (knowing how it felt to *me* to listen to him talk that way) and building on my experience with confrontation in other clinical settings, I told him:

> You know, Henry, I could be wrong about this, but I want to give you some feedback, based on the short hour and a half I have been with you. You have been speaking with a loud voice, using big gestures to make your point, and using fairly inflammatory language, like when you called your wife "crazy," "messed up," and said she "better get her act together" in the opening meeting, just before I interrupted. Remember? Now, I'm not here to tell you how to talk to people outside of this mediation, nor am I right now wanting to judge you for how you *think* about your wife, but I do want to tell you that as I hear you talk that way, if the communication were directed at me, I would feel put down, demeaned, and angry. I would either want to shrink away from you, or more likely, find a way to get back at you. In either case, I certainly wouldn't be very open to considering your proposals. Now, what's the point of my saying this to you now? I wonder if your wife might not be feeling some of the same things, and if so, it may say a lot about why she has been so intransigent on this whole issue of conservatorship.

The best confrontations are those that do not attack the other person (leading either to a defense or counterattack) but that use data (as did my report to Henry about the words he used and my own personal reactions) to let a party know how he or she is coming across to the adversary (see Resource A).

In order for confrontation to be effective, you will need to generate enough respect, trust, and rapport to get a hearing from the party. People who have had a great deal of experience in human relations, such as counselors and therapists, are already experienced in confrontation and can transfer this to mediation. Others can learn the skill. Whatever your background, remember that there may be opportunities to make brief confrontations along the way that may lead to a loosening of a position and an openness to other alternatives later. In the case mentioned above, my goal as mediator was to let Henry know that one of the contributing factors to the intransigence of his wife was his own way of communicating. If he could make changes in that, or make some recovery in the way he communicated with her, he might begin to get a different response.

Strengths and Weaknesses of Proposals. It is a tremendous service to a party in a dispute to have some outside person give an evaluation of the case. Indeed, some mediation models are built around the parties' desire to have this. For example, when the mediator is a retired judge, the parties will often ask for the judge's opinion on the case, in particular, "What might another judge or jury say about this case if we ever take it to trial?" This evaluation of strengths and weaknesses is then weighed by each side as the parties negotiate further with one another in the mediation process.

As a mediator, you will need to be careful about giving your opinion, since in doing so you set yourself up as a judge and can be viewed from there on as biased by the party who feels that his or her side did not receive your support. This holds true in caucuses as well as in joint meetings. The primary tactic should be assisting the party in identifying strengths and weaknesses, asking for the party's opinion of the strengths and weaknesses, and using probing questions to create doubt about fixed positions.

A defense attorney might say to you, for example, that liability is clear and there is a 90 percent chance that it will be shown that his client has no liability in this matter and that the case will be thrown out of court. Your reading of a deposition, however, and your listening to the opening statements, may point to an area of weakness in the case that is being overlooked or diminished by the defense counsel. Ask the attorney straight out about how he or she plans to deal with this aspect of the case. Continue to ask questions, in an interview fashion, though be careful that you do not lapse into an interrogating stance, which will lead to defensiveness on the part of the attorney and the possible perception that you are biased in favor of the other side. If your questions do lead the person to accuse you of bias, as they did once to me ("You're making me wonder whose side you're on here!"), then retreat and tell the person, for example: "I'm not on one side or the other; however, in the privacy of this caucus, as we examine the case together, I am trying to help you look at its strengths and weaknesses. So far, you've said that you have a 90 percent certainty of winning on the liability issue, but I haven't heard from you how you plan to handle the challenge that was presented by the plaintiff's side in the opening meeting."

If you as mediator believe that something is being glossed over, the shortest route to take is to say simply that you believe that the point is being glossed over and to suggest (again, in the privacy of the caucus and as a favor to this party) that the party take a look at this point before proceeding further. You might then ask what other ways there are to further evaluate the matter.

The primary purpose is to identify weaknesses and then to create openings for solutions to the problem beyond the original stated positions. It is not all uncommon in the end game of the mediation for the mediator to say to one party in private: "I am thinking of that issue that we identified two or three meetings ago, the weakness on liability, and I wonder if that's not something you need to take into account as you decide whether or not to accept the offer now on the table."

Competing Interests. Leverage in the end game, as we shall see in subsequent chapters, will rest on looking at several interests and not just one. If you wish to use maximum leverage in creating movement toward a new solution, then it is important to identify the competing interests along the way, as they occur. For example, in talking with a husband who is being particularly aggressive and abrasive in negotiations with his soon-to-be ex-wife in a divorce mediation, you might say in caucus:

> It seems clear that there are several interests here. One, of course, is to not pay her a penny more than you have to, especially since

you feel the way you do about the affair she had. And I have heard you say that you do not want to help her in the future, and this seems to grow in part from the anger you have about the marriage and recent events. But at the same time, you have expressed to me a clear interest in caring for your children and wanting a good relationship with them and wanting them to grow up in as normal an environment as possible. If their mother suffers as a result of these negotiations and feels she got a bad deal and if you keep the bitterness going, then you face the prospect of your son and daughter spending the next ten years with a mother who believes their father is continuing to mistreat her. Winning on one of your interests then means losing on the other.

Similar approaches can be taken in caucus with intransigent parties in religious or organizational disputes. I have seen religious factions argue strenuously that money should be taken from one budget item and put into a building fund for a new educational unit that would enhance their children's moral development and faith. Meanwhile, as they argue the case in caucuses and in public meetings, and as their children hear them argue the case at home and over the telephone, these same individuals unknowingly model an attack stance toward others in their congregation that contradicts the very religious ethic they wish to teach children in the new educational building! As a mediator, I am not at all reluctant to point this out in the caucus ("You say you want to win on this issue to build the educational unit, but your approach to winning and doing battle with the other side seems to be giving your own children a lesson that they will have to unlearn if they ever attend classes in the new building. Is that what you want?").

In the first caucuses, a mediation is likely to use each of these "loosening" techniques in a gentle and mild form. The key point is to take advantage of the opportunity at least to identify the contradictory interests at this stage, as a foreshadowing of impasse resolution later on.

• *Summarize frequently, and if necessary float test balloons for possible integrative solutions.* Active listening techniques can be used to summarize data generated along the way, interests that have been stated thus far, and a range of facts, alternatives, and possible solutions. In this first caucus, you will frequently find yourself saying things like: "Let's see what we have so far. I'm hearing this, and this, and this." Or, "There seem to be at least three key interests to be honored here." Or, "It seems you have a lot of information about the school situation, and arrangements for getting the children to and from school, though it seems that there are some real holes still on the topic of the expenses involved in taking care of the children at home."

Look for opportunities to float trial balloons for an integrative solution. Allow yourself, especially in the latter stages of the caucus, to offer "what if" questions to the party. Ask what might happen if the other side were to do this and this party were to do that and someone else were to do something else. Would this get people close, or at least on a path toward solution?

In my caucus with the wife concerned about her husband's alcohol abuse, I asked: "I am wondering, if by some circumstance he were to be sober—free of alcohol—and there were to be an assurance that he did not drink at all, would this make a difference to you?" Her reply in this case was, "Of course, but I do not think it will ever happen."

The latter remark was realistic, and it did not detract from the point. The key issue was that if it could be established that he was not drinking, then we might be able to go down a different path. As a mediator, I then began asking what it would take to establish this. An evaluation? Treatment? Attendance at Alcoholics Anonymous meetings? A certain time period of continuous sobriety? We would have to see at a later time.

Remember that the power of the possible solutions dimension of the Conflict Grid is that it lists solutions that will honor identified interests and square with other facts. This is what separates the mediation approach from that used by many lay people as they try to make demands on one another and impose their own solutions. The untrained negotiator will spend most of his or her energy arguing against the other person's position, and arguing for his or her own position. The seasoned mediator will begin to identify solutions in caucus that *both* honor interests and square with all facts. I frequently tell clients in caucus (especially in the latter stages) that we should treat this like an adult board game, where we are involved in the intellectual challenge of trying to create options that meet these criteria (honoring interests, and squaring with facts). In this very early stage, begin to propose steps that might help, bearing in mind the following:

- Consider small steps instead of large final solutions at this point (for example, agreeing on an evaluation for an alcohol problem instead of agreeing on a final "cure").
- Focus primarily on concrete behavior (for example: "If she were to provide her assurances to you in writing, would that help?" or, "If he were to promise to pick up the children every day promptly at 3:00 and no later than 3:15, would that work?").
- In this first caucus, instead of trying to focus on steps that honor both, or all, interests (because you may not have talked to the other parties yet), focus on small steps that will honor *this party's* interests (for example: "If an independent examiner, one that met with your approval, were to establish that the future medical expenses would be under $5,000, would this help you in coming to a final dollar figure?").

- *Close with a reminder of confidentiality, an open-ended inquiry about other topics, and a request for instructions on any messages to be communicated to the other side.* As a part of the educational process, repeat the confidentiality commitment that you made in the very beginning. A party may have opened up to you as a result of the rapport you built and the trust you established, and may need reassurance that whatever was said is going to stay with you. Give that reassurance again.

Also, invite the party to make any other statements that may not have been made up to that point ("Is there anything else you would like to tell me, or anything else that you would like to emphasize again?"). This is in the service of your gaining new information, and it also lets the party know that you truly do care about other concerns he or she has about the situation.

Finally, ask about messages that the party may want you to carry to the other side, or at least summarize what you believe to be your instructions. It may be that you have been asked to find out exactly how much was spent on a certain project, or maybe you have been asked to communicate an offer to the other person. Whatever the case may be, play it back to the person now and double-check to make sure you have your instructions clear.

- *Continue caucuses with the other party or parties.* Use the format described above with each party to the dispute. If you have two parties, you will conduct this caucus format twice. If you are meeting for an organizational mediation and have set up a series of open meetings for groups to attend, then you will use this same caucus format in each of these groups. If you are mediating a dispute involving municipal government, a neighborhood faction, and several other interest groups, you will use the same format in conducting caucuses with as many as four or five groups. It is only after you have conducted caucuses with each of these groups that you will make a decision about whether to convene parties for joint meetings or to continue with shuttle diplomacy.

Summary

The caucus is your first private session with each disputant. The parameters have been set in the opening meeting, though you can assume that there may still be distrust of the process even as you start the caucus. Open with the issue of confidentiality and close with the same reassurance. Maintain good eye contact; use active listening and summarizing to let the person know that you hear and care what he or she is talking about. With every utterance that comes from the party's mouth, every piece of paper put before you, every reference to the dispute, code the material in terms of the Conflict Grid: interests, other facts, BATNAs, and solutions. Do not be afraid to test perceptions or use confrontation to focus on weaknesses and strengths or invoke other interests to loosen the ground (you will thank yourself for it later), though go gently and do not push too far yet. Your main goal is to listen, and to understand what each person needs. Go for a little extra by testing the perceptions of each party concerning other parties' interests. How much does the party know, and how accurate is the party? Finally, wrap up each caucus by thanking the party for taking the time to talk with you, assuring the party that everything he or she has said will stay with you unless he or she asks you to communicate something to the other side later. Let the party know about the next step: you will talk to the other side and then make a judgment about getting everybody back together or continuing with shuttle meetings.

EXERCISE

1.   Take a preliminary look at the caucus exercise at the end of Chapter Eight.

Learning by Example: Two Caucus Stories

The flow of the conversation in any caucus will start with the party talking about the problem in any number of different ways, and you, as mediator, directing the party to focus on interests, other facts, BATNAs, and possible solutions. As indicated earlier, think of the whole process as filling in the blanks, or as painting by the numbers from a palette where one color represents interests, and another facts, another BATNAs, and another possible solutions. Or think of the conversation as a scavenger hunt where you have four categories of information you want, and you will be grading yourself as to how much information you get under each category and how accurate and precise it is.

Caucus with a Plaintiff in a Personal Injury Dispute

You are mediating a personal injury dispute, sitting in your first caucus and listening to the plaintiff's attorney and the injured party give further details on liability and damages. In the very beginning you will hear "what it will take to settle," phrased primarily in terms of positions and dollar amounts, and attacks on the weakness of the other side's case, with criticisms of what was said in the opening meeting by the other side. As you listen to all of this, code it in your mental Conflict Grid as "other facts," summarizing, clarifying, and ordering information as you go.

Along the way you may get a glimmer of other interests behind the position. Perhaps there was something in the way the insurance claims representative responded or did not respond to the plaintiff in the early going that caused an offense—a phone call not returned, or verbal behavior or some apparent attitude that put the client off—and that eventually led to a bigger lawsuit than might have occurred had there been a different beginning to the negotiation.

In the privacy of the caucus, you may hear even more about underlying interests. Perhaps the plaintiff wants money to get further job training if the injury precludes continuing in the same job. Note that a monetary award (one possible solution) is simply a way of honoring other key interests or matters of the heart, such as using the money to get training for new, remunerative, and satisfying work.

Be prepared for the parties (and their attorneys) to collapse categories so that the interests, other facts, and solutions are all rolled into one position that is put forward as the main event in the negotiation. For example, an attorney might say to the mediator that the case will settle for $150,000, and then defend this figure based primarily on (1) what a jury might award (future prediction of court proceeding) or (2) the strength of the liability argument (my client was not at fault, the defendant was at fault) and (3) damages to the client (she can no longer do the lifting required by her job).

Unless you have a way to break these various pieces into the categories represented in the Conflict Grid, you will have very little to go on in helping the parties to budge from their original positions on the way toward some common solution. Taking the example of the statements made by the plaintiff's attorney, consider the following:

• The $150,000 demand should be viewed in our model as simply one possible solution. The mediation tactic is to identify it as such and say: "Yes, I guess that would be possible, and that could be one way to settle the case; let's look at what gets you to that number, to see if that number is the right one or not."

• The prediction of what the judge or jury will award is, according to our model, one of the other facts. It is simply the attorney's prediction of what a judge or jury would do in a future judicial proceeding. Note that the other side will likely have a very different prediction; indeed, one of the services you can provide as a mediator is to identify these various predictions of what a judge and jury might do, or perhaps even to mediate the selection of an independent third party who would make such a prediction, perhaps a retired judge who will hear the facts of the case and give the parties a summary version of what they might expect in court; this latter approach is what is often done in minitrials and in settlement conferences conducted by retired judge mediators.

• The attorney's statement of damages is also one of the other facts, though in this case, it is one person's view of damages to put alongside the other person's view of damages (defense attorney or insurance company). The mediation tactic will be to record these various views of damages and perhaps move the parties toward selecting an objective standard that could be used to evaluate damages, perhaps an independent medical examination.

• Each side's view of liability falls under the category of other facts, including interpretations of law. The mediation tactic here is to (1) note in caucus the various interpretations of the law and liability, (2) assist the parties in an orderly presentation of data to back up their liability claims, and (3) assist the parties in identifying the probabilities of success (is there a 50 percent expectation that a judge or jury will rule in their favor on liability, a 90 percent expectation, or something else?).

• Note that in the preceding summary of the opening position on monetary settlement there is no statement of interests. While at first blush it might seem obvious that the person's interest is in getting money, think of the receiving of money as an action step that is intended to honor other interests, such as taking a vacation, receiving medical treatment, completing training for a new career, putting a son through school, buying a business, retiring early, or something else. Listen carefully in caucus and ask gentle yet firm questions regarding possible interests behind the money: "What will the money do for you?" "What needs will be met by having this amount of money?" Or conversely: "What needs will go unmet if you do not get the amount of money you have requested?" And further on down the line: "What other avenues (solutions) are available to you in meeting these interests?" "What minimum amount of money would you need in order to honor the interests that we have identified?"

• Typically, the way to find out what goes into a number is to assist parties in breaking the problem down into two main parts. First, you need to know what each party estimates the liability to be and that party's best guess as to the chance of convincing a judge or jury to agree with his or her view. Second, you need the parties' assessments of damages, including at least the following variables:

- Past and future medical expenses
- Past and future lost wages
- Pain and suffering
- Amount needed for the person to be "made whole," if possible, or to be put back on track in some way (for example, through employment training)
- Other key interests that were violated by the injury and must be honored in the solution
- BATNAs (court and litigation expenses and time involved in implementing a BATNA, as compared to a mediated solution)
- Possible solutions (including varying dollar amounts; structured settlements, through which money is paid out over time; interim steps, including independent medical examinations and justifications for dollars to be awarded as a part of settlement; or apologies from carrier, or from the person who is responsible for injury, to plaintiff)

Caucus with a CEO in a Corporate Dispute

Imagine you are meeting with a CEO in caucus, discussing her concern about a dispute involving two department heads. You ask open-ended questions, listen to the story, and use active listening and good eye contact to track the message and clarify what you are hearing. Along the way, you code everything in terms of the categories represented in the Conflict Grid. For example, suppose you hear the following in caucus:

> I have had it with these two people. There is no doubt that they both have a great deal to offer. Sue, for example, has been with this hospital for seven years, moving up through the ranks from nurse on through to vice president in charge of Risk Management. She is a methodical person, a hard negotiator, and has pretty good public relations skills—she would have to have been doing something right or she wouldn't have been in that position as long as she has.

But she does not abide fools lightly. And for some reason, she thinks Tom is one of those fools.

I think she's dead wrong about Tom. I have known Tom for six years, and as a matter of fact, I was instrumental in recruiting him for his position as CFO of our hospital three years ago. I think one of the reasons these two get along so poorly is that they are so much alike. They're both aggressive and very competitive. They do not know anything about building bridges, but they care a hell of a lot about protecting their turf. I think that each is a threat to the other.

I do not know what to do about these two, but I really do not want to lose either one of them. I can tell you one thing though, if it doesn't get better, I'm afraid one of them will have to go.

How would you code this statement in terms of the Conflict Grid? Reread it and ask yourself:

- What interests are represented?
- What other facts?
- What BATNAs?
- What possible solutions?

Let's compare notes. I read a number of other facts in this statement from the CEO: the number of years the two people have been in their jobs (seven and six, respectively) and their job titles (CFO, and vice president for Risk Management).

What about the CEO's stated perceptions about Tom's and Sue's competitiveness and their personalities? How do we code this information? I would suggest coding it as simply one of the other facts, since it is her stated view of these two parties. You might well talk to the patient representative, and she might have a different view of these two people. And the chaplain might have another view or interpretation. As a mediator, take all of these interpretations, from the CEO, from the chaplain, and from the patient representative, and code them as three views, three other facts that are ingredients of this dispute.

What about interests? Clearly, the CEO's interest is in having a resolution. She wants the problem to be solved. However, we do not hear a lot about the interests of these two parties. This is something you will need to explore in the caucuses. In the caucus with the CEO, however, you might well ask what *she* believes the interests of these parties might be. In doing this, you are picking up more information from her and possibly preparing yourself for what you might hear from the parties.

What about BATNAs? The CEO gives a clear impression of her own BATNA when she says that one of these people will need to go (be terminated, transferred, or whatever) if the two of them cannot work better with one another.

What about possible solutions? None have been stated yet.

Summary of the Flow of a Caucus

In the examples we have discussed in this chapter—a caucus with a plaintiff's attorney in a personal injury dispute mediation, and a caucus with a CEO in a health care corporate battle—your objectives as a mediator are the same. Invite the person to talk and use active listening and both open-ended and closed-ended questions to elicit information and refine it and to maintain rapport with the party. The party may take the conversation any number of directions. Do not worry too much about this. Simply follow along the path, collecting the information you must have along the way: interests, other facts, BATNAs, and solutions. If you find that the party is giving you little or nothing on any one of these dimensions, then inquire and redirect the conversation. Bear in mind that your key goal throughout is to fill in the blanks, or, in whatever way you can, get the information you need from this party on these four dimensions.

EXERCISES

1.   Read the following two caucus transcripts. In the first, the mediator is talking to Jack, a member of a process improvement team, and in the second, the mediator is talking with Dan, the team leader.[1] Summarize the Conflict Grid information from each party.

2.   Determine what other questions you would ask in each caucus.

Mediator: Jack, let me remind you that this meeting is confidential. I won't repeat anything you tell me without your permission. Now, tell me more about how you see this situation.

Jack: It's Dan, the team leader; he's the problem. He's got to go.

Mediator: You sound pretty sure about that. Help me understand how would that help you?

Jack: Well, at least our notes wouldn't get edited after the fact. And we wouldn't get interrupted. When we had a consensus, it wouldn't be sabotaged.

Mediator: Quite a list! Tell me more about the editing.

Jack: Well, he literally rewrites the minutes to suit himself. He leaves little or no time for anyone to see them. Then he sends memoranda to the Quality Council that reflect his view, not the group consensus.

Mediator: It seems like there are several things here that bother you. Changing the minutes is one thing, not providing time to discuss the corrections before the next meeting is another, and sending memoranda to the Quality Council that distort the consensus of the group is another.

Jack: Yes.

Mediator: How about the interruptions during the meetings?

Jack: Well, he just cuts off conversation if he doesn't like the way it's going. He humiliates people.

Mediator: In what way?

Jack: He calls people names.

Mediator: For example?

Jack: "Lame," "worthless," "lazy," stuff like that. "Pin-headed."

Mediator: So the name-calling is especially bad?

Jack: Yes.

Mediator: Anything else?

Jack: Well, he never believed in the quality philosophy to start with. We think he's just trying to kill the whole deal so he can go back to the way things used to be.

Mediator: So, as you see it, it's as if there's an underlying motive to almost sabotage the process, because he doesn't believe in it?

Jack: Yes.

Mediator: Jack, how do you suppose Dan views all of this?

Jack: The same old thing he always says. No teamwork;
             some people come late; blah, blah, blah.

Mediator: What's that about?

Jack: It may be that there's some truth to what he says, but
             his behavior is worse.

Mediator: I suppose you've already thought of this, but could it
             be that both sides need to make some changes in deal-
             ing with each other?

Jack: Maybe.

Mediator: What would it take to make this whole situation better
             for you and the other team members?

Jack: He needs to go, and I'll tell you this confidentially, I
             know at least two people ready to go over his head to
             make that happen if things don't change!

Mediator: So, he could be gone? But what if he stops, or put
             another way, what would need to happen for him to
             stay on, and for all of you to feel better about it?

Jack: Well, he's got to stop doing all the things we already
             discussed.

Mediator: The interrupting, the editing, the name-calling.

Jack: Yes. And we've got to know he's committed to the
             team concept and to this team's mission. We don't
             think he is.

Mediator: So, he would need to reaffirm or clarify his commit-
             ment to the mission?

Jack: Yes. And admit to us that he hasn't treated us right.

Mediator: Okay, let's think about this for a moment. Would you
             and the others be willing to do the same in return—
             admit error, and offer to make changes?

Jack: Depends what it is.

Mediator: I suppose you'll need to hear what he might ask,
             right? I would imagine he'll state some of the con-
             cerns he stated in the opening meeting.

Jack: Let's see what he wants.

Mediator: Okay. Have you told me anything I can't repeat to him?

Jack: No, I don't think so.

Mediator: All right, let me meet with him, and I'll get back to
             you.

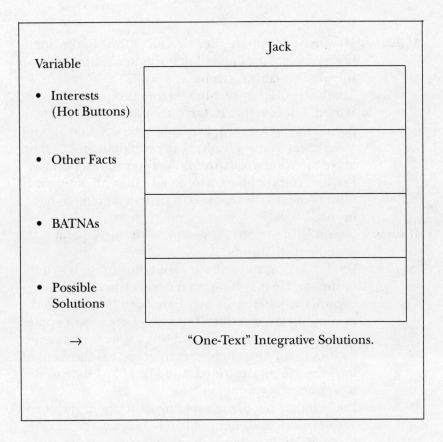

Variable

Jack

- Interests
  (Hot Buttons)

- Other Facts

- BATNAs

- Possible
  Solutions

→   "One-Text" Integrative Solutions.

Mediator: Dan, just to remind you, this meeting is confidential. I won't repeat anything you tell me without your permission. So, tell me how you see all of this.

Dan: It's a disaster. This whole project has just gone downhill fast.

Mediator: In what way?

Dan: Well, just what I said in the meeting. I don't think the team members take this project seriously. They don't act like they're committed to it.

Mediator: Some are late; some don't talk; some complain after the meetings; some dominate?

Dan: Yes. I can't get anything done in a timely manner. The buck stops here, so I have to take over when they can't get it done.

Mediator: That must be frustrating.

Dan: Well, it is.

Mediator: How do you suppose they view all of this? In the opening meeting, Jack implied that you were opposed to
the whole quality concept.

Dan: That's way overblown. Sure, before this project
started, I objected to it. But once top management
decided to go forward, I accepted the decision and my
assignment as team leader. I've been doing my best to
make the team work. And I'll tell you another thing,
I've been around here a lot longer than all of them! If
push comes to shove, some of them are going to be
history.

Mediator: So you have options for dealing with this, separate
from the mediation?

Dan: You bet I do! Can I tell you about one thing? It's the
facilitator. He may have been a bad choice. He can't
control the meetings. I may have been heavy-handed
in running the meetings, but when I see some people
dominating the meetings and when I see recommendations that I don't believe truly represent the views of
the group, I get frustrated, and I feel like I have to do
something.

Mediator: I'm getting a picture of building frustration, and then,
at some point, you felt you had to take charge. Maybe
they need to hear more about the impact of their
behavior on you—the frustration, for example.

Dan: I'd like them to hear it.

Mediator: Maybe that could happen in a joint meeting. Let's
look closer at what steps you believe would improve
the situation, before you meet face-to-face.

Dan: Well, I think the whole team has to clarify its commitment to the original mission. The people on the team
have to start behaving like team members—showing
up on time, making their suggestions in the meetings
instead of later; they need to speak up—that sort of
thing. Also, we have to have a new facilitator.

Mediator: How would that help?

Dan: Well, if we had a facilitator who could control the
group and edit the minutes, I wouldn't have to. I

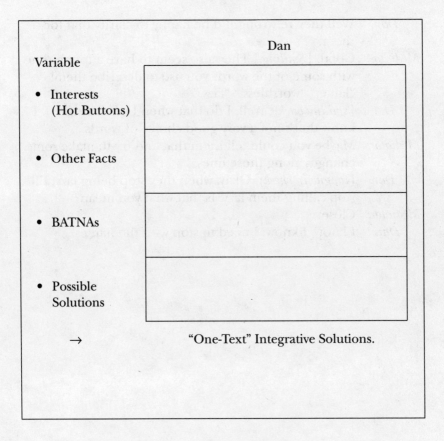

Variable	Dan
• Interests (Hot Buttons)	
• Other Facts	
• BATNAs	
• Possible Solutions	
→	"One-Text" Integrative Solutions.

don't know how to replace him without causing more problems at this point.

Mediator: Some of the team members have suggested training, perhaps for everyone, including the facilitator? Do you think that might help?

Dan: Maybe. We could try it.

Mediator: Anything else?

Dan: That's about it.

Mediator: I'd like to tell you about a few other things I hear from them.

Dan: Good, have at it.

Mediator: As I hear it from them, both sides may need to affirm their commitment to the team. For example, they think you don't want the team to work.

Dan: Well they're wrong. I'd be happy to clarify that for them.

Mediator: Good. [*Smiling.*] They also seem to have a tough time with some of the words you use to describe them: "lame," "worthless," "lazy."

Dan [*smiling back*]: Well, I do that when I get frustrated. I know that's not a very good choice of words.

Mediator: Maybe you could tell them that and try to make some changes along those lines.

Dan [*tongue in cheek*]: Okay, when they stop being lazy, I'll stop calling them lazy. Is that what you mean?

Mediator: Close.

Dan: I know, I know: I need to stop with the names.

Chapter Nine

Generating Solutions and Drafting a Trial Agreement

You and each of the key parties in a dispute have just completed caucuses, which involved at least two meetings (and many more if you are mediating a large multiparty dispute). Along the way, you have taken notes as the disputants have opened up to you in these private meetings. You have heard a great deal about interests since you have probed as best you can to find out what drives the dispute for each person. You know a full range of other facts such as various reports of the amount of money available, readings of the law, deadlines, and timetables that the parties have introduced. You have also heard about the BATNAs for each party, so you have a sense what each might do if this entire mediation breaks down and no settlement is reached. Finally, you have perhaps heard more solutions than you can possibly keep track of. Along the way, you had ideas of your own, some of which you tested on the parties to whom you were speaking at the time; others you simply recorded in your notes.

You have finished all these meetings, and the big question now is, What do I do next? You can begin your answer to this question by reviewing your notes and translating them into a one-text worksheet, before moving forward with the next round of joint meetings or shuttle diplomacy.

Compiling the Worksheet

Fisher and Ury popularized the "one-text" or "single-text" approach to bringing order out of the usually chaotic process of disputing. They describe the American mediating team at Camp David, which shuttled back and forth between the Israeli and Egyptian cabins and eventually drafted a document of steps that seemed (to the mediators) to honor the interests discovered and facts identified, then invited each party to critique the document. As the document was subjected to individual scrutiny of the parties, the mediators amended it, and carried it to the next party, following the same process of critique and revision, until the final product passed muster with both sides. The resultant one-text agreement was a written representation of a series of integrative solutions to which the parties could agree in resolving their dispute.

Consider also the classic stories (related in Chapter Two) of the children fighting over the orange and the graduate students disputing over whether the window should be up or down in the library. In the former case, the one-text agreement might include as its first point that the orange be peeled, that the inside be given to one child and the outside given to the other. Added to this might be an apology from each child to the other for unkind words exchanged during the dispute, plus some sort of forgiving statement that lets each know that the other is willing to put the dispute behind him or her at this time. The graduate students might simply settle for an agreement on the windows that are to be open, and, depending upon how well or badly they had treated one another, dispense with apologies. In both of these situations, the mediators (parent and librarian) would likely put nothing in writing, though they might verbally summarize the agreement.

For our purposes, think of the one-text statement as an agreement that may be either written or stated verbally. Its chief defining characteristics are the following:

- It forms a single summary that identifies the steps the parties have agreed to take to solve the problem.
- Its steps meet the three-part test of (1) honoring, or at least not violating, key individual and mutual interests; (2) squaring with other known facts (for example, organizational policy or state law); and (3) being better than the parties' respective BATNAs.
- Its individual steps are designed to be translated into a to-do list to carry out the agreement (see Chapter Fourteen for sample one-text agreements).

The Preliminary One-Text List

Look back over your notes, and pay particular attention to anything that refers to possible solutions (in the coding scheme listed in Chapter Seven, review points marked by marginal arrows). Make a list of the solutions identified earlier, as if you were completing a one-text worksheet like the one shown in Exhibit 9.1.

Pastor Versus Choir Director

Here is an example of how a one-text worksheet takes shape. A mediator had just completed caucuses with a senior pastor and a choir director who were in dispute over the kind of music (traditional or modern) that would be included in worship services. The two had been estranged for a number of weeks, following a particularly ugly verbal exchange that included the senior pastor slamming down the telephone after an argument. After caucuses with each person, the mediator wrote down the following as steps that might open the door to reconciliation:

Exhibit 9.1. The One-Text Worksheet.

Party and Action Step

1.

2.

3.

4.

5.

6.

7.

8.

Party and Action Step

1. Apology from the senior pastor for the telephone incident.
2. Discussion of the parties' differences on music, followed by brainstorming by the two parties on ways to create a mix of modern and traditional music in the main worship service. Could they also negotiate the musical forms for other worship and group activities in the church's calendar?
3. Discussion and agreement on the part of both the senior pastor and the choir director on authority regarding worship format (recognition of senior pastor as "chief liturgist"?), plus development of mechanism so that choir director's input will be taken into account.
4. Mutual commitment to discuss the music program with each other on a regular basis (perhaps at regularly scheduled meetings) and to bring up concerns to one another, instead of allowing them to be swept under the rug only to emerge later as a bigger problem.
5. A formal "consensus building" or "dispute resolution" clause for their working agreement, if possible. In any case, include coaching on steps they might take to achieve consensus so that only in extreme circumstances would there be a worship activity in this church that did not have the full support (following discussion and negotiation) of these two key parties.
6. Exploration of the communication problems (other blowups? patterns?), and steps to improve communication; possible forgiveness exchange in light of apology (above) and new plan for the future.

The success of any or all of these steps would depend, of course, upon whether or not each party would be willing to try them! Each step grew directly from caucus discussions, which included ventilation regarding sins of the past, active listening by the mediator, and extensive probing and note taking to complete the Conflict Grid for each party.

Personal Injury Claim

A woman injured in an automobile accident went to mediation, along with her attorney, and confronted the insurance company's claims representative and defense attorney regarding her claims for damages. She demanded not only past medical expenses and lost wages but also awards for pain and suffering and future loss of earnings. After caucuses with each side, the mediator had learned that liability was not in dispute, as police reports found that the insurance carrier's insured was clearly at fault. However, there were numerous other questions regarding whether or not there would be data to support the plaintiff's claim. After two caucuses, the mediator summarized her own one-text worksheet as follows:

Party and Action Step

1. Medical documentation from the plaintiff to the insurance carrier to justify past expenses.
2. Documentation from plaintiff's employer regarding time away from work and wages lost.
3. Possible independent medical examination (separate from the physician the plaintiff had already visited, claimed by the insurance carrier to be a "plaintiff's doctor"), to justify her having taken time away from work in the past, her current inability to work, and the effect she predicted on her future earning capacity.
4. Direct statement by plaintiff to insurance carrier regarding nature of injuries (there has been no face-to-face communication thus far, and claims representative is highly suspicious of this client; furthermore, both attorneys would like to see how good a witness this plaintiff might make).

FASHIONING A ONE-TEXT AGREEMENT DO'S AND DON'TS

DO	DON'T
Begin formulating possible one-text items from your first notes on the case.	Neglect to think in one-text terms from the very start.
Use action verbs to capture each point and describe specific behaviors the parties will take to implement the agreement.	Allow the agreement to remain vague.

Remember that your primary conceptual framework is the Conflict Grid, which allows you to unbundle the problem (interests, facts, BATNAs, solutions) before you seek to create one-text items that will work for all parties.

Fail to draw on the components of the problem that you have already defined through caucuses and joint meetings.

Consider several options for reaching partial agreement, when full agreement is not possible:
- Agree on some points, and agree to disagree on others.
- Defer some points to higher authority.
- Implement some measures now, and wait on others.
- Introduce objective standard as a guide for selecting among options.

Take an all-or-nothing approach, assuming that if the parties cannot agree on all or most points, then no agreement will be possible.

Build in an agreement about follow-up (when, where, convened by whom).

Leave this to chance.

Include a dispute resolution clause.

Neglect this opportunity to help the parties prevent future disputes by agreeing to manage conflict through direct talks or mediation.

Using the Worksheet

As these two examples indicate, the one-text worksheet simply identifies a series of steps that might lead the parties out of the mire of their current dispute and onto a path toward possible solutions. In completing the one-text worksheet, do not be guided too much by whether or not the parties will in fact be successful in carrying out the steps. Instead, use your own private knowledge (after all, you're the only one who has heard about the interests of *each* party) to create a list that you think might lead in a fruitful direction, toward integrative solutions. Also, do not worry about which step would need to come first. In some cases, this will be obvious, for example, when restitution and apologies are offered before forgiveness is given. In other cases, the parties themselves, in the joint meetings, will help determine the order. The main objective is simply to make a list of the steps that will need to be taken in order to help the parties move forward.

EXERCISES

1.   Using the caucus information about Jack and Dan from the previous chapter, sketch a preliminary one-text worksheet along the lines described in Exhibit 9.1.

Party and Action Steps

1.

2.

3.

4.

5.

6.

7.

8.

Joint/Shuttle Meetings

After a round of caucuses that involves meetings with each party, and after review of your notes to begin a sketch of a possible one-text agreement, the next phase will involve either further shuttling back and forth between the parties, joint meetings, or combinations thereof. The next three chapters cover mediator decisions in planning these meetings (Chapter Ten), a standard format for talking about data in each meeting (Chapter Eleven), and the resolution of impasses (Chapter Twelve).

Chapter Ten

Planning the Next Round

Growing from the one-text worksheet, the next question is, How might we best explore, test, revise, and eventually reach agreement on the one-text list? Through individual meetings, and if so with whom, or through joint meetings? The rule of thumb after the first round of caucuses is for the parties to do as much of the work themselves as is humanly possible. This means that joint meetings in which the parties transfer their own messages to one another will be the treatment of choice, unless some aspect of the dispute or limitation of the parties argues otherwise. The mediator in the church situation described in Chapter Nine made the following plan:

> First, I will talk with the choir director alone, asking for permission to discuss her feelings about the telephone incident with the senior pastor. [This request for permission assumes that this particular permission was not covered at the close of the first conference.] I will also ask if the other items on the one-text worksheet would be helpful to her. The next meeting will be with the senior pastor, presenting the one-text ideas and possibly coaching him about the upcoming joint meeting—I need to find out whether he agrees that an apology is warranted, and if so, how he plans to apologize. Next, I might bring the parties together for a joint meeting to address the issues on the one-text worksheet.

If you have any doubt about which meetings should occur first, try this test. Imagine the parties sitting together in the room and talking about the various points on the one-text list. As you imagine this conversation, notice anything that seems to be awkward, or explosive. If you discover any such point, such as someone who is about to apologize but may do so in a way that results in a put-down of the other party instead of a true apology, then you know immediately that you will need to include a private coaching caucus and an individual meeting with that party, *before* the joint meeting.

There are other considerations in deciding which meetings to schedule:

- *Are the parties equipped and prepared to meet with one another face-to-face?* If not, meet separately to coach the parties about what will happen in the meeting and how they can negotiate in a constructive manner.
- *What approach will take the least amount of time?* If the parties are ready to talk with one another, joint meetings will always go faster than private meetings with the mediator going back and forth in shuttle diplomacy.
- *Are there physical constraints to having joint meetings?* For example, parties living in different cities may find it too difficult to get together.
- *Would telephone conference calls help the parties, or a combination of telephone conference calls and individual caucuses?*

Exhibit 10.1. Next Round of Talks.

What meetings (individual or group) must be scheduled and with whom in order to explore, revise, or implement the steps on the one-text worksheet?

Who Should Attend	*One-Text Item (Agenda)*
1.	
2.	
3.	
4.	
5.	

In sum, the review of your notes, the creation of a one-text worksheet, and the planning of the next series of meetings marks a critical juncture in the mediation process. While you will clearly have discussed possible solutions with each party in caucus, this is your first opportunity to begin putting everything together and to find out if there is truly an integrative path that might be possible. Think of this step as the caucus you have with yourself. You might even want to review your notes with a colleague, or if you are a new mediator, with a supervisor. This is the time when you may discover that certain interests are still unclear to you. You may have heard one party talk at length about what he or she wants, or in particular, what he or she will not do, and still find yourself confused as to what really drives the dispute for that person. If so, put question marks on your one-text list and make sure you include another individual meeting with that party to explore interests further. Have new parties been identified, and should you schedule caucuses with these individuals or groups? At this point, you can use a variation on the rule of thumb that you used in identifying parties at the start of the mediation: plan a new contact with anyone whose participation will be critical to implementing the one-text agreement and/or anyone who could derail the effort if he or she is left out.

EXERCISES

1.   Using the preliminary one-text worksheet in the previous chapter, list the next round of talks for the mediation between Jack and Dan.

	Who Should Attend	*One-Text Item (Agenda)*
1.		
2.		
3.		
4.		
5.		

Next Round of Talks for Mediation Between Jack and Dan

2.   Whom else might you need to speak with after meeting with Jack and Dan?

Chapter Eleven

Using the SOS Model (Summaries—Offers— Summaries)

Picture yourself bringing the parties into a room together after a round of caucuses, or walking into a room to meet a party for a second caucus after you have met with the other disputant (and the party knows you have done so). You likely now have far more information about interests, other facts, and everything else on the Conflict Grid than either of the parties has alone. All eyes are on you. Since the parties do not have the information that you have, they are likely still stuck in their disputing mode, and feeling defensive and suspicious of the other side, even though you may have loosened the ground considerably in the caucus. There is the possibility that all your progress in opening the door to new ideas in the caucus and building real bridges between yourself and the parties may disappear as soon as they see each other in a joint meeting or, indeed, as soon as they hear you say anything, even in caucus, that has to do with the other side. Almost reflexively, they may go back into a disputing mode: retreating to established defensive positions and attacking everything they hear. After all, they "know" what the other side is like. As they view it, the mediator may have some interesting ideas, but— again as they view it—the ideas probably will not work. What, then, can you do to keep this reflexive response from carrying the day?

Moving Toward Solutions

This chapter presents a model designed to advance the process by helping the parties assimilate and talk through the data they have presented during private caucuses. The model can be used in joint meetings or in private shuttle meetings with one party at a time. It involves alternating between summaries and offers, with a final summary in each session to cement the progress that has been made. I call it the *SOS Model,* a memorable acronym, which in this case stands for summaries—offers—summaries.

The SOS Model provides a method for the mediator to facilitate progress along each of the three dimensions of the mediation process: awareness/empowerment by each party in expressing his or her own interests, needs, and concerns; understanding/recognition of the other side in terms of Conflict Grid categories; and possible agreement/reconciliation among the parties. Having heard from the parties privately, and with their permission, the mediator will summarize progress made, and use the grid categories to encourage the parties to engage one another by offering information (facts or self-disclosures of feelings), questions, and if appropriate, the solutions of apology, restitution, plan for the future, and forgiveness.

Summaries

The mediator using the SOS model in a joint meeting might proceed as follows: "I wonder if you don't need to address one another directly about some of the things that you have summarized to me in our private meetings. How about taking turns talking to one another right now, focusing on at least two issues: (1) your own statement of what happened and how you felt about it and (2) remedies that have special importance to you."

A more directive beginning is for the mediator to open by presenting a general outline of items on the one-text worksheet as a start in helping the parties set an agenda. For example, the mediator might also proceed as follows: "As I listened to each of you in our private meetings, I took notes on significant themes that you each want to address. With your permission [granted ahead of time by each party], I can summarize them now as a possible agenda for our meeting. First, you both expressed a desire to get closure on that unpleasant telephone interaction that occurred last week. Second, there is the issue of job descriptions—what should they be? Third, there is the issue of budget cuts, and what to do about them. Would either of you like to add to the list, or correct anything?

[Assist parties in completing the agenda.] Should we start with the first item?"

Offers

As the parties begin to talk, they will offer information, feelings, and opinions on each topic. As mediator, you will use active listening to generate clarity in terms of Conflict Grid categories. This part of the meeting will also give an opportunity to the party who is not speaking to listen to the other side's views, interests, and concerns. Your role at this point is to serve as a coach or facilitator for the parties in this exchange. Throughout, you will continue to focus on at least two areas for each item on the one-text agenda. First, the parties will talk about the problem, describing its history as well as their own feelings, interest in resolution, concerns, and possible solutions. Second, the parties will make offers for what they are willing to do to solve the problem.

The parties may offer trades to one another ("I will do this for you, if you will do that for me"). They may offer their own solutions, such as: "Let's get more information about this, before we decide"; "Let's have a neutral third party review this, and then we can renegotiate"; "Let's use an objective standard to help determine the worth of the piece of property, before we decide how to dispose of it." They may offer to split the difference or compromise in some other way, with each giving a little bit in order to help reach an agreement.

However, the parties may also just go right back into their dispute. These "negotiation fireworks" are not at all uncommon at this juncture, and you can approach them in one of the following ways:

- *Allow some ventilation* (as long as it does not violate the ground rules against name calling, personal attacks, and threats). The objective is to allow the parties to "get it out" as a first step toward accomplishing something on the one-text list, such as recognition of wrongdoing and apologies.
- *Interrupt the parties,* imposing control on the verbal interaction, allowing only one person to talk at a time ("tell your side") on the way toward accomplishing something on the one-text list.
- *Reframe the outburst* to encourage consideration of the standard solutions, such as acknowledgment of wrongdoing and apologies.

- *Separate the parties* by meeting with each in caucuses to find out what the party needs most at that point and why the flare-up has occurred and to coach the party about going back into the meeting.
- *Stop the parties from talking* and coach them both together on how to get back on track.

As mediator, you might offer your own paths for resolution (such as the steps described in the boxes below for valuing a piece of property and for dividing household furnishings). Disputants often have no idea of how they might resolve major differences, and steps such as these, offered by the mediator, can provide a path for sorting through information and interests and creating mutually agreeable solutions.

Summaries

Following the parties' own guided discussion, give another summary of your own on what the parties have accomplished so far, are accomplishing even as you speak, and have yet to accomplish. Just as active listening is a hallmark of caucus behavior (clarifying and understanding interests), so summarizing is the hallmark of this phase of negotiation. Identify any agreements that have been made thus far. If you cannot summarize an agreement and record it for the parties' benefit, then you can summarize the interests and summarize the progress that the parties are making and what they have yet to accomplish. For example, a mediator might give the following summary:

> I am hearing a good and honest discussion about how you each felt about that incident last Friday. I know you have different views about it. Bob, your intention, as I understand it, was to be heard, and to not let the conversation be broken off. Mary, you had a very different need, and were afraid to talk to Bob, lest he "blow up" again.
>
> Is this a fair summary? [If they nod yes, continue. If either balks, ask for clarification or correction.] Okay. Then, let's talk about what you each need now in order to go forward. [Focus on standard solutions from the Conflict Grid.] Having acknowledged some of these behaviors, are apologies in order?

Summaries focus on what has happened and what should happen next. The mediator above focused on what had already occurred, but then pointed out the way to the next step, which was offering apologies. Once this next step was completed, the mediator could proceed, using the same SOS steps with the next item on the agenda.

Steps for Valuing a Piece of Property

1. Identify the property (by name, address, and so on) to be discussed.

2. Identify other information about the property (deeds, location, physical description).

3. Invite statements of personal interest in the property ("It's the home I grew up in, and I'd like to stay there"; or, "It's the home I grew up in, and I can't wait to leave it," and so on).

4. Ask for values already given to the property (personal opinions, appraisals, tax records, and so on).

5. Ask about previous attempts at bridging the gap in the different valuations and the success or failure of these attempts (for example, hiring an appraiser, the parties' arguing with one another, or whatever).

6. Ask what the parties most need to settle the matter, and listen carefully to their responses (for example, one person may need a particular objective standard while the other may not trust experts, especially since experts were first mentioned or imposed by the other side).

7. Based on answers to the previous question, propose alternatives for valuation: use of a mutually agreed-upon third-party evaluator (realtor, appraiser); use of the average of two such appraisals; use of a mutually agreeable third party to make an appraisal with an agreement ahead of time that the appraisal will be binding; or use of the third party's appraisal as simply an advisory to the parties, after which mediation will continue.

8. Implement steps for receiving third-party opinion (including determining timetables and who is to bear the cost and reconvening the parties to continue mediation).

---

9.   Receive the report from the third-party evaluator and ask if the parties can agree on the appraisal; if not, meet with each in caucus.

10.   If caucuses are necessary, invite information and use impasse resolution techniques (Chapter Twelve).

11.   Reconvene to affirm agreement (or declare impasse).

12.   Adjourn.

Shuttle Version

In an individual meeting under the shuttle diplomacy model, the opening summary might begin with a statement about what the party you are addressing has already said to you and then turn to what the other side has said, which you will now report, after having received permission to do so. For example, listen to a mediator talking to the injured driver and the driver's attorney in the incident discussed earlier (in Chapter Nine).

> I have just finished my meeting with the claims adjuster and the defense attorney, and I have been asked to communicate the following to you. First, they report understanding, based on the statements you asked me to communicate with them, that you are concerned about getting reimbursed for the past medical expenses and lost wages and that you view your future job prospects as very limited due to this injury. They understand that you have confidence in the recent medical examination. They have several other concerns, however. First, as they report it, they do not have accurate documentation on medical expenses or on lost wages. Also, they will need more information on the limitation that the injury will pose for you in the future.

In this individual meeting under the shuttle approach, the mediator would finish the summary and then go on to offer recommendations from the one-text worksheet regarding next steps that might be taken to exchange new information or perhaps to allow the parties to receive a new independent medical examination, or to take the other steps that were listed. The mediator would follow with another summary of what was to happen next. This might include bringing the parties together for the next meeting in order for them to negotiate, for example, the selection of someone to perform the independent medical examination. Or the mediator might continue with the shuttle approach, using the SOS model as a guide for all individual talks, until an agreement is struck on all items listed on the one-text worksheet.

CHECKLIST FOR DIVIDING HOUSEHOLD FURNISHINGS

1.   Assist the parties in creating one master list of all items to be divided (possibly merging separate lists or delegating one party or the other to make the lists and bring them to mediation). Consider also taking photographs of property or using any other steps to ensure that every piece to be divided is on the list.

2.   Ask the parties to talk about particular interests, matters of the heart, or other emotional investments in any piece of property. If the parties are reluctant to do this with one another, use a brief caucus.

3.   Help the parties choose a method to value the property, such as its fair market value (what each item would receive if sold) or its replacement value to the party (what it would take to go out and replace the item, for example, a new sofa to replace the one given up). Assign a monetary number to each piece of property.

4.   Go through the lists, item by item, asking which party might prefer to have that item in his or her column, and make the preliminary check mark showing that the item should go in that person's column if and only if the parties readily agree that it should. In this first round all items over which there is little or no dispute are disposed of.

5.   Go through the list again, this time taking items in dispute and again inviting the parties to bargain or trade, one taking one item, another taking another, on an item-by-item basis. Look for opportunities to group items. ("This chair goes with these other pieces of furniture in the den, and I would like to have them together." Such statements may generate a response like, "Fine, the same holds true for me for the small tractor and the equipment in the barn.")

6. Continue in this way, moving past items on which the parties are not able to make a preliminary trade.

7. For the items remaining on the list, mediate division, using:

- Caucuses to see what is important to each side (where is the person's particular investment?).
- Open discussion of interests with the other party in the joint meeting, with the hope that through discussing interests, the parties may move toward creating solutions that will honor interests for both parties.
- Alternative ways to honor interests (once they have been identified) besides possessing the particular item on the list (for example, "If I cannot have the painting, can we arrange for me to get another painting in some other way as a part of the overall negotiation after this list has been divided?").
- Each party's buying particular items from the other party.
- A coin flip or another third party.
- Linking any dispute over an item from this list to other unfinished items in the overall negotiation (for example, "I do not mind yielding on this item, if I can have my wishes on some other issue unrelated to this list").
- Giving disputed items to a third party, for example, a child or a friend.
- One party's taking the item (for example, a boat) while the other party retains the opportunity to use it.

8. Calculate the monetary amount for each party's list, to determine if the amounts are equitable or not, and include these amounts in other negotiations (for example, in divorce mediation, if one party gets 40 percent of personal property and the other 60 percent, include the monetary values as a part of the overall negotiation so that this difference is recognized in other monetary negotiations).

9. Review final list. Adjourn.

Refining the One-Text Agreement

The SOS Model can be used as a guide for shuttle diplomacy and also for joint meetings. (See Chapter Sixteen for a more detailed version of the joint session model applied to interpersonal conflict resolution.) The objective is to build on the information gained in the first round of caucuses, and then, through joint meetings and shuttle diplomacy, to transfer responsibility for fashioning the one-text agreement to the parties themselves. Private meetings may be used to coach parties on how to negotiate, and to test certain refinements in the one-text agreement that need to be reviewed privately (giving the parties greater degrees of freedom to move from an initial position to new common ground). Joint meetings provide the parties with their primary opportunity to encounter one another directly; to address the concerns, pain, and problems from the past ("getting it off their chests"); and to hear and perhaps understand the plight of the other side better. The process then allows the parties to propose solutions, take responsibility for outcomes, and make commitments to one another. The mediator's role is typically one of facilitator and coach.

EXERCISES

1. Using the information from the exercises in Chapters Eight, Nine, and Ten role play both a shuttle and joint meeting approach with the two parties Jack and Dan.

    a. Bring the parties together for a joint meeting, using the SOS Model to facilitate their talk with one another.

    b. Conduct shuttle meetings, going back and forth between the parties, bringing them together at the end for the closing meeting.

2. Discuss with your colleagues the differences between the two approaches, as well as advantages and disadvantages of each in this case.

| **Resolving Impasses**

Beginning mediators often view an impasse (or even the threat of an impasse) as an alarming situation, one fraught with the potential failure of the mediation process. Conversely, if you talk with seasoned veterans who have been through many battles on the way toward resolution, you get a distinct impression that impasses are what mediation is all about! This is when the parties show their true colors. The parties or their attorneys may dig in to fixed positions or retreat from what appeared to be an emerging common ground. This is when the parties truly need a good mediator. Hence my first word of advice: take a deep breath and let it out slowly—the situation is about to get very interesting!

We can begin with a few assumptions about impasses:

• While the dictionary defines *impasse* as a "deadlock" or "predicament affording no obvious escape," the word may have different meanings to different parties at different times in the process. To one party, the statement "we are at an impasse" might mean that all hope of resolution is lost, but to another, it might simply be a negotiating ploy to threaten the other side (a way of saying, "Give me what I want, or else!").

• In a true impasse, the parties are stuck on positions that, as they now stand, cannot be reconciled; the mediator's strategy will therefore be to help people move away from these positions, either toward one another or toward some alternate path. All of the strategies discussed in this chapter focus on ways to achieve this movement.

• Remember that impasse is one of the two possible outcomes of any mediation, the other being agreement of some kind. Given the stakes of not agreeing (high cost of avoidance, power plays, and higher authority resolutions), in most mediations it will be well worth the effort to break the deadlock. However, do not be afraid to declare an impasse at the end if all efforts at resolution fail; the parties can then pursue their respective BATNAs.

In planning your strategy, consider the following steps in dealing with any impasse:

1. Ask yourself: Why is the impasse occurring at this particular time? What function does it play for each party?
2. Use one or more of the impasse resolution strategies (described below) in an attempt to create movement and resolve the impasse.
3. If you declare an impasse and end the mediation process, leave the door open for future negotiations and the opportunity to reconvene the parties if circumstances change.

IMPASSE AS "LOGJAM"[1]

It might be more productive for you to use a word like "logjam" instead of "impasse" to describe the time when the parties seem to be stuck in positions, unable to move forward. The metaphor of a logjam—timber stuck for a time and not moving in its journey along a river—has hope, in that a logjam is amenable to influence, whether by removing a log, moving one or more logs, or adding more timber or water. Experiment with the images you use for problems like impasses, bearing in mind that some words may actually add to a problem instead of helping solve it.

Impasse Function

The psychology of individual and group dynamics holds that all behavior—even impasse and deadlock behavior—serves a particular function for the individuals and members of the group. When your parties reach an impasse, your question should then be: What function does this impasse play for these parties right now? Why is this party, or the attorney, saying no to the proposal on the table? Or, Why has this party retreated to his or her earlier position?

On first glance, it may seem to you that the impasse behavior is a negotiating ploy, a tactic to gain advantage. The person prepared to walk out of the talks, or the one who says, "This is our last meeting; we'll see you in court," may simply be attempting to get the other side to back off from demands.

A deeper analysis, however, may reveal that the deadlock behavior (whether a tactic, or truly a deadlock declared by one side) occurs because that party *perceives* that the offer on the table will not meet his or her needs and that the earlier position will. You can ask about this in an individual caucus, or it may be clear from the information you already have. In either case, answer the following questions when an impasse is raised by either party or begins to cross your own mind:

- Why is this occurring right now? Is it a negotiating ploy? Is it for some other advantage? How does this person expect that threatening impasse will achieve the advantage?
- How do the parties perceive the proposal on the table now as a method for meeting their key interests, and how do they perceive their earlier proposal?

Resolution Strategies

When you face an impasse in the proceedings, there are at least five kinds of action that you can take. You can (1) go back to basics, (2) change the negotiation mix, (3) challenge the party or parties, (4) support the party or parties, or (5) change the deal on the table. This section will consider these options in detail.

Go Back to Basics

Your first thought in facing an impasse should be: Have I missed something from my earlier analysis of the dispute? In particular, ask the following:

- *Are there other parties who are sabotaging the mediation?* I once conducted a divorce mediation where the parties would agree to certain items one week and then return the next week to back off from the agreements. After this happened twice, I discovered that they were each involved in lengthy consultations with their respective mothers, who, not having been a part of the process, were derailing the agreements reached in mediation. The solution turned out to be an invitation for telephone caucuses with both mothers. Perhaps one or more of your parties is engaged in key consultations such as this with family members, spouses, or others who have an interest in the outcome.

• *What interests might we have missed?* Does this party have an interest in keeping the dispute going? Are there satisfactions gained for this party by engaging in verbal combat on a regular basis? Can this be exposed, or can an underlying interest or need be met in some other way?

• *Are there some other facts or parameters of this dispute that we have not yet identified?* I learned during one corporate mediation that one of the parties with whom I had direct caucus meetings during the day was returning to his home in the evenings to drink bourbon and rethink everything. The alcohol-induced rethinking—and telephone consultations with associates—led to the unraveling of many proposals. We learned to steer all of our telephone consultations away from evening hours and to anticipate his second-guessing with new questions of our own *before* he left the daily meetings.

• *Is the party's BATNA truly becoming more attractive than a negotiated agreement, and if so, why?* You may need to help the parties do a new cost-benefit analysis to examine what will happen if they do not reach agreement in mediation.

• *Are any of the standard solutions missing in the deal now on the table?* Apologies? Restitution? Plans for the future? Forgiveness? Think of the situation from the point of view of the party who is retreating or digging in, and ask yourself: Does this person need an apology from anyone? Is there something in the restitution or making up for past wrongs that is incomplete? If we improve the deal somewhat, might the integrative path become more attractive? Does this party believe that the whole thing will unravel again in the future—and is the fear possibly warranted? Or is it possible that everything is in place, but this particular person simply has no concept of how to let go of the dispute, no way to put the matter behind him or her, possibly through forgiving what has occurred?

The first approach must be to remember that the heart of an impasse is the same as the heart of the dispute. We simply reserve the word impasse to talk about deadlocks that occur later in mediation, while we often refer to disputes as the occasions that prompt mediation to begin. If you find yourself stuck or if the parties are digging in, then go back to the Conflict Grid and ask again all of the questions you raised in your first meetings with the parties, to see if something has been missed. It is possible that by addressing the missing factor now, you will be able to help the parties move toward common ground for integrative solutions.

From Positions to New Solutions

The impasse often takes the form of one party or another stating a position from which they will not budge. As the diagram in this box indicates, a back-to-basics approach can include four sets of statements or questions designed to create movement from fixed positions to new solutions via underlying interests. The circled numbers in the diagram correspond to the following paragraphs and indicate the flow of the conversation between the mediator and one of the parties in caucus:

1. The party states a position (P_1), and holds fast to the position, saying the other side will simply have to adjust to it. The mediator's standard sentences here include the following: "Let me see if I heard you correctly. You are saying that . . . [restate the position, whatever rationale the party has given]. Your view is that this will work not only for you but also should be acceptable to the other side."

2. The mediator turns the conversation from positions to interests (I_1). "I imagine you could hold the line in that way, and it is possible, of course, that the other side will come around. However, before testing that, let me ask a few questions. What are the interests behind the position you have stated? Put another way, what are you trying to accomplish, or what are you trying to honor, by taking this position?" The objective here, of course, is to transfer talk from the positions back up to matters of the heart. If these basic interests can be described, then it will be possible to move to the third phase of the inquiry.

3. The mediator invites talk about new solutions, or positions $(P_2, P_3, \ldots P_n)$ in order to honor the interests (I_1). "I see your interest now in [saving face, not being made to look like fool, getting into this new market by June 1, or whatever the party has stated], but I wonder, just for discussion's sake, what other steps, besides the one you have mentioned (P_1), you could come up with here that would also help?" Continue probing, brainstorming, pushing for the creation of alternatives [some sensible, others less realistic, all with a goal of getting something on the table].

The path set out in paragraphs 1, 2, and 3 is the mediator's back-to-basics approach for moving from a position through interests and on to new solutions. Another approach is to shift the discussion to competing or equally important interests.

4. "I understand that by taking this position (P_1) you might honor these interests (I_1) and that perhaps there seem to you to be no other good solutions $(P_2, P_3, \ldots P_n)$. I would like to ask, however, does not what you have advocated here (P_1) conflict with other interests you have identified to me that are also important $(I_2, I_3, \ldots I_n)$?" Examples of competing interests $(I_1$ versus $I_2, \ldots I_n)$ are saving face but also losing a job (and financial security), and winning out over an ex-spouse in postdivorce litigation but creating so much bad will between parents that children suffer.

In sum, the back-to-basics approach begins with acknowledgment of position(s) taken by one or more parties, but then moves back up the grid to interests, and then to new solutions—or to competing interests as a way of generating new solutions. The intention is to bring some dissonance or instability to the current positional stance, thereby opening the door to new options.

Moving to New Solutions

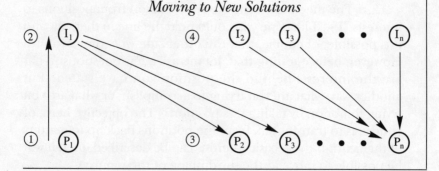

Change the Negotiation Mix

Consider any sampling of the mediation literature or of presentations by mediators at professional meetings or even of war stories at case conferences, and you will pick up a veritable laundry list of strategies that can be used on the spot in any caucus or joint session in order to jolt the parties and help them move away from fixed positions. While the preceding back-to-basics strategies aim at going under and around fixed positions by looking at interests, facts, and other important material, change-the-mix strategies aim at adjusting the mediation process itself. Consider the following methods:

• *Use humor.* The heart of humor during a crisis or conflict is that it changes the perspective of the parties, allows for the physical relief of laughter, and lets people figuratively "get out of character" for a period of time. If humor is your gift, then use it. However, bear in mind that jokes directed at the parties will backfire and that the best humor is that which pokes fun at the mediator or the mediator's plight. (For example, one mediator tossed a Laurel and Hardy line to a co-mediator at a point during a joint meeting when one of their suggestions had fallen flat. To the delight of the parties, he said, "Now, Stanley, here's another fine mess you've gotten me into!")

• *Take a break.* If you're up against a wall and going nowhere, it makes sense to stop the process entirely and suggest that people stretch for a few minutes and come back.

• *Take a walk.* Building on the concept that fixed positions can be literally associated with a place in the room, invite the parties to take a walk and get out of the room for a while. The change of scenery may lead to a change in perspective.

• *Stand up and talk or pace.* This works on the same principle as taking a walk, though it is done in the room. Get out of your own chair, stroll to the window, and look out, or sit in a different part of the room, putting your feet up as you talk, inviting brainstorming, and letting the movement of your body model a loosening up of ideas and perhaps positions.

• *Suggest caucuses with key outside parties.* It may be that caucuses with attorneys for each side, or other key individuals, will lead to information that will shake the negotiation mix in a different direction.

- *Flip a coin.* This variation on the outside-input or outside-standard theme simply involves deferring a decision to the chance outcome that the flip of a coin produces. Typically, this works when there is an interest in saving some of the time and money that might go along with expensive negotiations and when each side can in fact live with the other side's winning the coin flip.

- *Use caucuses to separate the parties.* If the parties are not doing well in joint meetings, move toward separate meetings to see if you can get a different result.

- *Buy time by adjourning the process for a while.* This is a variation on taking a break; consider suspending the negotiations for a period of days.

- *Bring outside standards to the negotiating table.* One of Fisher and Ury's key principles of negotiation involves the use of objective standards to resolve differences and bring parties together. Many alternative dispute resolution techniques are based on the principle of the parties getting input from some outside arbitrator or a retired judge or from a minitrial, where the parties watch their attorneys argue, as a way to add new information to the negotiation. The parties could agree to consult a third person, or any other source (for example, a blue-book to help them decide how to value a car).

- *Defer to higher authority.* Sending one or more issues to an arbitrator or other higher authority may be a way of preserving agreement on all the other issues.

- *Include outside parties such as attorney advocates in the process.* By adding one or more individuals to both sides, you may be able to get the new parties to offer ideas that will sway your intransigent party.

- *Isolate one or more parties for a time.* Just as adding parties to the negotiation process changes the mix, so isolating some parties for a period of time can do the same thing. I once suffered through several caucuses where a particularly intransigent individual monopolized the conversation, putting me in the awkward spot of either living with the disruption or confronting him and alienating him. The solution turned out to be to go for more productive work in private meetings with certain individuals and then caucus with this individual alone to test ideas before bringing them to the larger group caucus.

CONFRONTATION EXAMPLE

I have found that the safest confrontations are those where I can use data that comes from my own experience with the party. I once conducted an organizational mediation where one of the central parties had been accused by his subordinates and associates of lying and other forms of shading the truth. As they told it, he would give one version to them face-to-face and then give an entirely different version to others, often with little similarity between the two. It seemed that he did this more for political expediency (trying to get everyone onboard) than for any self-serving or malicious reasons. In any case, it was hurting his credibility with his colleagues. Halfway through the mediation, I had received permission to share this with the party, and had done so, though neither the party nor I had truly come to grips with the problem. The party had not even admitted wrongdoing, to say nothing of exploring apologies or remedies for change. And then the moment of truth presented itself. The party was telling me his plan for setting up a meeting between himself and another party, one that would include me as mediator in the meeting. He stated, "I will just tell them that this is your idea and that you would like for us to get together to talk."

The only problem with this statement was that it was *not* my idea. I responded: "I can't help but notice that your plan is to frame it to the others to make it look like my idea, when in fact, it is your idea and not mine. Is this what your associates were referring to when they said that you sometimes 'shade the truth?'"

He paused, acted as if he were caught for the moment, and then said, "Yes, you're right. I guess I do that, don't I?"

There may have been other ways and other opportunities to confront him, but there was none better than doing so with data that were immediately available to both of us. These data were far less arguable than other information would have been, and the point was much more easily made.

Challenge the Parties

Mediators in all walks of life use caucuses as times to challenge and confront parties as a means of creating movement. Challenges might take the following form:

• *Costs.* If you see a party ignoring the cost of the proposal he or she is espousing, then say so. Remind the party of the litigation costs in going to court. Remind an intransigent spouse in divorce mediation that the price of winning a particular point may be hurt feelings and anger that interfere with her parenting relationship with her children.

• *Strength of a case.* Some parties have a difficult time evaluating the strength of their cases, and others evaluate their cases in an unrealistic manner. If you sense this is happening, perhaps you can give input on the strength of the case or arrange for advisory arbitration from some mutually agreeable party to evaluate the case.

• *Negotiating style.* More than once I have told individuals in caucus that their negotiating style is interfering with getting a yes from the other side. This challenge to the negotiating style is best coupled with supportive coaching, discussed in the next section.

RESPONDING TO VERBAL ATTACKS

Many a mediator who walks into the middle of a fight with a view to helping the parties resolve a problem runs the risk of being verbally attacked and accused (rightly or wrongly) of misunderstanding the parties, mishandling the process, taking sides, or any of a number of other errors. When this happens, what can you do?

Having watched numerous skilled individuals deal with verbal attacks, here is what I have learned from master mediators:

• Treat all verbal attacks upon you or your work with respect. Painful though it may be, you have an opportunity to correct a wrong and improve the relationship. Instead of immediately defending yourself, treat an attack as a diagnostic opportunity to gain more information.

• Acknowledge the attack and ask questions first. For example, "I'm sorry to hear you feel that way. What happened here to make you draw that conclusion about me?" Two good things happen when you follow acknowledgment with a question. First, you get yourself off the hot seat. Instead of having to defend your situation (which you probably will not do too well with the limited information you have), you put the question back on the attacker, which puts him or her in the position of explaining the situation. Second, as the party talks, you have an opportunity to hear more information about interests, events, and other material that will be useful to you.

• Use active listening to continue to clarify and refine what the party is saying, again resisting any tendency to defend yourself just yet. (For example, "If I'm hearing you correctly, you have real questions about my approach, particularly since I spent over an hour in caucus with the other person and spent much less time talking with you. Also, you feel that I showed bias in the meeting by asking challenging questions about your numbers and not about the other side's numbers.")

• Once you feel you have a handle on the situation (the reasons for the attack or protest), respond as appropriate. For example:

Acknowledgment and apology. "I see what you mean. I wish I hadn't done it that way, and I hope you will accept my apology. How about if I . . ."

Clarification. "You know, that's not what I intended; what I was trying to do was . . ."

Remember, always, that you are the expert on your intentions (views, feelings, inner thoughts, motives), even though the *behavior* that occurs is open to interpretation by everyone in the room. This means that there can be two or more interpretations of the behavior. Your approach can be to clarify your intentions ("I didn't mean it to happen this way") and still acknowledge that the behavior contradicted your intention ("I can see now how it looked to you").

• Finally, take the lead in proposing that, if possible, you now go forward, learning from the matter while putting it behind you. This may be the sort of modeling of constructive acknowledgment of wrongdoing and problem solving that the parties likely have not been able to do themselves. If you model this as a mediator, you are at least behaving in a manner congruent with the mediation model, and at best, you may be priming the pump for the parties' own cooperative behavior regarding the substantive issues.

In summary, treat the attack with respect. Acknowledge the attack, ask questions, and use active listening to clarify what you are hearing. Make a distinction between intentions (private, internal data) and behavior (external data that can be interpreted in many ways). Make acknowledgments and apologies as appropriate and then make some proposal or overture for going forward.

Support the Parties

It is useful to remind ourselves that movement from one position to another involves risk. It is not unlike crawling along one branch of a tree and then reaching over to move to another branch. In doing so, you have to leave one spot, grab new branches for support, and live with the fear that the branches may not support you and that you might even have to make a jump or leap, with the hope or plan of catching onto another limb, before you are safe again. All of this usually must be done without a safety net! There are many things you can do to support and encourage parties as they make these seemingly risky and fearful moves. Consider the following:

• *Coach on negotiation strategy and communication skills.* Tell the party having a difficult time getting agreement from the other side that the abrasive and demanding presentation is a part of the problem. You do not need to give an entire course on negotiation and communication skills, though you can use your own expertise in this area to diagnose the problem the party is having. Perhaps the party needs to be coached on how to lead with the presentation of interests (using the "I" statements discussed under self-disclosure communication skills in Resource A) and on how to use active listening to show the other side that his or her interests are being heard.

• *Offer new concepts.* I once debriefed with a party who told me that when the mediator suggested that certain steps would certainly allow her to maintain her dignity while others would not, this helped her turn a corner in planning her strategy. See if your party needs coaching with a new concept.

- *Validate feelings.* In caucus, you can say to a party, "If I had gone through something like this, then I would be angry too!" The validation of feelings may be the support that the party needs to move from the angry feelings branch to the solutions branch.

- *Interpretation of the other side.* Perhaps you can take a side-by-side approach with one party in caucus and share notes on how you both interpret behavior from the other side. This is a powerful form of support (not bias) and may be just what the party needs in order to process the data and move forward.

- *Pep talk.* Think of all the pep talks given by coaches as they help players move into competition and it becomes clear that disputants often need the same sort of encouragement as they move into new territory. Do not be afraid to offer it.

Change the Deal

The problem may not be with missing basics (for example, interests, key facts, and the like), nor with the negotiation process, nor with the need for confrontation or support of the parties. The impasse may lie in the fact that the integrative proposal—the deal on the table—really is inadequate. This is the time when your own intellectual creativity is called into play, and everything you know about problem solving will be needed. If you are stuck viewing the problem in only one way, you may need to change your own negotiation mix and take a big break from the problem, ask a colleague to consult with you between caucuses, or do whatever else is necessary to find a new way to look at the problem.

See if any of the following might help the parties move out of their deadlocked positions onto a common path:

- *A partial solution to a complex problem.* The most obvious form of this occurs when two parties agree to a solution to one part of the dispute and defer the rest to resolution by higher authorities. It may be that staff of two government agencies can agree to solve one part of the problem that is within their purview, while sending the rest of it up the chain of command or to the courts.

- *Procedural solutions separated from substantive solutions.* Most disputes involving parties that will have a future relationship will have both substantive and procedural dimensions. The conflict rests not only on what we should do about this particular problem now (substance) but also how we will handle similar problems in the future (procedures). Perhaps the parties can agree on one even if they cannot agree on the other. The other could be postponed for discussion at a later date or sent to higher authorities.

• *Trades.* If the parties have not already proposed this, perhaps you could suggest that each gives the other some or all of what is wanted in exchange for getting something back.

• *Compromises.* Mediators who fashion integrative solutions know that compromises are one of the weaker forms of outcome; nonetheless, they are acceptable. Perhaps each side will say yes to getting a little less of what he or she wants in exchange for getting something instead of nothing.

Declaring Impasse

As was mentioned earlier in this chapter, impasse is one of the two outcomes in any mediation. If the preceding strategies do not lead to movement toward agreement for your parties, then do not be afraid to declare an impasse and end the mediation at that time, leaving the door open for negotiations to begin again at a later date. In declaring an impasse, you can include the following in your final analysis of the situation:

• *A face-saving statement about why the impasse has occurred.* Though you may feel like blaming one side for throwing a monkey wrench into the process, if you wish to leave the door open for future negotiations, it will be better to frame the impasse in such a way that neither side loses face. (For example, "We have gone through a number of mediation sessions together, and at times, the two sides seem to have had a meeting of the minds on possible solutions. Efforts have certainly been devoted toward reaching agreement, but it is clear now that you are at an impasse. You each have different views as to why this is the case, and I do not see any point in reconciling these views at this time. It could be, however, that this will change in the future, at which time we might resume the mediation process.")

- *An explanation of how to initiate mediation again.* Invite them to call you, or suggest that you can, if they agree, mark a date on your calendar to call both sides for follow-up to see whether or not they wish to reconsider mediation.
- A *reminder of confidentiality.* If the parties are on their way toward resolution through the courts, remind them of the confidentiality provisions that protect your notes and testimony.

Summary

The threat of impasse is at the heart of any mediation process, just as the reality of a dispute is at the beginning of any mediation. The same principles used for analyzing disputes and assisting the parties in creating integrative solutions constitute the first step in impasse resolution—go back to the basics. Beyond this, there are numerous strategies that can be used in an attempt to get the parties to reexamine interests and move from fixed positions toward common ground or toward one another. If these steps are successful, then you will be on a path toward testing the emerging agreement (discussed in the next chapter) or declaring an impasse while leaving the door open for renewed negotiations at a later date.

EXERCISES

1.   Select one of the role plays in Resource F. Assume that the mediation has progressed through one round of caucuses and shuttle/joint phases and that the parties have now been convened for the closing meeting. Then have one party renege on the deal because some important interest has been neglected or because there has been some change since the previous round of shuttle or joint meetings. The job of the mediator is to resolve the impasse using any of the techniques described in this chapter.

Note to the obstructionist: Write down on a piece of paper the reason you are reneging on the deal (review this chapter to get ideas on reasons for digging in and forcing an impasse). If the mediator is successful in discovering the reason, you should respond appropriately to these overtures by moving forward with a revised agreement. If the mediator is not successful, you should continue to force an impasse.

2.   Complete a second or third round of the preceding role play, switching roles so that all participants have a chance to be the mediator in the impasse resolution mode.

Closing

Some mediations seem to close themselves, as when a claims adjuster and plaintiff's attorney agree on a particular amount of money to settle a personal injury claim. In many other cases, however, the closing will require more mediator guidance. Bear in mind that your primary objective is to help the parties reach a new understanding or plan for the future to which each can say yes and then begin immediately to implement. The closing phase of mediation may occur in the round of shuttle meetings or in the joint meeting following caucuses. It includes three key checkpoints: testing the agreement or declaring impasse (Chapter Thirteen), putting the agreement in writing (Chapter Fourteen), and wrapping up the process (Chapter Fifteen).

Chapter Thirteen

Testing the Agreement

You have just finished your final round of talks with the parties (either in caucuses or in joint meetings), and you have written notes that make up a one-text agreement. Or you may have outlined the agreement on a flip chart, summarizing what the parties have agreed to. Before drafting a written record of the agreement, it is a good idea to subject the agreement to several tests. You will do this again once the agreement is committed to writing, but now is the time to begin challenging what you and the parties have created together.

Key Questions

Can you expose weaknesses or areas that will surely lead to failure or derailment in the months ahead? If so, far better to expose the problem now, when you have a chance to fix it, than to let the parties walk unknowingly into a future that is wired for failure. Consider the following:

- *Are the most critical interests of the key parties and their constituencies honored by this agreement, or at least not violated by it?* Suppose you have been mediating a church dispute where the parties are divided over how to allocate next year's budget: the conflict is over devoting more money to benevolences and helping the poor versus building a new educational wing. The parties may well have begun the dispute in an all-or-nothing mode; that is, determined to build or not build the new facility. You have assisted them in identifying the interests that have provided the driving force for this positional bargaining, and now you have a new integrative solution on the table, namely, a new building (albeit a less expensive one than that originally proposed by the group that sought it), coupled with resources committed to developing a participatory educational curriculum that involves adults and children in implementing outreach programs through the new facility, plus an agreement by both sides to actively participate in implementing both aspects of the agreement. The first test question is: Does this plan truly honor the underlying interests of each of the parties?

To begin to answer this question, you can go back to your Conflict Grid notes from the early caucuses. Look at the marginal check marks (for key interests) to see if they are honored by this agreement. Also, ask the parties directly in open meetings, and in private caucuses, if necessary, whether or not this deal will in fact honor those interests.

Do not be afraid to play devil's advocate with each party. For example, you might address this question to those who want the new building: "How sure are you that you will be satisfied with the building, which as it turns out is not nearly as large as the one you wanted in the beginning?" Or, "Let's have a closer look here: how are you going to justify this agreement to your spouses tonight, when, after all, this is less than you were pushing for in the beginning?" The idea in questions such as these is to see if the parties themselves can see the link between the new integrative one-text plan and their underlying interests. If they cannot explain the link, or something seems to be missing, then take time to explain how the plan does in fact meet the interests—or get to work with the parties on amending the plan.

- *Does the agreement square with other facts?* Have another look at the Conflict Grid data. Given the budgetary constraints, organizational policy, relevant laws, and other variables, how does the agreement measure up? A mediator once helped a divorcing couple fashion a mutually agreeable joint managing conservator arrangement regarding their children, only to find that one provision violated the newly revised family code and therefore needed to be changed.

- *How will the agreement be received by other key parties and their constituencies?* Go back to one of the first principles of the opening phase of the mediation, identifying parties and their constituencies, and ask this question again: Do we now know of any other parties who could help this agreement along if we include them in the review or who could derail it in some way if we exclude them? If you know of these parties and their interests, then look at the agreement on the table through their eyes. If you were these other parties, would you oppose the agreement or support it? If the former, what needs to be changed?

• *Imagine the deal going forward, and see where it leads.* Picture the parties implementing the solution as it now stands to see if you picture it holding up or falling apart. Suppose your parties are two business partners who also have spouses who know each other and are good friends. Is there something in their relationship, or in the realities of everyday living (for example, contact these families will have at upcoming birthdays, religious holidays, or other events) that surely must be taken into account in testing the agreement? Two negotiating parties may well agree to go their separate ways, not anticipating how they will handle an upcoming family-oriented holiday. As a mediator, draw on your own experience in living to picture the parties moving forward through holidays, birthdays, court dates, and changes in economic or family circumstances; see if this exposes other points that need to be negotiated.

• *Ask the parties for a critique.* Central to the one-text procedure described in the previous chapter is the idea that the parties themselves critique the one-text agreement and tell why it will or will not work for them or someone else. Invite more of this critique in the testing phase right now. Ask the parties: What have we missed here? If you picture yourself living with this agreement, what obstacles do you anticipate? Have we addressed them sufficiently, or do we need to have another look? What else could we build into the agreement to make it work well for you and your people? How about the other side—do you think this will work for them, or not? What do we need to do to increase their chance of success, as well as yours?

• *What do the parties' attorneys think of the agreement?* If the parties have been represented by counsel during the mediation sessions, then the opinions of the attorneys regarding legal protections for each party will have already been covered as a part of the ongoing mediation process. In most divorce mediations, the parties will receive consultation from attorneys along the way, and a final review of the agreement by attorneys should be included in the final test of the agreement. The parties can carry a draft of the agreement to the attorneys, or they can discuss the main points of the agreement with their attorneys to receive the attorneys' input, before the mediator dictates a formal draft. As mediator, you can encourage the parties to invite critique by their attorneys and to interview the attorneys regarding the areas of the agreement that concern them the most. The attorneys have been hired to provide legal advice, and also—by virtue of their experience—to anticipate obstacles that might not have been covered during the mediation caucuses and joint meetings. Whether the attorney gives verbal comments (which the parties should record in note form) or a detailed letter, each point the attorney makes should be incorporated in the mediation process and treated as a test of the agreement, leading to negotiation of changes when necessary.

Summary

Think of the testing phase of the process as your attempt to assist the parties in trying to shoot the agreement down, before it suffers a similar onslaught from outsiders after the mediation is over. Do not be afraid to look one of the disputants in the eye and say, "You are agreeing to this now, but what will you do ten months from now when you are sitting around having a beer with one of your friends and he tells you you are crazy for having said yes to this deal?" If your party cannot give a credible answer (summarizing how his interests are covered in the current agreement and how his losses would be far greater if he pushed for more), then initiate more talk about interests, the merits of the current solution, and possible revisions. Bear in mind that the psychology of dispute resolution is such that both parties are trying to develop a *cognitive handle* for the situation—a way of thinking about, looking at, or describing the experience that they can then carry into the future. As you test the agreement at this stage in the mediation process, think of your role as helping the parties prepare a verbal summary of what they have accomplished and defending it not only to themselves but also to others with whom they will surely discuss it in the future.

EXERCISES

1. For this exercise, use your notes from the exercise at the end of Chapter Eleven regarding a possible one-text agreement between Jack and Dan. Compare your notes with the transcript of the caucus at the end of Chapter Eight, and then answer the questions raised in the present chapter (for example, are the most critical interests of the key parties and their constituencies honored by this agreement?). Make notes on any changes that would need to be made in the agreement to honor the interests and facts identified in the caucuses.

2. As a variation on the theme, ask a partner to play the part of Jack or Dan and then verbally list the main features of the agreement, giving particular attention to which items to list first and which second. Do you notice any differences when you begin with items that seem to favor the party with whom you are speaking, as opposed to starting with items that seem to honor the interests of the other side? Discuss the differences with your partner.

Chapter Fourteen

Putting the Agreement in Writing

Clearly, some mediations will not need a written agreement. Take an interpersonal dispute involving two office workers, for example. If the ground rules state that what is said in mediation is confidential and nothing will be put in either party's personnel file, then the outcome might be verbal exchanges of apologies and commitments to try a new way of relating in the future. In a case like this, the closest the parties might come to a written agreement is to ask the mediator to keep his or her own notes, in order to have something to refer to at follow-up time.

However, most mediations will involve some sort of written record regarding the agreement, information that will serve either as a guide for a new working relationship or as a record for the attorneys to use in drafting legal documents. In a divorce mediation, for example, the memorandum of agreement will need to cover all points required for the attorneys drafting an agreement incident to divorce, for example, property division, child support, conservatorship agreement regarding children, and other issues. The discussion in this chapter focuses on a generic format for mediators who are drafting memoranda of agreement that can be used by the parties, whether in preparation for creating further legal documents or not.

General Principles

Consider the following guidelines in drafting a memorandum of agreement:

- *While the private mediation conversations are confidential, the one-text agreement will be public.* Make sure the agreement saves face for the parties. For disputes involving government agencies, the agreement will become a part of the public record. Similarly, a divorce mediation agreement will be entered with the court and will therefore be public. The same is true of a written agreement involving business partners (the copy taken away by one party will be shown to other friends, who will then have the written version of the mediation outcome).

The rule of thumb, therefore, is to concentrate on *solutions* and honorable *interests* in the written draft, and to exclude problem analysis or other points that can be embarrassing to one party or the other. Most one-text agreements list solutions and agreements for future behavior. For example, an agreement might state: "Bob will take primary responsibility for marketing and will schedule weekly meetings to brief other departments on new ventures." This is clearly going to be easier for Bob to live with than the statement: "Bob agreed that he had been acting unilaterally and had failed in providing timely communication to his colleagues, and he agreed to correct the situation with monthly meetings."

- *Since the agreement needs to pass muster with each of the parties, tilt toward their words in drafting the mediation agreement* (unless words from one party are offensive to another). For example, a CEO may be concerned that an errant department director has not been acting like part of the management team but more like an independent entrepreneur. He may want the term "manager," or "vice president," to show up in the draft instead of "director" (the latter meaning, to this particular CEO, more independence). If you had been able to mediate an agreement on the CEO's words in the caucuses, then make sure that they appear in the draft. Other phrases may have meaning to both parties, and they should be included even though they may not be the mediator's choice of words. The risk in this approach, of course, is that the document may begin to look like the proverbial camel—the horse that was put together by a committee. I once had a CEO tell me that a mediation agreement I drafted was filled with convoluted language, an affront I absorbed in public, reminding him in private that the agreement reflected the wishes of at least fifty people (representing five major groups), and that this was the hazard of any mediated agreement. His preference, of course, would have been for cleaner language that primarily reflected his view, an attitude that had contributed to the dispute that required mediation in the first place.

- *Strive for simplicity in choice of words and grammatical construction.* Keep documents as simple as possible. Some one-text agreements will involve only a listing of behavioral steps, which are then initialed by the parties, while others will involve many paragraphs. Go for the fewest number of words whenever you can.

- *Check the document to make sure it is positive about the solution, behavioral (stating who will do what), and specific about timetables for the completion of each step.* The best way to frame the negatives that were discussed in mediation is by discussing the interests of the parties. For example, you might say in the introduction to the agreement, "Having discussed their interests in fiscal integrity, cooperative working relationships, and the development of new markets, the parties have agreed to the following . . ." The three interests you list are code words, with each construct likely aimed at one particular party. For example, the CEO who was angry about the fiscal irresponsibility of a weak COO will read this phrase in the agreement as a reflection of all of his own feelings, even though they are not spelled out in the memo. In order for the CEO to say yes to the agreement, he will need to *read* that his main interests have been addressed. Your intention in drafting it this way is that the phrase "fiscal integrity" will be a summary phrase to let the CEO know that these interests were discussed and represented in the final agreement. Likewise, other parties should be able to read their own interests into the other key phrases, with none of the parties taking offense at the list.

- *Until the agreement is finally signed, try to use only a single copy for shuttle talks and revision.* Nothing will confuse or derail a mediation more than distributing ten copies of an untested agreement to people, each of whom then adds editorial comments, leaving the mediator with the task of trying to reconcile ten different versions. A far better approach is to carry one copy from party to party, inviting input and making changes along the way. If you are meeting with a large group, put the one copy on an overhead screen, invite discussion, and mediate revisions with the group.

Format for the One-Text Agreement

There can be wide latitude in the drafting of one-text agreements, though you may find it useful to include the following elements:

• *Consider addressing the agreement as a memorandum from the mediator to the parties.* This will allow you to present your own summary of what the parties have agreed to, for their consideration and review. They can then initial the agreement if it meets with their approval, after making changes in meetings with you.

• *Begin with an introductory summary of the issues being mediated,* followed by a statement of the interests of the parties in reaching agreement and working together.

• *List the behavioral commitments,* organized according to the parties who will take responsibility for implementation; that is, list the steps to be taken by the executive director, the steps to be taken by the management team, and so on.

• *Include a dispute resolution clause* (see discussion of dispute resolution clauses, below), through which the parties agree to discuss differences with one another first, using mediation as a backup method for resolving future disputes.

• *Include steps for follow-up.* If the parties agree to meet in six months to review progress, specify when the meeting will be and who will convene the parties.

• *Consider including a to-do list* as an appendix, to specify exactly who will do what and by when. This list will be useful to the parties in evaluating progress and follow-up.

DISPUTE RESOLUTION CLAUSES

In most drafts of mediation agreements, there will be some provision for future dispute resolution. This provision can provide a model for the inclusion of mediation in other contracts that the parties may have with one another as a part of business or organizational relationships. The central feature of any such clause is an agreement to (1) talk with one another or to negotiate as a first step in conflict resolution and (2) use mediation by a mutually agreeable third party as a second step, before resorting to litigation or other methods. Sample dispute resolution clauses follow.

Motorola Clause[1]

Illinois law governs this Agreement. Motorola and Customer will attempt to settle any claim or controversy arising out of it through consultation and negotiation in good faith and a spirit of mutual cooperation. If those attempts fail, then the dispute will be mediated by a mutually-acceptable mediator to be chosen by Motorola and Customer within 45 days after written notice by one of us demanding mediation. Neither of us may reasonably withhold consent to the selection of a mediator, and Motorola and Customer will share the costs of the mediation equally. By mutual agreement, however, Motorola and Customer may postpone mediation until we have each completed some specified but limited discovery about the dispute. The parties may also agree to replace mediation with some other form of alternative dispute resolution [ADR], such as neutral fact-finding or a mini-trial.

Any dispute which we cannot resolve between us through negotiation, mediation or other form of ADR within six months of the date of the initial demand for it by one of us may then be submitted to the courts within Illinois for resolution. The use of any ADR procedures will not be construed under the doctrines of laches, waiver or estoppel to affect adversely the rights of either party. And nothing in this section will prevent either of us from resorting to judicial proceedings if (a) good faith efforts to resolve the dispute under these procedures have been unsuccessful or (b) interim relief from a court is necessary to prevent serious and irreparable injury to one party or to others.

Convening Clause[2]

A variation on the negotiation clause theme is the use of a "convening meeting," through which the parties are brought together to choose both a process for dispute resolution (mediation, arbitration, or something else) and a provider of the process. The following is an example of this clause:

Should any dispute arise between the parties to this agreement, we shall first attempt to resolve it through direct discussions in a spirit of mutual cooperation. If our efforts to resolve our disagreement through negotiation fail, we agree to attend a convening meeting to discuss the possible use of alternative dispute resolution (ADR) to resolve our differences.

If we cannot resolve our dispute through some form of ADR within three months of the demand by any party for a convening meeting, either of us may then submit the dispute to the courts within _____ (state) for resolution. Nothing in this section will prevent either of us from resorting to judicial proceedings if interim relief from a court is necessary to prevent serious and irreparable injury to one party or to others.

Sample One-Text Agreements

The boxes in this section contain examples of one-text agreements from two situations. One concerns a couple settling a postdivorce dispute; the other involves a research and development dispute.

Postdivorce Modification

Sue and Tom came to postdivorce mediation with a dispute regarding child care for their two small children. The residence arrangement called for the children to live with each parent for two weeks, alternating throughout the year. A child care worker approved by both parties was to be hired by Tom and was to take care of the children after school in each home. Problems arose when the worker did not meet the specifications of care required by Sue. After discussing the matter in mediation, which included an interview with the child care worker, an agreement was reached and drafted by the mediator for review by the parties. Notice that this agreement begins with a paragraph on assumptions, which provides a context (areas that are not to be changed by the agreement) as well as a face-saving summary for the parties as to why the dispute began. It continues with a straightforward list of behavioral agreements that identifies steps to be taken by each person. The agreement also includes a statement about future conflict management and follow-up.

MEMORANDUM

TO: Sue Doe
         Tom Doe
FROM: Mediator
DATE: Month/Day/Year
RE: Draft of Mediation Agreement

I am writing to summarize agreements reached in mediation regarding child care arrangements. It is my understanding that you will take this draft to your attorneys for review before our next meeting. In the meantime, if there are any questions concerning this draft, please contact me.

Assumptions

Sue and Tom expressed clear differences of opinion regarding the performance of the current child care worker, though both agree that they would like to make certain adjustments in the situation. They also understand that some of the difficulties experienced since the time of their divorce are due to the fact that they have not had a regular mechanism for communicating with one another on a regular basis regarding the children, child care arrangements, and other issues. This means that some problems have escalated into disputes. Their hope is that by creating better mechanisms for communication now, they will be able to prevent other matters from growing into problems in the future. Finally, both Sue and Tom agree that they wish to honor the other elements of their divorce decree, for example: Tom will continue to pay for child care services; they will continue under a joint conservatorship arrangement; and they will maintain residence and visitation arrangements negotiated at the time of their divorce.

Agreements

Having discussed recent difficulties regarding the child care arrangement, Tom and Sue have agreed to make the following changes:

    1.   Instead of the previous approach of hiring one person to maintain care of children in two different homes

(switching when the children move), Tom and Sue have agreed that each person will hire a child care person for his/her own time in the home where the children reside.

2.   As a courtesy to the other parent, Tom and Sue agree that they will not hire a child care worker who has not first been interviewed by the other parent; furthermore, they will discuss decisions regarding hiring with one another, with a view to hiring individuals in each home who have the approval of the other parent; Tom will continue to pay the salary for both child care workers (per the previous child support arrangement); this means that under the new arrangement he will increase his support payment to Sue by $250 per month;

3.   In order to encourage similar standards for the care of the children in both homes, Tom and Sue have agreed that they will create uniform job descriptions that will be used for the worker in each home. They will experiment with these job descriptions for three months, and at that time, review any changes based on performance in each home. Tom and Sue agree that they will seek child care workers who can make at least a one-year commitment.

4.   In order to facilitate communication between parents regarding all aspects of child care, and in order to correct for some communication difficulties that have occurred in the past, Tom and Sue agree to the following mechanisms:

a.   A periodic phone call. They will talk with one another Thursdays at 9:00 P.M. to discuss routine matters regarding the children.

b.   Quarterly face-to-face meetings. Now scheduled for the first Tuesday of each quarter, at a time and place of their choosing, possibly in the mediator's conference room, the purpose will be to discuss such matters as summer camp and other arrangements regarding the children; the first meeting will occur May 7; subsequent meetings will occur each quarter (July, October, January, April).

c.   "To Mom" and "To Dad" folders. To be created by Tom and Sue, and to allow for transfer of information regarding the children to one parent or the other at the time of visitation. Information will include a calendar of activities.

    d.   An agreement to use these three communication mechanisms as the first approach, and to make phone calls to the other parent only for matters that cannot fit into one of the previous categories.

    e.   Future conflict management. Sue and Tom agree to talk to one another as a first approach to dealing with any future problems they have on any aspect of child care; if they cannot reach a mutually satisfactory agreement, then they will seek mediation to resolve the differences, with each party agreeing to pay for one-half the mediation fee.

    f.   The mediator will schedule a conference call with Sue and Tom in two months to evaluate progress and make any adjustments that the two may require.

Research and Development Dispute

The CEO of a medical research and development consortium fired its medical director, who had been hired to serve as a liaison between the administrator and the medical research staff. Infuriated by this action, the medical research committee—a group of five physicians elected by the medical research staff to oversee research assignments and policies and protocols—met in emergency session and stopped just short of a vote of no confidence in the CEO. A few physicians engaged in behind-the-scenes efforts with the consortium's board of governors to have the CEO removed. Influential board members responded that this was a "personnel decision" and that the board would take no action at this time. Angered by the board's rebuff, and aware of ongoing negotiations with a major pharmaceutical company thinking of acquiring an interest in the consortium, some physicians began a letter-writing campaign to board members detailing alleged "gross negligence" by the CEO.

A board member suggested mediation, to which the parties agreed; the mediation involved two months of joint meetings, caucuses, and shuttle diplomacy. It included caucuses with the CEO, medical research committee, board of governors, selected research staff, and attorneys representing all parties. While the original demand of the medical research committee was that

(1) the medical director be reinstated or (2) the CEO be fired, the situation changed when the medical director made it clear that he did not wish to return. The focus of the mediation turned to the performance of the CEO and the question of whether or not he should be allowed to remain with the consortium.

The integrative solution, one acceptable to the CEO, board, medical research committee, and other interested parties, was for the CEO to invite an organizational review by an outside consultant and for all parties to make several interim agreements to resolve the immediate crisis. The organizational review step was a compromise through which the CEO was allowed to stay on but agreed to subject his policies and procedures to the scrutiny of outside experts. The long-range problems were not solved by this interim step, but the parties were willing to stop the warfare and focus on a common path toward long-term solutions (outside input by mutually agreeable third-party consultants). The CEO kept his job, while the medical research committee gained a mechanism for leverage that avoided continued public haggling. The agreement also included provisions whereby the medical research committee agreed to work with the CEO instead of going over his head to the board of governors and to continue with all of its oversight responsibilities.

MEMORANDUM

TO: CEO
           Medical Research Committee
           Board of Governors
FROM: Mediators
DATE: Month/Day/Year
RE: Mediation Agreement

We are writing to summarize agreements reached during recent mediation sessions. These agreements grew from a series of individual and joint meetings involving all of you, and can serve as a blueprint for steps to be taken during the coming months. For convenience, the agreements are grouped according to individuals responsible for implementation. They are also summarized as a to-do list in Appendix A to this memorandum.

CEO

The CEO agrees to take the following steps:

1.   Following agreement with the Medical Research Committee and the Board of Governors, the CEO will recruit a management consultant (hired after input from all parties to this agreement). The consultant will be engaged to conduct an organizational review of policies and procedures related to the relationship between the administration, the Medical Director, and the Medical Research Committee, and provide a report to all three sets of parties regarding changes (if any) that might be made to improve their working relationships. It is the intention of all parties that the organizational review include input from medical, administrative, and support staff of the consortium as well as from the Board of Governors.

2.   The CEO will implement certain interim steps as follows:

a.   Work with the Medical Research Committee in creating a selection process for a new Medical Director.

b.   Meet with the Medical Research Committee at its next meeting to (1) exchange information on termination of the Medical Director and (2) create a mechanism for input by the Medical Research Committee to the organizational consultants.

3.   With the chair of the Medical Research Committee, prepare a memorandum to be circulated to department heads regarding the outcome of mediation and the planned next steps.

Medical Research Committee

The Medical Research Committee agrees to take the following steps:

1.   Participate fully in the planned organizational review conducted by the consultants.

2.   Cooperate with the CEO in fulfilling the terms of the agreement (above).

3.   Assist the CEO in further defining the role of the Medical Director and in the recruitment process for a replacement.

Board of Governors

The Board of Governors agrees to take the following actions:

    1.   Meet with the CEO and Medical Research Committee representatives to review the results of the comprehensive organizational review.

    2.   Consider changes in Board policies based on the comprehensive organizational review, particularly regarding the appropriate role of the Board when conflict exists between the Medical Research Committee and the CEO.

Follow-Up

The Medical Research Committee, the CEO, and the Board of Governors will participate in follow-up to evaluate progress at three- and six-month intervals following the signing of this agreement. The mediators will schedule the follow-up meetings.

Dispute Resolution Clause

The parties agree to attempt to resolve any dispute arising out of this agreement through direct discussions with one another in good faith and a spirit of mutual cooperation. If attempts to resolve a disagreement through negotiations fail, they agree to submit the matter to mediation conducted by a mutually acceptable mediator. The parties agree to select a mediator within 21 days after written notice by one of the parties demanding mediation.

_____   _____
CEO   Medical Chief of Staff

_____   _____
Chair, Board of Governors   Date

Appendix A: To-Do List

CEO

STEPS	BY WHOM	TARGET DATE	DONE DATE	COMMENTS
1. Recruit management consultant to conduct organizational review.				
2a. Create a selection process for a new Medical Director.				
2b. Meet with Medical Research Committee.				
3. With Medical Research Committee representative, draft and distribute memorandum to department heads.				

Medical Research Committee

STEPS	BY WHOM	TARGET DATE	DONE DATE	COMMENTS
1. Participate in planned organizational review.				

2. Cooperate
   with CEO in
   fulfilling the
   terms of the
   agreement.
3. Assist in
   further
   defining role
   of the Medical
   Director and
   in recruitment
   process.

Board of Governors

STEPS	BY WHOM	TARGET DATE	DONE DATE	COMMENTS
1. Meet with CEO and Medical Research Committee to review the results of the comprehensive organizational review.				
2. Respond to any changes in Board policies proposed in organizational review.				

EXERCISES

1. Using the guidelines presented in this chapter, draft a one-text agreement for the mediation involving Jack and Dan, discussed in the previous chapters.

2.   With partners playing the roles of Jack and Dan, ask one party to review the agreement and provide feedback on changes, or errors. Revise according to the input of the party. Repeat the process with the other party until both sides agree to the draft.

Note to parties: Review the transcripts from Chapter Eight and the narrative for this case in Resource F, and critically evaluate the draft given you. If you wish, take the role of a stickler on at least one point, arguing for language that helps you but might be offensive to the other side. In the debriefing, evaluate the mediator's ability to help you move toward language that will work for you as well as the other party.

Note to all: Debrief on the strengths of the approach taken by the mediator in preparing the draft and the weaknesses in this particular round, and make suggestions for improving performance in the future.

Chapter Fifteen

Wrapping Up the Process

At first glance, it might seem that adjournment would be one of the least important parts of mediation. After all, the main work has been completed, a solution is at hand, very likely committed to writing, and there seems little left to do. This is actually true in many cases: for example, where the primary outcome is a monetary settlement, as in personal injury mediation. However, if the parties must share a future business or personal relationship, then adjournment becomes a marker event in ending the dispute and in beginning the new relationship under the mediated agreement. On the low end, the process may be accomplished with a simple handshake, and the mediator wishing the parties success in moving forward. On the high end, the mediation may end with a formal ceremony for the signing of the agreement, just as international agreements are marked by formal signings, including press coverage.

Elements of Adjournment

The ceremony you choose will depend on the nature of the dispute and the needs of the parties. In planning adjournment, consider the following points:

- *In most cases, you will simply declare the process to be at an end.* That is, you will say something along the lines of, "We are adjourned," to mark the end of mediation.
- *Make your own closing statement* (just as you began with an opening statement). Praise the parties for their efforts at exploring the parameters of the dispute, in creating integrative solutions, and in committing to going forward in carrying out the agreement.

These closing words are an important part of the adjournment ceremony since they lift the parties from the disputing trenches to a higher plane of agreement and bring out the best in the parties as they go forward together. This is not to say that you are denying the uglier aspects of the dispute; but having fully recognized and analyzed the dispute, you are encouraging the parties to move forward now with the solution. For example, a mediator might say:

> It is clear that you have both been through a great deal of stress in dealing with this problem. And we know that you still may have your own very different views as to what some of the root causes are here, though the important part is that you have looked at the underlying interests on both sides and have taken very significant steps in creating solutions that can work for both of you. I commend both of you for your efforts; you have already accomplished a great deal by getting the agreement to this point. Now the hard part begins, as you carry it out. I am confident that you can make the agreement work. [Perhaps say something about the key features of the agreement and how they honor the well-focused interests defined earlier in the mediation process.] Even though I do not believe you will need it, you also know that you can initiate a mediation session to deal with any future differences you may have. We have a follow-up meeting scheduled for [date], at which time we will see how things are going, and make any adjustments required.

• *In all disputes where there is to be a future relationship between the parties, consider some behavioral event that allows them to participate in the process of reaching agreement and beginning the implementation process.* This behavioral event parallels the rituals that have been used throughout history (bar mitzvahs, baptisms, marriages, graduations, promotions, and funerals) to mark the end of one phase of life and the beginning of another. At a minimum, the parties may initial an agreement and shake hands. For mediations that involve religious groups, a religious ceremony or worship service may provide the marker event that is needed. The Episcopal Church, for example, has a Service of Reconciliation in *The Book of Common Prayer*.[1] For large public disputes, a press conference following a signing will be the indication to the public that the hatchet has been buried and that the parties will cooperate with one another in the future. In choosing the behavioral ceremony, be guided also by the circumstances surrounding the beginning of the dispute. If, for example, a dispute involving members of a school board was played out in the press, then it is almost mandatory that the resolution be played out for the public at a press conference, even if it is only a reading of the agreement and a question-answering session with the parties stating their support of the agreement.

As you did in testing the agreement (Chapter Thirteen), think of any party with knowledge of the dispute who might need to be informed of the outcome or included in the ceremony. It may be that as a part of the adjournment process, the mediator will suggest that the parties invite various constituents to a final meeting. The advantage could be that the constituents can benefit from seeing and hearing the parties say yes to the agreement in one another's presence.

FOLLOW-UP CHECKLIST

In planning for follow-up, consider the following:

1. Be sure to specify who will schedule the follow-up meeting. For example, the mediator may call the parties three months after initialing of the agreement, or one of the parties could take responsibility for this. Specify who will call whom and by when.

2. Follow-up can be carried out through telephone consultation, face-to-face visits, or a combination of both. If a face-to-face meeting is planned, the mediator should talk privately with each party (perhaps by telephone) prior to the meeting in order to hear a candid and confidential appraisal of the progress, problems, and other needs of the parties.

3. In conducting the follow-up meeting, use the one-text agreement as a guide to evaluate progress, especially the to-do list, and go over each point, determining whether or not the steps have been carried out. For any failure, encourage the parties to talk about why the failure occurred (was it owing to neglect or error, for example, or was the step itself less realistic than the parties had hoped).

4. As an overall guiding focus for the follow-up conversation, encourage the parties to talk about three main headings:

- *Progress made thus far (the positives).* The parties can take credit for gains, which can strengthen their resolve to deal with any problems that remain.
- *Problems, difficulties, or failure experienced.* This is the heading under which the parties discuss all of the negatives, including any accusations that the other side reneged on the agreement or did not carry out the steps promised. It is important to discuss this in terms of behavior ("So, it appears that you did not meet for your monthly meetings from January through March, even though you did have one meeting in December. Is that right?").
- *Next steps to be taken.* Translate every problem the parties identify into a possible action step for change, or a tightening of the agreement.

5.   Treat the entire process as a feedback loop on an agreement that was fashioned in the context of a dispute and now, in the natural order of things, needs to be tightened, refined, or perhaps changed in significant ways.

6.   Encourage the parties to learn from the time between agreement and follow-up, and use caucuses, if necessary, to help the parties face squarely any inconsistencies (for example, agreeing to something that they cannot carry out).

7.   Consider scheduling additional follow-up, at other specified times, which can be completed by the parties themselves or with the assistance of a mediator.

Summary

Proceeding under the assumption that reaching an agreement through mediation will be new and therefore foreign to many disputants, offer guidance to the parties on how to end the process, just as you offer guidance to the parties on how to begin a process of negotiating to reach agreement. Treat it as your opportunity to lift the dispute from the lower level of a fight to a higher level of working together to implement the plan, and as your opportunity to reinforce and encourage the parties for their cooperative behavior thus far and their commitments for the future. Be creative in finding some behavioral manifestation (one that squares with the parties' cultural, social, and religious values and that also is appropriate for the nature of the dispute) that lets the parties participate in the ending of the dispute and the negotiations, and then move forward under the new agreement.

EXERCISES

1.   Think back over your own experiences (including those from your reading, television watching, and theater going) of closing ceremonies following the resolution of disputes. These experiences might involve international peacemaking as well as the resolving of disputes involving business partners, neighbors, or siblings. What behaviors did you observe in the closing ceremonies, and how effective were they in affirming the resolve of the parties to go forward under a new arrangement? What would you have preferred to exclude or include in the closing ceremonies?

2.   Write an outline of the points you would like to see covered in the closing face-to-face meeting between Jack and Dan. What would you do to encourage the behaviors you believe to be important?

3.   Structure a role play involving Jack and Dan in the closing meeting. As the mediator, structure the agenda to allow the parties to review the agreement and conduct the closing behaviors you have identified as important.

Note: For a variation, have one party throw in a monkey wrench at the end through a verbal barb or other statement that indicates possible noncompliance. In the debriefing, evaluate the mediator's ability to deal with this added situation.

Variations

The resolution of a conflict can come in at least two forms. The most common is an agreement or commitment to implement certain steps after the mediation or negotiation is complete. For example, when an insurance carrier and an injured person agree that the carrier will pay a certain amount of money to resolve a personal injury dispute, this is an agreement for something that will happen later (money changing hands), after the mediation is over. Similarly, if two department heads in a large corporation agree to make certain procedural changes to improve their working relationship, their commitment is for some future behavior, after the mediation is over.

A second form of conflict resolution is of the "here and now" type. This is more immediate than (1) restitution or (2) commitments for the future (two of the standard solutions in mediation described in Chapter Two), and involves apologies, recognition and acceptance of responsibility for past errors or wrongdoing, immediate forgiveness of wrongdoing, and a commitment to go forward without carrying the heavy baggage of blame regarding the past. Counselors often refer to this as *interpersonal peacemaking*. Chapter Sixteen presents an outline for facilitating the verbal exchanges that may occur in single-session interpersonal peacemaking events. The format can also be used as a guide for representatives from two or more groups to talk through any set of past wrongs on the way toward resolution of a conflict. The remaining chapters in this section discuss other standard variations on the five-step model: skipping the opening face-to-face meeting (Chapter Seventeen) and using informal mediation (Chapter Eighteen).

Chapter Sixteen

When Interpersonal Peacemaking Is Needed

Harold, a department director, has been verbally abusive to Lois, a team leader, on at least three occasions over the past two years; a recent event was a last straw for Lois.

Jack filed a complaint with the city to get Tim to clean up his yard, and is seething over the shouting match that occurred between the two of them last weekend.

Assume that your mediation of either of the preceding cases has already covered Steps 1 through 3, that is, first contact, opening meeting, and caucuses. It is now quite clear to you that for the parties to resolve their differences, they will need to talk through their differences with one another in a joint meeting. How might you proceed?

Talking Things Out

The steps that follow do not need to occur in the order given. Indeed, you may find that the parties skip around a great deal, and at times, you will feel more like a follower than a leader. At the same time, it is important to have the following components in mind so that you can assist the parties in touching each of these bases.

We can begin by stating the objective: *peacemaking meetings are designed to encourage individual recognition of past behavior that has hurt or offended the other side.* Such meetings allow the parties to take responsibility for the behavior (though not the particular reaction of the opponent) and to exchange apologies, commitments for future change and/or restitution, and forgiveness, as a means of interpersonal reconciliation.

The meeting will involve at least two people, but it could also include a small group. It will cover the following mediation steps:

- Create an agenda.
- Identify "sins" of the past.
- Clarify past behavior and intentions.
- Discuss what each person wished had happened.
- Focus on options for resolution.
- Invite offers.
- Confront as necessary.
- Summarize and plan documentation.

Create an Agenda

Begin with the assumption that your parties may know little or nothing about how to talk through some major event that has hurt them in the past. Your first job will be to give your own summary of the task at hand. It might go something like this:

> It is clear from our discussions so far that some events from the past are still with you, getting in the way of your going forward in your working relationship. I'm thinking, Sue [turning to Sue], of the reaction you had when you heard that Helen had "snooped" through your papers, including sitting at your desk and checking your computer files last summer. [Turning to Helen.] Helen, you told me why you did this, and have expressed your regrets, but the two of you have not had a chance to talk this through with one another until right now. In your private meetings with me, you each have expressed an interest in doing this in order to clarify what happened, and you hope, to put the matter behind you.
>
> Here's what I would like to suggest: first, I will ask you each to take turns giving your own summary of what happened and why. I will ask you to listen to the other person without interruption. This may be hard. If you would like, feel free to take notes on things you want to remember to say when it is your turn to talk.
>
> After you have each had a chance to speak, I will make some

other suggestions on ways the two of you can sort through what happened and reach some resolution now.

With an introduction along these lines, you are able to draw on your private conversations with the parties (already having gotten their permission to discuss the matter in the joint meeting) and to put the topic squarely on the agenda. You do not need to give the parties a complete list of all the things you will ask along the way, though you must give them enough to get them started and enough to let them know that they will each have a chance to talk. Once you have done this, you can turn to the first person, and let her begin.

Identify "Sins" of the Past

Treat each opening statement as the speaker's opportunity to talk about his or her perception of the problem. As you turn to the person, you might begin with something like this: "Sue, I wonder if you could tell your side of the story. In particular, tell your understanding of what happened and also your own reactions to the events."

After Sue has finished her statement, invite the other party to make the same opening statement regarding events from the past and personal reactions. Your own comments at this point should serve to offer objective summaries, sometimes reframing to make the statement of the past more palatable to the other side. For example: "So, you are mentioning a couple of concerns here: the fact that the report arrived on Tuesday instead of Monday, and your own interpretation of this that somehow it meant that she didn't care about the pressure you faced in putting the whole project together on time."

Your goal is to get each person to focus on behavioral events and on personal reactions to these events. If the conversation gets heated later, you may coach the parties on the fact that the only cases where they are truly expert are those regarding (1) their own memory of events and (2) their internal feelings, thoughts, and reactions about these events (as described in the box below).

TALK ABOUT THE THINGS YOU KNOW BEST!

People involved in interpersonal fighting often make assertions about the other person ("You're crazy") and engage in mind reading ("You don't like me"), instead of moving more constructively to the information on which they are most expert. Do not be afraid to coach the parties at this point:

> Wait a minute! May I suggest that you each talk about the information you know best—first, your memory of past events and, second, your feelings about those events. Start by talking about the events as *you remember them happening.* We might well have two different versions of the events. That is fine. I do not want you to try to *reconcile* your memories right now. Instead, it will be helpful to the two of you to put on the table the two versions of the events.
>
> Also, how about telling each other how you each reacted to the events? If you felt angry, hurt, or upset, say so. For example, José, can you tell Louis about the feelings you had and the interpretation you gave to the written evaluation you received in the mail?

In some cases, it may be quite important to know what in fact did happen in the past. For example, in a personal injury dispute, police reports on who arrived at the intersection first and who went through the red light are important in determining liability, which has a critical bearing on the outcome of the mediation. However, in many interpersonal disputes, either there is no way to go back to find out who is correctly assessing what happened or, more often than not, to do so would entail a great deal of time and expense. The alternative approach, and one that works well in interpersonal peacemaking, is for the mediator to coach the parties to "agree to disagree" about their versions of events. The parties will likely not come to such a conclusion themselves, and that is why they may need to be coached toward this approach, perhaps as follows:

> I want to make a suggestion. Instead of trying to get clear on

who is correctly stating what "really" happened last August, for
the time being, let's proceed with two versions of what happened. Let's put them both on the table, and treat each with
respect. In addition, let's talk about your personal reactions
(feelings and interpretations) to these events, as you each summarize them, and put that on the table as well. Then, with
these two versions and these stated feelings and interpretations
available, let's see what we have, and what will be needed to
help the two of you go forward.

Clarify Past Behavior and Intentions

Once each side has given a version of events, invite each person,
again taking turns, to ask questions of clarification about what happened and also about intentions. More often than not, the parties
will hear things that they did not know were true, or more likely,
they will hear a version that they do not believe. Frame this in a
constructive light with a statement such as the following: "Now that
each of you has heard the other give her version of the events, I
can imagine that you have questions for each other. Now is the
time to ask them. If something is unclear, or if you believe someone's interpretation is off base, ask about this. Sue, would you like
to begin?"

As at the beginning, you are giving the parties a mental and
verbal *set,* or *map,* for the conversation. You want them to ask questions of clarification and to offer answers. As they do this, use your
own reflective and active listening skills to summarize what is being
said (see Resource A). Your objective at this point is not to solve
the problem or even to bring the parties closer together but simply to assist them in sorting through the information and, in a
sense, arranging it on the table. It might be useful to use words
such as the following:

I see a number of things on the table right now. Sue, you have given
your version of what happened last summer. And you have done the
same, Helen. In some ways, they overlap, though there are some
differences, such as [state the differences]. Also, Helen has said
that her intention was not to snoop, but that she was afraid of what
Sue might be doing to get back at her, and that led to her looking

through the materials. Helen, you have said, however, that you do see how Sue interpreted this as snooping, and you can see how this would have bothered her. Helen, you have stated your reasons for looking through the materials. As I heard it, you were alarmed at the way Sue had been acting, and you also were responding to a rumor from another party that Sue was collecting information on you and might use it to report to your boss, to get you transferred. [Turning to Sue.] You stated that this was not your intention, but that, as a matter of fact, you thought that Helen was trying to get your job, and you were simply trying to keep notes to protect yourself should there be some sort of investigation or challenge to you later.

So we have your own summaries of what happened, and you each helped your cause by stating some of what your true intentions were. Have I summarized things correctly so far?

Again, note that your goal at this point is simply to identify information, not to reconcile people or stated views. This step of summarizing reports of events, internal reactions, and intentions is critical to what follows.

Discuss What Each Party Wishes Had Happened

This is the point in the process at which you will open the door for parties to discuss their regrets. Some parties will do this voluntarily, and others need to be encouraged—if not asked directly—to at least brainstorm ideas on this topic. For example, you might say: "As I listen to this, I wonder if you each do not have some regrets over what happened. If it could happen all over again, what might each of you do differently? What might you have preferred the other person did differently?"

Note that you are inviting talk on two topics from each party: what the party could have done differently, and what the party wishes the other side had done. Do not be surprised when each of the parties begins by talking first about what the other should have done, pointing a finger of blame. However, do not let it stop there. Allow one party to start by putting the other party's house in order—you did ask for comments along those lines—but insist that the speaker go on to talk also about what he or she might have done differently.

Continuing with the example in the previous paragraphs, you might hear the parties making these points:

- Helen says she regrets looking through Sue's papers and getting into her computer. She will likely say this with a phrase added that justifies why she did it; no matter, at least she is expressing the regret.
- Sue says she wishes she could have talked to Helen and worked things out, instead of fearfully keeping notes to protect herself should there be an investigation.
- Both Helen and Sue express regrets that others in the office contributed to the problem by saying things privately to each party that encouraged paranoia about what the other party might think of her.

This is a very important part of the process of interpersonal peacemaking, since it allows people to talk about what might have been. Many individuals will mistakenly assume that what might have been is not worth talking about, saying, "What's past is past," and that it is "water under the bridge." As a matter of fact, many times disputants will not talk about the past at all for these very reasons.

Counselors and therapists know, however, that emotional pain, hurt, and behavioral intransigence are often rooted in disappointment about what might have been, in feelings of anger over injustices from the past, or in feelings of anxiety that what happened in the past might happen again. As a mediator, your job is to uncover these "might have been" or "wish I'd done" sentiments, so that you can build on them when you get to apologies, forgiveness, and moving forward. Without these statements, you will not have the tools you will need later on in the conversation.

Focus on Options for Resolution

This is the time when you might prime the pump for using the standard solutions: apologies, restitution, plans for the future, and forgiveness. If you have not already done so, pick one or more of these standard solutions, and tell the parties how it might apply here. You might even go so far as to point out the limited number of ways for dealing with such situations, and give your own summary as follows:

You know, in my experience, there are really only four ways you can put something like this behind you. And, even more, you might need one or all of them in order to really get the job done. First, for example, one or both of you might apologize to the other for something you have done that may have caused hurt. This would be your own personal statement of regret. Second, another party might make some new plan or commitment to not do certain things in the future, or to do certain new behaviors, to keep the working relationship on track. A third way, of course, is to make restitution for some past wrong. That may not seem like it applies to you here, and it may not, but it is something that can be done. You can't take events away, but in some cases you can make up for something with a form of restitution. The final way, of course, is to forgive the other party for what you perceive to be wrongdoing. Without necessarily making this a complex theological or philosophical issue, the concrete meaning of forgiveness is this: if you forgive someone, you agree that you will no longer hold this issue over that person's head, or over both your heads. Instead, you will let it go, and move on. This is not the same as "forgive and forget." You *will* remember what happened, so do not try to forget it; however, you can choose, as a willful act, to forgive a wrong done to you.

As you can well imagine, these four solutions are often linked with one another. For example, it might be easier for you to forgive something if the other person has apologized. Or you might be willing to forgive something if you have some good-faith commitment from the other person that the two of you will try to do something differently with one another in the future.

Now, having said this, which of these might apply to your situation? Who would like to start?

Summarize all four standard solutions to the parties, so that they do not get hooked on the inadequacy of a partial solution. For example, parties who have been through disputes will tell you straight out that apologies mean nothing to them as long as they live in fear that the same offense that caused the conflict might well happen again. Also, parties will tell you that no amount of money can take away what happened or make something right that was wrong. To this, you will be on firmer ground if you quickly agree, and note that they can't change what happened, but they can make willful decisions now about how they will react to what happened and what steps they will take. Standard solutions give them an outline of what they might consider.

Invite Offers

Inviting offers follows quickly after considering options. This is the time when you ask the question, "Who would like to start?" Here, your role is that of facilitator and coach. In your earlier caucuses, you may well have taken the opportunity to coach each party about how to make an apology or offer forgiveness or about the parameters of a plan for the future. If you have not done this, and the parties need assistance, you can coach them in the meeting, or if you feel that doing so would cause one to lose face (for example, by being asked for an apology when it is hard for him or her to give it), you could suggest a private round of caucuses at this time. My recommendation would be that you take care of all of the coaching needed prior to this meeting so that you will not interrupt the flow.

As the parties make their offers, listen to the package that is emerging in the flow of the conversation. Are all of the standard solutions being covered? Is anything being left out? If so, say so to the parties, and let them know that you think the process is incomplete.

Confront as Necessary

Do not be surprised if one or more of the parties shows tremendous resistance to offering or accepting one or more of the standard solutions. After all, these people have been involved in a dispute. The wounds may run very deep and the parties may have no experience with moving through such difficult topics. As stated earlier, you can coach the parties on how to go through the process. For example, you may need to coach them on how to make an apology. I am quick to remind parties that they should apologize only for things for which they truly feel apologetic. An apology may be something as simple as: "I am sorry for the impact that my behavior had on you. I didn't mean it to hurt you that way, but it is clear that it did hurt you. And I am sorry for the hurt that you experienced." Notice how carefully worded that apology is. A party can make such an apology in good faith, and with good result, even when the party feels that his or her behavior was justified.

Beyond coaching the parties, you may need to confront them with the following consequences of not taking steps toward one another:

- *Mutual harm.* If each party carries a wound or hurt into the future, this will affect any future relationship between them. It will cause a drain on emotional energy and may derail business and other activities.
- *Individual debilitation.* Nurturing a hurt and keeping a dispute alive can interfere with the individual's personal functioning.
- *Impact on other parties.* Children, co-workers, other constituents in political and governmental settings—there is usually someone who may suffer if the parties do not work things out.

Such confronting may best be done in private caucuses, but it could come during the joint meeting. The general rule of thumb is that if the confronting will not cause one party to lose face but, instead, puts the focus for movement on both parties at the same time, then do it in the open meeting. If it could expose one party too much, then do it privately.

Summarize and Plan Documentation

The wrap-up for an interpersonal peacemaking meeting is for the mediator to summarize what has happened and help the parties test the agreement for the future. If there are particular commitments regarding restitution and plans for the future, these will be included as a part of the written one-text agreement (see Chapter Nine), though the apologies and forgiveness will likely not be a part of any written record. Instead, they become a part of the verbal record and memory of each of the disputants. As mediator, you will likely have been summarizing all along during this meeting, and at the end, it will be time to give a final summary of what has occurred. The watchword for summaries such as this is to see that statements are accurate and behavioral, save face for the parties, and at the same time, give a clear path for the future, separate from whatever has been done toward healing in this very meeting.

You might say something such as the following to the parties described in the example used above:

> I do believe that the two of you have made considerable progress toward dealing with these difficulties from last summer. We all know that you can't take away what happened. Nor should I or anyone else ask you to simply "forget it." As a matter of fact, for the past hour we have gone through deliberate attempts to try to remember what happened, but we have done so with a special approach: we have asked you to talk about what happened, to clarify your intentions, and we have given you a chance to ask questions and get answers.
>
> We've also gone a step further: I've invited you to talk about your regrets and what you might wish had happened. In addition, you've each made apologies to one another, and more than that, you have made commitments about how you want to handle things from now on. For example, you have agreed to talk directly with one another about any concerns about your working relationship, and to use me as a backup mediator if you should ever need that. Also, you have gone on record with one another as saying that you will support one another in your respective jobs. You have agreed further to have weekly meetings with one another to talk about the work flow, and to find ways to include each other as backup for projects that require extra time. Also, you have agreed to do a daily check-in with one another on the work for that day, to make sure that everything gets covered.
>
> Finally, I have heard you say that you are willing to "let go" of some of those things that took place last summer. You agreed to think of this as forgiving one another. You are now ready to go forward without letting the dispute of last summer be a part of your working relationship. I commend you for this, and I wish you well in the months ahead. We agreed also to get together for a follow-up meeting once a month for the next two months, and then thereafter only as needed.
>
> Are there any other questions, or is there anything else either of you would like to say?

At this point, the parties may repeat something that has already been said, or not. A handshake would be appropriate at this time. There may be no written record of the apologies and forgiveness portion of the agreement, though the other parts may be put in writing (see Chapter Fourteen).

Summary

Interpersonal peacemaking on relationship issues can be approached during a single meeting, assuming that there have been caucuses with each party prior to the meeting to frame the issues for the joint discussion. In the private caucuses, you can help define and frame the problem, foreshadow possible solutions, and coach the parties on issues they may have to confront in the joint meeting (for example, if confronted with wrongdoing will they be prepared to apologize?). During the meeting itself, you can follow the steps outlined above, but do not worry too much about the order in which they are covered. The most important point is that the bases are touched in some way or another, since each may be critical to the final outcome.

EXERCISES

1.   Set up a role play involving a two-party dispute. For example, use the SouthCo case from Resource F. Using the agenda in this chapter as a guide, conduct a joint meeting with the parties, guiding them through the agenda for exploring the problem and encountering one another.

Note to each party: Have your grievances ready, and allow yourself to engage in tried-and-true disputing behavior such as interruptions and attacks. However, respond to any direction from the mediator that appropriately turns your attention to more useful paths: for example, discussing behavior from the past instead of engaging in a personal attack of the other side.

Note to mediator: Think of this task as guiding the parties and redirecting any behavior that smacks of a verbal free-for-all toward the steps involved in this chapter (not necessarily in the order given). For example, suppose Party A says something like, "You don't care about my future here, and you never did." You could respond, "Could you say that another way? Tell Party

B what happened in the past that has led you to conclude that she doesn't care about your future here. Be specific." Similarly, if Party B says something like, "Well, that's your problem!" in response to an attack, the mediator might suggest another direction: "It seems that you obviously don't like something about what he just said, could you say what it is that bothers you about his narrative of past problems?"

2.   As a variation, if the parties cannot successfully follow the agenda offered by the mediator, conduct brief caucuses with each party to coach them on the agenda and how they can best make use of the format you are offering for this meeting.

Chapter Seventeen

When Face-to-Face Meetings Won't Work

One standard variation on the five mediation steps is to dispense with the opening face-to-face meeting and move directly to caucuses with each party. There are at least three sets of circumstances when this might be appropriate: a joint meeting to start may be physically impractical, it may cause great discomfort to the parties, or it may keep serious talks from getting started at all. The following examples describe a specific situation of each type.

"I Won't Leave My Wife's Bedside!"

The head nurse asks a hospital patient representative to speak with Mr. Jones, the husband of a terminally ill cancer patient. He has been spending the majority of his time with his wife in her hospital room. Last night, Mrs. Jones was transferred to a critical care unit where families are permitted to visit for fifteen to thirty minutes every two hours. Due to the patient's anxiety over being placed on a ventilator, the staff made an exception to the rules and allowed Mr. Jones to remain by her side most of the night. Mr. Jones's complaint today is that the staff is now asking him to visit only at the scheduled times. He feels he has encountered a rigid nurse who enforces rules without regard to patient or family needs. The staff states that Mr. Jones's continual presence is interfering with their ability to provide the very best care for Mrs. Jones. One of the things most irritating to Mr. Jones has been the manner in which the nursing staff has approached him.

In this case, it would be impractical and inappropriate for a mediator to attempt to convene an opening meeting with Mr. Jones and one of the nursing staff. He likely would not want to leave his wife's bedside even for a mediation to solve the problem, and it would be inappropriate to conduct the mediation at her bedside. The most logical approach would be for the patient representative to speak privately with Mr. Jones at the bedside or in the corridor nearby, answering questions regarding mediation, explaining what the patient representative might do to solve the problem ("Perhaps I can talk to the nursing staff . . ."), and then moving directly to an inquiry to elicit Conflict Grid data (Step 3). Similarly, the first talk with the nurse could well move through first contact and opening meeting steps, then to Conflict Grid data collection (Step 3) again.

"I Won't Be in a Room with That Man!"

What does an ombudsman do in helping an employee decide what steps to take in dealing with sexual harassment in the workplace? Certainly, we can conceive of circumstances where it would be inappropriate to require that the victim and the alleged offender meet each other face-to-face. The most helpful and protective approach would be to do a full inquiry into the problem first, and then decide whether or not to propose a face-to-face meeting. Indeed, the entire mediation may be completed without the parties confronting one another directly. The mediator might respond to an inquiry by covering the questions under first contact (Step 1) with one party, then defining the ground rules and what the mediation option would be, eliciting a yes to going forward with the inquiry with this one party (Step 2), and then proceeding to ask questions and listen for important information that would be covered in the caucus (Step 3). After completing the same series of steps in one visit with the other party, the ombudsman would be in a position to know what the best next step might be—very likely it would be to shuttle between the parties, or depending upon what content emerged, to consider face-to-face meetings after exploration and coaching the parties on the meetings' purpose.

"We Can Only Get Together for a Day!"

If the parties live in different cities and can schedule a day for mediation but no more, the most sensible approach would be to conduct caucuses with each party on the telephone before the parties arrive for the one-day mediation. In this case, you would cover the first contact (Step 1) and caucuses (Step 3) with each party on the telephone, and then schedule the opening meeting (Step 2) to start the day when they all arrive in town. The opening meeting might be very brief (face-to-face discussion of the mediation process, how they will use it, ground rules, signing the agreement to mediate). It would be followed by joint discussions or shuttle meetings (Step 4).

Points to Remember

In skipping the opening meeting, you are moving past a formal step but not neglecting its content. Often, you will be collapsing Steps 1, 2, and 3 together into one event. In your first contact, you will answer all the questions that might be raised about the mediation process (Step 1), and explain what the process will be, including a summary of the ground rules, which you would ordinarily have given in the opening meeting, and then elicit a yes to going forward under the ground rules (Step 2). Since, at this point, you still will not have a commitment from the other side that mediation can go forward, you will tell the party with whom you are speaking, "I will see if [the other party] is interested in mediation when I talk to him." Then, still in that first visit, go forward with the inquiry regarding interests, facts, BATNAs, and possible solutions. In proceeding in this way, you maintain the integrity of the process by covering all the steps, while showing flexibility in not inappropriately bringing the parties together for a face-to-face meeting when circumstances require an adjustment.

EXERCISES

1. Considering your own experience in conflict management, list two or more situations where it would have been

appropriate to skip the opening meeting and go directly to caucuses.

2.   Identify the other changes in the five steps that might be required by the conflict situations where you are called upon to serve as mediator.

3.   Select a role play from Resource F and complete a mediation situation without using a formal opening meeting.

Chapter Eighteen

When Informal Mediation Can Help

Informal mediation is a standard variation that is frequently used by managers, team leaders, administrators, and consultants to organizations. Each of the following is an example of informal mediation at work:

- A human resources counselor assists a supervisor and employee in resolving a conflict over a performance evaluation.
- A hospital administrator talks to a physician about a complaint of rude treatment of the nursing staff.
- A strategic planning consultant helps a chief executive officer and others on the management team reach agreement on key features of a five-year plan.

This chapter will define the chief parameters of informal mediation, with a view toward suggesting ways that you can draw on the mediation model to enhance a wide range of other business and personal activities.

Defining Characteristics

Informal mediation has the following characteristics:

1. *The term mediation is seldom used.* The mediator simply performs the functions, without a formal title.

2. *The mediator might not use all five steps.* Instead, one or more parts of the model come into play to help two or more individuals reach agreement.

3.   *The goal is the same as that in the formal process:* a one-text integrative solution that honors the interests of the parties, squares with the available facts, and provides them with a solution that is better than their respective BATNAs.

4.   *The parties to a dispute must still work out their own solution,* as in formal mediation. This means that informal mediation can avoid the triangles that sometimes operate in the workplace when two individuals complain about their conflict to a third party but never deal directly with one another. While informal mediation may certainly involve private meetings with the parties, the ultimate objective will be to get the parties talking with one another and fashioning their own solution.

Informal Mediation in Action

The remainder of this chapter will summarize some of the most common examples of informal mediation in work and organizational settings.

Conflict Grid Talk During a Meeting

By far the most frequent (and the easiest) use of the mediation model in the workplace is for a manager to employ Conflict Grid categories in making a contribution to any discussion of a work-related problem. Imagine a conflict in the marketing department of a computer manufacturing firm when the subject on the table is whether the production department can deliver a product in time to fulfill the requirements of the new marketing plan. Absent an integrative model to analyze the problem and create solutions, the discussion runs the risk of deteriorating into accusations, turf battles, and excuses based on personalities. An alternative approach is for the manager to use Conflict Grid categories in asking questions and influencing a discussion: for example, Who are the key parties? What are their underlying interests? What facts will they bring to the table? What are their BATNAs? and so on. Without ever using the word mediation, and without ever conducting a caucus with any of the parties, a single manager can raise strategic questions about underlying interests and move the group toward fashioning solutions that not only do not violate these interests but, in fact, honor as many as possible.

Team Building

Astute managers can use the mediation model to understand the needs and interests of individual workers and to fashion ways to include these needs and interests in overall team efforts. What is the real reason one or two individuals go their own way and do not act like team players? An informal mediation model might involve holding individual visits with each (while taking a walk or over coffee or lunch), asking open-ended questions, and listening for underlying interests that are not being met by the current direction of the group.

Performance Evaluations

Managers are clearly involved in a negotiation process in attempting to achieve compliance of employees in meeting performance objectives. But what happens when an employee complains to the personnel department about unfair treatment by a supervisor? While some human resources departments offer formal mediation as a part of grievance procedures, others also use the mediation model as a part of their ongoing human resources responsibilities in talking with supervisors and employees. In this case, the human resources manager is not an agreed-upon neutral third party (indeed, the human resources manager functions in the chain of command and is seen by employees and supervisors as working for the organization), but he or she can use elements of the mediation model to assist the supervisor and employee in reaching an agreement. Individual meetings with the parties serve the function of caucuses in the mediation model, and an inquiry using Conflict Grid categories can be used to identify obstacles to performance and to create new solutions.

Troubleshooting

Whether the context is a government agency, a business, or a school, religious organization, or construction company, conflicts among people can be expected to occur as a part of the ongoing work process. Informal mediation can provide a model for analysis and for the creation of solutions that will enjoy the support of the parties who must carry them out. In some cases, the person assigned the troubleshooting function may use the word mediation to describe the process ("I am going to talk with each of you to try to understand what it will take to solve this problem. Think of me as a mediator, if you like. But the main thing is that we find some solution that works, and find it soon"). Depending upon the circumstances, the troubleshooter can use as many aspects of the formal mediation model as are appropriate, for example, honoring confidentiality of communications and structuring joint talks using elements of the interpersonal peacemaking model from Chapter Sixteen.

Organization Development

Most of the standard functions of organization development (OD) specialists (whether in-house or outside consultants) involve working with individuals and groups to assist them in some aspect of the change process. As anyone involved in such an effort can attest, there can be numerous obstacles to going forward, and one large set of obstacles involves conflict between individual and organizational goals. OD specialists, therefore, can use the mediation model, sometimes even structuring a process along the lines of the standard five steps, though perhaps using different terminology to describe the phases, all with a view to using Conflict Grid categories to analyze problems and create integrative solutions.

Strategic Planning

What is a successful strategic planning process if not an effort aimed at bringing key individuals in an organization together around a single plan? This is exactly the function of the one-text integrative solution in the mediation model. Most planners will conduct individual interviews with managers as a part of the early stage of the planning process, which provides them with an opportunity to use the Conflict Grid (in this case called a *collaboration* or *planning* grid) to collect data, and sketch possible options for the final plan. Some organizations will use formal mediation to resolve interpersonal and philosophical obstacles before spending money to hire consultants to undertake an expensive strategic planning process.

Summary

There are numerous opportunities in any organization for people to use aspects of the mediation process on an informal basis to help individuals and groups resolve problems and reach integrative solutions. There is nothing sacred about the five steps or about the term mediation. The key distinction is that when the term mediation is used, it will be important to honor all of the ethical guidelines that go along with mediation (see Resource C), and to clarify ground rules for the parties (as is done in the opening meeting). The parties must know the framework the mediator will use before they say yes or no to participating in the process. This does not prevent managers from using pieces of the mediation model to assist them in achieving other goals under other titles, for example, consultation, strategic planning, team building, or supervision. In these latter cases, the "truth in advertising" is that the main process is supervision, team building, strategic planning, and so on, though the process is enriched by using aspects of the mediation model to achieve goals.

EXERCISES

1.   Consider books you have read and television programs, movies, or plays you have seen in which one or more of the characters was serving as an informal mediator. Write out a critique of the informal mediator, using the five steps as a guide. For example, to what extent did the informal mediator use Conflict Grid categories to analyze the problem, or use impasse resolution techniques to break a deadlock, or use communication skills (Resource A) to help the parties understand the situation and move forward toward a solution?

2.   Considering your own experience as a manager, employee, parent, or neighbor, identify situations where you have already served as an informal mediator. What did you do

that contributed to your success or failure, based on principles you now understand from previous chapters in this volume?

3.   Using the categories identified in this chapter as a guide, determine the situations in which you anticipate serving as an informal mediator. How might you use elements of the model to enhance your performance?

Epilogue:
The Mediator's Calling

If you are new to the mediation process, this discussion of the five mediation steps will likely have brought you to the same conclusion that many others have reached: "I have been doing this all along!" The reality is that mediation draws on communication skills, analysis of problems, and initiative in problem solving that successful people have used throughout the ages in work, community, and home settings. At the same time, the five-step model should bring added clarity to your work in very complex situations, where the stakes are high and the parties are as willing to blame or make a scapegoat of the mediator as they are their adversaries. In a continuation of the coaching stance I have taken throughout this volume, I would add a few words of advice and encouragement as you begin to apply the model to your own situations.

1. *Enhance your learning by looking for the numerous applications of the model outside the formal mediation process.* I once heard a lecturer on behavior modification for mental health professionals admonish the audience: "These principles will *not* work on your own children and pets!" I would like to suggest that the mediation principles, while perhaps limited with your pets, could certainly be applied at home. We all have conflicts with our children, spouses, neighbors, and co-workers. Continued use of the Conflict Grid will sharpen your skills in listening to disputants and in finding ways to assist in creating integrative solutions to honor their interests.

2. *Join mediation organizations to share experiences, support one another, and increase skills.* Most states now have associations of mediators, as do most local communities. Whether through your local dispute resolution center; your county, state and national bar

associations; or organizations such as the Society of Professionals in Dispute Resolution, the Academy of Family Mediators, the Association of Family and Conciliation Courts, or subgroups in the national associations for psychologists, human resources professionals, and other managers, find colleagues who are also engaging in mediation on a regular basis. Exchange notes, attend continuing education seminars, and you will find that your own skills will grow.

3.   *Share in the spadework and creative efforts required to confront issues of licensing and certification in the future.* Many of your colleagues from various professions (such as law, behavioral sciences, community dispute resolution, and academia) are already hard at work confronting the issue of whether or not mediation is a process that can be certified and licensed. Some controversy exists around whether mediation can survive as both a social skill and a professional discipline, and colleagues on several sides of this issue are diligently working to fashion integrative solutions. Join the effort, and apply the mediation model to what you do. Listen carefully to the interests represented by those who fear that licensing and certification will restrict participation and also to the interests of those who lobby for some structure to bring order and client protection to the field alongside other disciplines. There is no better place to test the limits of our model than on issues that involve our own day-to-day reality and practice.

4.   *Invite and share in an organizational and anthropological critique of the mediation field.* Not all cultures view collaborative conflict resolution (and peacemaking) with the same value, nor do they view the merits of mediation the same way as you may.[1] While holding fast to your current applications of the mediation model, expand your horizons through cross-cultural communication and initiatives to learn how the model may need to be changed for use by others in cultures different from your own.

5.   *Use the mediation model for prevention.* Remember that mediation is one form of collaboration (alongside negotiation), and that collaboration occurs every day, well before there might be a conflict or dispute. Whether under the main heading of problem prevention or enhancement of human relationships, you can double both your effectiveness and your own learning by applying the principles of mediation to the planning process and to all negoti-

ations at the start of a relationship, long before there is any possibility of a dispute.

EXERCISES

1.   Make a list of steps that you might take to enhance your skills as a mediator.

2.   Consider your own perspective on conflict management throughout the world. What are the areas where you have the greatest interest in seeing mediation grow?

3.   What can you do to encourage this growth?

Resources

Resource A:
Communication Skills Review

Seasoned mediators know that communication skills are essential for building rapport with the parties and for gaining critical information regarding interests, feelings, and other facts of the case. While the primary focus of this book is on mediation, the following review of basic communication skills will be useful for beginning mediators.

The Level I and Level II communication skills identified in this resource can be used to help you work the Grid during caucuses, and also to help you coach parties toward analyzing problems and creating solutions. To appreciate the role of communication skills in mediation, we can look at analogies from sports and music. Communication skills are to mediation much as the skills of running, throwing, hitting, and catching are to baseball, or as the skills of playing notes on a scale (including sharps and flats!) are to musical performance. In the case of a baseball player, the specific skills of running, throwing, and so on are required in order to play the game and are prerequisite to knowing the finer points of how to throw a player out who is stealing home or how to make a double play. Similarly, musicians, once they have learned how to play particular notes, are then in a position to make true music by combining notes into chords. Likewise, mediators must know *how* to communicate before they can help parties through the process of dispute resolution.

In human affairs, it is often the parties' failure to execute good communication that has led to conflict and created a need for mediation. The mediator can help in two ways: first, by modeling good communication skills and, second, by coaching the parties in how to communicate better with one another at certain points in the mediation process.

Verbal Versus Nonverbal Communication

While most people think of communication as being a verbal exercise, it is equally true that body language (gestures, facial expressions, body positioning) all serve as strong indicators of what parties are thinking and feeling. In most cases, the parties are unaware of their nonverbal communications. Communication specialists such as psychotherapists and counselors are careful to notice contradictions between verbal behavior and nonverbal behavior. For example, a party might say, "I'm fine with that," at the same time clenching his fists or gripping the arm of the chair tightly.

No one can know for certain what nonverbal behavior means to the person who is communicating. The primary objective is therefore to observe nonverbal behavior and compare it with the verbal message, noting contradictions and discussing them with the party. Watch for nonverbal behavior of the types listed here, and explore the implications of the suggested messages.

- Posture and body position:
  Slouching—tired or bored with the process
  Body position turned away—turned off by the message or the speaker
  Moving in chair—anxious about the message being heard, or eager to talk
  Arms folded and crossed—"Show me," or an attitude of disbelief
- Facial expressions:
  Direct eye contact—agreement, especially if accompanied by a head nod, as if listener is tracking the communication
  Scowl—disapproval
  Narrowing and squinting of eyes—criticizing or rejecting the message
- Voice volume and speech:
  Loud and rapid speech—anger or anxiety
  Slow speech, low volume—discouragement, sadness, depression

Research on nonverbal communication is not at a point where mediators can be given clear guidelines on what a particular behavior means—and our knowledge may never get to that point, given the amount of individual variation. Party A may speak loudly in anger while Party B's loud reply may reflect a hearing deficit. Your best course is to simply use nonverbal behavior as a second data source, comparing it to the verbal message to see if there is a good fit or not. If there is wide divergence between the verbal and nonverbal message, ask the party what it means. For example, a mediator might say to one of the parties in caucus: "Tom, I hear you say that you can agree with the proposal, but as I look at your face when you talk, you don't seem very enthused about the idea. The words say yes, but your gestures say no. What's going on?"

Do not fall into the trap of trying to tell the party what the gestures mean, but simply observe the contradiction and "play back," or reflect, what you observe. Then ask the party for clarification. In most cases, this will lead to an admission of ambivalence, or some other breakthrough, to give more precise meaning to what the party's communication is intended to be.

Level I Communication Skills

Three basic skills are essential for building rapport and gaining needed information from the parties: *active listening, self-disclosing,* and *questioning.*

Active Listening

Active listening is a method through which the mediator focuses entirely upon the speaker's communications and internal frame of reference (that is, what is known of the speaker's feelings and other views) and then reflects back to the speaker what has been heard, to check understanding of what has been said. In active listening, the focus is not on the listener's view or opinion but rather on the speaker's content. Active listening in mediation has the following characteristics:

- The focus is on interests, feelings, perceptions, desires.
- The listener's statements are reflective and often empathic; they "play back" what the listener has heard.

- The listener's statements frequently deal with the other person's view, feeling, or report of the situation.

Sample Sentences

Here are some statements that characterize active listening and some that are the opposite of active listening.

Active Listening	Opposite
• If I understand you correctly, you believe that . . .	• That doesn't make sense . . .
• You seem to be concerned that . . .	• Let me tell you how I see it . . .
• It appears that your view is . . .	• That may work for you, but remember this . . .

Standard Applications

Use active listening whenever you are trying to generate more information from a party. Active listening primes the pump, so to speak, and encourages more talk. For example, a mediator might say, "If I hear you correctly, you are bothered by at least three things here [list them accurately]." If you are accurate in your summary, using the party's own words, you will get a head nod, and the party will very likely feel that you have really heard what he or she has been trying to say. If you are off base in any way, the party will let you know, either with a nonverbal gesture (quizzical look) or with a clear no or a correction. In this case, the process is also helped, since you are able now to refine your understanding of what the party is telling you.

Self-Disclosing

Self-disclosing is a communication skill that focuses on the speaker's feelings, thoughts, or beliefs. It has these characteristics:

- It uses "I" statements to communicate "my" interests, views, feelings.
- It deliberately gives the listener more information about data that would otherwise be known only by inference or guess. For example, you might be able to infer from my behavior

that I am angry; however, since anger is an internal state, you will know much more if I also *tell* you that I am angry, and why.

Sample Sentences

Here are some statements that indicate self-disclosure at work, and others that are the opposite of self-disclosure.

Self-Disclosing	Opposite
• I am concerned about . . .	• The whole thing costs way too much . . .
• It seems to me that . . .	• Everybody knows that . . .
• My interest is . . .	• There's no way you'll get agreement on . . .
• I am worried . . .	• Keep doing that and [threat] . . .

Standard Applications

In mediation, your goal will be to get the parties to self-disclose as much as possible—to you in caucus and to one another in joint meetings—regarding interests, feelings, views, and preferences. In most disputes, the parties are so frightened of one another, believing (often correctly) that information they disclose may be used against them by their adversary, that self-disclosure will be perceived as a high-risk behavior. You will very likely, therefore, invite self-disclosures in caucuses, to pave the way for further discussions between the parties during joint meetings.

Sometimes, you will need to model self-disclosing behavior to the party in caucus. For example, you might say, "I have still not heard what you really want on this issue, though, as I put myself in your shoes, I can imagine that I would feel upset over what has been said and quite worried that unless something changes, my job would be at risk. Are you feeling anything like this?"

Questioning

Questioning is a basic communication skill aimed at eliciting and clarifying data. There are two basic types of questions and three time dimensions.

- Open-ended questions (who, what, where, why, when, how) can be used to generate data.
- Closed-ended questions (those yielding a yes or no answer) can be used to refine and clarify statements and test commitment.
- Both types of questions can focus on the past, the present, or the future.

Open-ended questions are standard fare in mediation, and open the door for the mediator to hear information that can be used to fill out the Conflict Grid. In addition to the who, what, where, why, when, and how questions, mediators can also probe with statements that declare the mediator's interest in information, followed by a question, For example, the mediator can say, "I really want to know how you feel about this matter. Could you tell me how you react to the proposal as I have presented it to you?" While the question invites a yes or no answer, a yes answer leads naturally to, "Go ahead and tell me." If the answer is no, the mediator might then say: "Help me understand why you would rather not talk about that."

Sample Sentences

Here are some examples of open-ended and closed-ended questions.

Open	*Closed*
• What other information might be needed in order to assess damages?	• Did you get an appraisal?
• Who else expressed an interest in this problem?	• Did you tell them you would be late?
• How do you see this situation?	• How long have you worked here?

Standard Applications

In the early going of any mediation, when the goal is to generate as much information about interests and other facts as possible, open-ended questions will be the order of the day: "What happened to make you feel this way?" "How have you coped with this situation so far?" and the like. Once information is available, and the parties have begun to sort through interests, facts, proposals, and various solutions, then you will frequently ask closed-ended questions such as: "Will this proposal work for you, or not?" "If she agrees to this payment, and also makes these changes in the procedures for doing business from now on, will you agree to put the matter behind you, and to support her in these efforts?"

In sum, the three Level I communication skills—active listening, self-disclosing, and questioning—are used by negotiating parties to clarify information from the other person, the speaker, and the world surrounding the problem. Mediators will use all three communication skills themselves and will also model and coach the parties on using these skills in generating needed information. The diagram below summarizes the focal points of the three Level I skills.

Level II Communication Skills

Once information has been generated through active listening, self-disclosing, and questioning, another series of communication skills can be used to translate, expand, and channel the information. Level II skills include *reframing,* to give a different perspective on any piece of information; *brainstorming,* to generate possible solutions based on the information available; and *confronting,* to control the negative impact of a negotiating style.

Reframing

Reframing involves changing the wording, concept, or description of a piece of information to make it easier to understand or accept. It has the following characteristics:

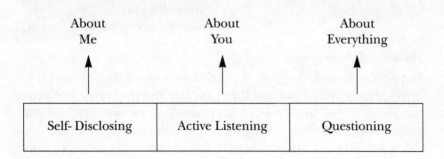

- It is a translation exercise through which the mediator changes the communication by moving it from one language to another, with the hope that in the second language, the content may be more palatable to the other side or more conducive to collaborative problem-solving.
- It is a useful technique for moving from positions to interests.
- It is especially useful for unloading or defusing intense situations by using a different word or term to describe something that one party may have stated in a particularly obnoxious fashion.

Sample Sentences

Here are some types of statements you may hear from mediation parties, and some things you can do to reframe them to move the mediation forward. The first two try to change poisonous language into a more useful form, and the second two address a shift in basic concepts.

Original	*Reframed*
• The guy's an absolute jerk.	• By that you mean, he is often late, he interrupts people, and he doesn't seem to listen.
• She's a total loser.	• Could you tell me how her performance falls short of the mark?
• I can't get my way.	• Maybe you'll have better luck if he gets something out of it, too. How about trying for a win/win?
• He's selfish.	• Maybe he's also apprehensive about his performance, and worried about failure.

Standard Applications

Disputants frequently get into logjams because of the way they perceive each other or the way they perceive the problem. The standard use of reframing is to give another perspective on the problem (for example, pointing out that the stress of a move into a new building is as much a causal factor in things not happening on time as is the "laziness" of a subordinate). Any reframe must be data-based in that the new concept must be supported by available facts.

As the sample sentences indicate, reframing can take two primary forms. One is to change or eliminate loaded or poisonous language. The other is to change an entire concept. For example, one party might refer to an idea as "silly" or another person as "crazy." The reframing approach is to reword the offending statement so as to focus on the key characteristics or behaviors that seem silly or crazy while editing out the offensive language. Reframing language should not weaken or diminish a criticism but should focus on solving the problem rather than attacking a person.

As an example of a concept change, consider an international leader mediating for the release of hostages in the Middle East. He challenged the leader of a country holding the hostages to consider a different view of the release of the hostages. He told the leader in question not to think of the release of the hostages as "giving in to pressure" but, instead, to view it as a "bold new move" for international diplomacy. Not capitulation, but leadership. A new frame that in this case opened the door to the release of hostages.

Brainstorming

Brainstorming is a Level II communication skill that aims to generate possible solutions to a problem that has already been defined in terms of interests and other supporting facts. Brainstorming has the following characteristics:

- It asks "what if" questions.
- It allows ideas to be put forward without critique. Instead, brainstorming saves the critique for later, so that the communicator will not hold back for fear that fresh ideas will be attacked early on.
- It is particularly useful for creating integrative solutions that might honor the interests of both parties in mediation.

Sample Sentences

Brainstorming deliberately evokes ideas, while the opposite approach cuts them off. Here are some typical examples:

Brainstorming	*Opposite*
• Let's see how many ideas we can generate, without criticizing any one of them at the start.	• That will never work!
• What if . . .	• He'll hate the idea.
• What could you recommend about this?	• Forget it!

Standard Applications

Brainstorming is typically used in the closing phase of each of the early caucuses in mediation, when the mediator asks the party to identify possible solutions based on what has been said so far and what is known so far about the interests of the other side. It is quite common for the parties to have stopped the brainstorming process and to be imposing positions or demands on each other by the time they get to the mediator. Frequently, the mediator will need to make an argument for brainstorming. For example, the mediator might say: "I know you have told me you see no other solution to this problem, but let's try an experiment. Let's pretend that some benefactor will give all of us $100,000 for each idea we can generate, no matter how crazy, and that we have five minutes to earn as much money as we can. You have each heard what the other person needs here, and we know about the other constraints on your company; now, what steps might the two of you take to solve this problem?" Creative problem-solvers know that workable solutions often grow from what start out as wild and crazy brainstorming ideas. As a mediator, you may need to structure time for brainstorming to open the door to possible workable solutions.

Confronting

Confronting is a communication skill used by mediators to encourage one or more of the parties to stop a particular negotiating behavior that is destructive to the process. It is typically done in caucus, though in some cases it will occur in the joint meeting. Confrontations that attack ("You don't know what you're talking about") typically lead to defensive behavior from the other side ("I do too know what I'm talking about") and to a counterattack ("You are the one who is missing the point!"). Disputing parties often need assistance in confronting one another.

One approach is to use a *when-I-because* sequence. This will include the three elements of behavior (what the other person is doing that bothers the speaker), the speaker's reaction to the behavior (often a feeling), and reason for the reaction (a justification of some sort). In this sequence, the mediator encourages a party to cover the following points:

- *When* [state the behavior, for example, "When you come in late to these meetings . . ."].
- *I* [state personal feeling or reaction, for example, "I get upset"].
- *Because* [state reason, for example, "because it looks to me like you don't care about what we're trying to do here"].

A when-I-because statement gives the other side clear information as a part of the confrontation, which lets him or her know what behavior might need to be changed in the future in order to get a different reaction from the listener. The information then lays the groundwork for negotiation regarding behavior.

Sample Sentences

Confrontation can be either constructive or destructive to the mediation process. Here are some examples of both approaches:

Effective Confrontation	*Opposite*
• When these reports come in a day or more after deadline, I get frustrated because it makes me think you don't care that I need them on time.	• You don't give a damn about the impact of your late reports.
• When I read that memo with its criticism of my work, I felt humiliated because there wasn't a single reference to anything I was doing right.	• You don't care about me.

- When they changed the meeting time, I got suspicious (and I decided to be careful of these people) because the last time they did that it meant they did not want to work out anything anyway.

- These people can't be trusted.

Standard Applications

Confronting points out a negative in the person to whom it is addressed so it can be risky to do in joint sessions, where it might appear that the mediator is siding with one party over the other. In the privacy of a caucus, confronting can be a very useful technique for the mediator to help one of the parties change destructive negotiating behavior. For example, a mediator might say to a CEO during a private caucus:

> Bob, I certainly can't speak for your colleagues, but in the privacy of this room, I want to let you know how I have reacted as I have watched all five of you talk during these recent meetings. I've noticed that the first words out of your mouth are often negatives, such as, "That won't work," or, "We tried that," or something else. If I imagine for a moment that I am one of your subordinates, here's how I might react: "When I hear the negative as your first response, I get discouraged, and reluctant to bring ideas to you, because, after all, I'm looking for at least some support for what I am trying to do."

Summary

Communication is the bedrock of negotiation and mediation. Many disputes occur because of the disputants' own poor communication skills. Mediators can model constructive communication skills and, at times, coach parties individually or together on ways to enhance communication so as to achieve understanding and create solutions.

Resource B: Sample Ground Rules and Forms

The parties to any formal mediation should be provided with written ground rules, information about the mediator (a résumé), an agreement to mediate, and any other descriptions of the process that may help the parties understand how mediation differs from the alternatives.

The forms in this resource are used by Chorda Conflict Management, Inc., and can serve as a guide for you in drafting your own forms. In-house mediators (for example, mediation teams relating to employee relations or human resources departments) must address issues of confidentiality and how mediation relates to other components of an in-house grievance process. The forms in this resource are generic and can be edited and revised for use in commercial, corporate, organizational, and family settings.

MEDIATION GROUND RULES

Introduction

The purpose of these ground rules is to define the mediation process and to serve as a guide for the parties in deciding whether or not to use mediation to solve a business problem or resolve a conflict.

Section 1: General Principles

a.   *Definition of Mediation.* Mediation is a process through which a third party assists two or more other parties in reaching agreement on any issue. Mediation may be used as a part of a planning process (before there is a problem or conflict) or as a method for formal dispute resolution. Mediation is to be distinguished from arbitration and litigation, in which third parties (judge, panel, jury) decide the matter for the parties.

b.   *Outcome(s).* The objective of mediation is for the parties to reach agreement on steps to be taken to go forward with a plan, solve a problem, resolve a conflict, or settle a dispute.

c.   *Structure of the Process.* The Mediator will provide information to the parties who inquire about mediation (through telephone contacts with all parties, including follow-up with written materials) and then schedule a joint opening meeting. The remainder of the process will include a combination of individual, confidential caucuses (private meetings with each party), joint meetings, and/or shuttle meetings until the parties reach either an agreement or an impasse. The process may be stopped at any time by the Mediator's declaring an impasse or by one or more parties stopping participation.

Section 2: The Role of the Mediator(s)

a.   The Mediator will provide information to the parties regarding mediation, clarify ground rules, and structure a process for balanced discussion of the issues.

b.   The Mediator will strive to maintain an impartial stance, and will disclose any relevant biases or conflicts of interest to the parties.

c.   The Mediator will also explain fees, confidentiality, and other aspects of the process required for the parties to make a decision regarding participation.

Section 3: Role of the Parties

a.   By participating in the mediation process, the parties agree to work with the Mediator and with the other parties in defining interests, generating relevant background information, and creating possible solutions.

b.   Since participation is voluntary, the parties are not bound to accept any solutions proposed during mediation. Similarly, the parties may at any time terminate the process, and pursue other options for dispute resolution.

Section 4: Attorney Representation and Consultation

a.   The parties may seek independent legal consultation at any time during the mediation process.

b.   The parties may also be represented by counsel during the mediation.

Section 5: Confidentiality

a.   The Mediator will maintain the confidentiality of all information produced during the mediation process, and will not disclose information to anyone outside the process without permission of all parties.

b.   By participation in the process, the parties waive their right to subpoena the Mediator in any subsequent litigation, and waive the right to require the Mediator to produce documents generated during the mediation.

Section 6: Agreement to Mediate

By signing the Agreement to Mediate, the parties indicate their willingness to abide by the mediation rules throughout the duration of the mediation process.

Section 7: Fees

The Mediator will charge an hourly fee, which will be shared equally by the parties, unless arranged otherwise at the start of mediation.

Section 8: Cancellation

If a party desires to cancel a mediation appointment, he or she will notify the Mediator (and, if applicable, other parties) not less than 24 hours prior to the scheduled session. Otherwise the Mediator will be entitled to compensation for the canceled mediation session.

Section 9: Mediation Outcome and Termination

If the parties reach agreement, the Mediator will draft an agreement for review and signature by the parties.

Any party or the Mediator may declare an impasse, at which time the Mediator will assist the parties in exploring next steps after the mediation, as well as conditions under which the parties may resume mediation.

Section 10: Interpretation of Rules

The Mediator shall interpret these Rules[1] in accordance with his or her sole discretion and determination, and such interpretation shall be binding upon the parties during mediation.

Agreement to Mediate

The parties listed below wish to reach an agreement on one or more issues. For this purpose, we make the following initial agreement:

1. The topic(s) to be the subject of mediation is (are):

   _____

   _____

2. The mediation process has been explained to me; I have read and agree to be bound by the Chorda Mediation Ground Rules.
3. I understand that mediation does not take the place of independent legal advice and, if necessary, will seek my own legal counsel on the issues under discussion.
4. Other stipulations:

   _____

   _____

Signed on the _____ day of _____ 19 _____ .

_____   _____
Party   Party

_____   _____
Party   Party

_____
Mediator

The Mediation Process

The mediation process includes the following:

(a) First Contact (telephone or face-to-face): The mediator explains the process, ground rules, and fee arrangements and answers questions.

(b) Opening Meeting (face-to-face or telephone conference call): The mediator invites each party to offer a brief summary of the issue(s), and assists all in planning the agenda. All parties sign an Agreement to Mediate.

(c) Private Meeting: The mediator meets with each party individually (confidential caucus) to elicit further detail on important interests and facts.

(d) The mediator continues with individual meetings (shuttle diplomacy) and/or joint meetings, as needed.

(e) Throughout the process the mediator assists the parties in identifying interests and options, and cooperating with one another to secure additional information (for example, appraisals, testimony of experts), all with a view to reaching a mutually agreeable solution.

(f) If more time is needed, or if the parties require further data before reaching an agreement, additional meetings may be scheduled.

(g) Once an agreement is reached, the mediator assists the parties in planning all steps for implementation, including drafting a memorandum of agreement.

(h) If the parties reach an impasse, the mediator assists them in deciding whether to schedule further mediation or to pursue other avenues for resolution.

Resource C:
Ethical Standards

Ethical Standards of Professional Conduct for Members of the Society of Professionals in Dispute Resolution[1]

Application of the Standards

Adherence by SPIDR members to these standards is basic to professional conduct. SPIDR members commit themselves to be guided in their professional conduct by these standards. The SPIDR Board of Directors is available to advise members about interpretation of these standards. Other neutral practitioners and organizations are welcome to follow these standards.

Scope

It is recognized that SPIDR members resolve disputes in various sectors within the disciplines of dispute resolution and have their own codes of professional conduct. These standards have been developed as general guidelines of practice for neutral disciplines represented in the SPIDR membership. Ethical considerations relevant to some, but not all, of these disciplines are covered by these standards.

A. *General Responsibilities*

Neutrals have a duty to the parties, to the profession, and to themselves. They should be honest and unbiased, act in good faith, be diligent, and not seek to advance their own interests at the expense of the parties.

Neutrals must act fairly in dealing with the parties, have no personal interest in the terms of the settlement, show no bias toward individuals and institutions involved in the dispute, be reasonably available as requested by the parties, and be certain that the parties are informed of the process in which they are involved.

B.   The Neutral's Responsibilities to the Parties

1. *Impartiality*—The neutral must maintain impartiality toward all parties. Impartiality means freedom from favoritism or bias either by word or by action, and a commitment to serve all parties, as opposed to a single party.

2. *Informed Consent*—The neutral has an obligation to assure that all parties understand the nature of the process, the procedures, the particular role of the neutral, and the parties' relationship to the neutral.

3. *Confidentiality*—Maintaining confidentiality is critical to the dispute resolution process. Confidentiality encourages candor, a full exploration of the issues and a neutral's acceptability. There may be some types of cases, however, in which confidentiality is not protected. In such cases the neutral must advise the parties, when appropriate in the dispute resolution process, that the confidentiality of the proceedings cannot necessarily be maintained. Except in such instances, the neutral must resist all attempts to cause him or her to reveal any information outside the process. A commitment by the neutral to hold information in confidence within the process also must be honored.

4. *Conflict of Interest*—The neutral must refrain from entering or continuing in any dispute if he or she believes or perceives that participation as a neutral would be a clear conflict of interest. The neutral also must disclose any circumstance that may create or give the appearance of a conflict of interest and any circumstance that may reasonably raise a question as to the neutral's impartiality.

The duty to disclose is a continuing obligation.

5. *Promptness*—The neutral shall exert every reasonable effort to expedite the process.

6. *The Settlement and Its Consequences*—The dispute resolution process belongs to the parties. The neutral has no vested interest in the terms of a settlement, but must be satisfied that

agreements in which he or she has participated will not impugn the integrity of the process. The neutral has a responsibility to see that the parties consider the terms of a settlement. If the neutral is concerned about the possible consequences of a proposed agreement, and the needs of the parties dictate, the neutral must inform the parties of that concern. In adhering to this standard the neutral may find it advisable to educate the parties, to refer one or more parties for specialized advice, or to withdraw from the case. In no case, however, shall the neutral violate section 3, above, Confidentiality, of these standards.

C. Unrepresented Interests

The neutral must consider circumstances where interests are not represented in the process. The neutral has an obligation, where in his or her judgment the needs of the parties dictate, to assure that such interests have been considered by the principal parties.

D. Use of Multiple Procedures

The use of more than one dispute resolution procedure by the same neutral involves additional responsibilities. Where the use of more than one procedure is initially contemplated, the neutral must take care at the outset to advise the parties of the nature of the procedures and the consequences of revealing information during any one procedure which the neutral may later use for decision making or may share with another decision maker. Where the use of more than one procedure is contemplated after the initiation of the dispute resolution process, the neutral must explain the consequences and afford the parties an opportunity to select another neutral for the subsequent procedures. It is also incumbent upon the neutral to advise the parties of the transition from one dispute resolution process to another.

E. Background and Qualifications

A neutral should accept responsibility only in cases where the neutral has sufficient knowledge regarding the appropriate process and subject matter to be effective. A neutral has a responsibility to maintain and improve his or her professional skills.

F.   Disclosure of Fees

It is the duty of the neutral to explain to the parties at the outset of the process, the bases of compensation, fees, and charges, if any.

G.   Support of the Profession

The experienced neutral should participate in the development of new neutrals in the field and engage in efforts to educate the public about the value and use of neutral dispute resolution procedures. The neutral should provide *pro bono* services, as appropriate.

H.   Responsibilities of Neutrals Working on the Same Case

In the event that more than one neutral is involved in the resolution of a dispute, each has an obligation to inform the others regarding his or her entry in the case. Neutrals working with the same parties should maintain an open and professional relationship with each other.

I.   Advertising and Solicitation

A neutral must be aware that some forms of advertising and solicitation are inappropriate and, in some conflict resolution disciplines such as labor arbitration, are impermissible. All advertising must honestly represent the services to be rendered. No claims of specific results or promises which imply favor of one side over another for the purpose of obtaining business should be made. No commissions, rebates, or other similar forms of remuneration should be given or received by a neutral for the referral of clients.

Resource D: Mediation of Disputes Involving Domestic Violence

Report of the Academy of Family Mediators (AFM) Task Force on Spousal and Child Abuse[1]

This report is for educational purposes only and is not intended as an AFM policy.

Family violence, which is mostly perpetrated against women, and its impact on children, continues to pose serious questions for dispute resolution professionals and the practice of mediation. Women's advocates, mediators, mental health workers, lawyers and the judiciary are increasingly working together to better understand the complex consequences of family violence. Collaboration is increasing among mediators and advocates from victims' networks.

Some critics consider divorce mediation to be inappropriate in cases where domestic violence is an issue because of the fear of retribution, the absence of trust, and the imbalance of power between the parties. They argue that mediation may not protect parties from coerced settlements and from subsequent intimidation and violence; they believe litigation is preferable to mediation in these cases.

For cases in which there is abuse, a question often asked is whether the legal process—including arrest, protective orders, and litigation—is adequate to restructure a post-separation parenting relationship which will work in the best interests of all involved. This subject continues to be a topic of much debate.

These guidelines address some of the issues involved in determining which cases may be appropriate for mediation and offers recommendations regarding ways to safeguard the physical safety and legal rights of all parties.

Basic Guidelines for Mediators

- Family mediation cases in which there is or has been domestic violence are complicated and can be dangerous to the participants and the mediator. Therefore, beginning mediators and mediators not trained or experienced in domestic violence should not accept referrals of these cases but rather should refer them to an experienced mediator or to another appropriate resource. Another choice would be for an inexperienced mediator to co-mediate with someone who has considerable professional experience dealing with domestic violence.
- If the abuse history or potential for violence is sufficient to jeopardize a party's ability to negotiate without fear or duress, the case should not be mediated.
- There should be no mediation concerning the violence itself. For instance, an offer to stop hitting in exchange for something else should not be tolerated.
- When safety is an issue, the mediator's obligation is to provide a safe environment for cooperative problem solving or, when this does not seem workable, to help the clients consider more appropriate alternatives.
- Above all, the mediator must promote the safety of all participants in the mediation process.

Guidelines for Assessing Whether Mediation May Be Appropriate

A. Prior to commencing mediation, screen all clients for a history of abuse to determine which cases are inappropriate for mediation, which require additional safeguards in addition to or instead of mediation, and which should be referred to other resources.

  1. Conduct initial screening separately with the parties. This could be done a variety of ways. For example, screening could take place within a brief telephone or face-to-face interview, or with a written questionnaire. Using a structured questionnaire, basic information can be gathered which includes details about any history of abuse. If screening is not done separately, a victim may be unwilling to reveal the presence of violence and/or may be placed at risk for revealing the violence.

2. Screening should continue throughout the mediation process.

B. Whether couples enter mediation voluntarily, or because it is mandated by statute or court/local rule, matters of safety, free choice, and informed consent require special consideration, especially in situations where domestic violence is a factor.

   1. Mediators and mediation services have an ethical duty to assure that mediation occurs in a safe environment and that the process goes forward only if both parties have the ability to mediate safely, autonomously, and free from any intimidation. The parties must be capable of reaching outcomes satisfactory to both of them voluntarily, and with informed consent. If these conditions cannot be met, mediation needs to be terminated safely and appropriately.

   2. In order to assure safety and freedom from coercion, it is important that the courts not view a party's request to waive the mediation requirement as evidence of a lack of cooperation.

   3. In jurisdictions in which there is mandatory mediation, it is especially important that there be separate screening. In addition, the following options should be made available:
      a. separate sessions
      b. the presence of a support person
      c. an exemption from the mediation requirement

C. Clients should be strongly encouraged to consult with attorneys prior to mediation and certainly before an agreement is finalized.

D. Mediators must be knowledgeable about domestic violence. Training for mediators should include the following:
   1. Issues related to physical and psychological abuse and its effect on family members
   2. The impact that family violence (including witnessing violence) has on children
   3. Effective techniques for screening, implementing safety measures and safe termination
   4. Referral to appropriate resources, in addition to, or instead of mediation
   5. Sensitivity to cultural, racial and ethnic differences that may be relevant to domestic violence

E. When a decision is made that mediation may proceed,

mediators need to assure standards of safety, voluntariness, and fairness. When mediators have concerns, they should inform their clients that they are not neutral about safety.

The following are recommended procedural guidelines:

1. Obtain training in domestic violence and become familiar with the literature.
2. Never mediate the fact of the violence.
3. Never support a couple's trading non-violent behavior for obedience.
4. Set ground rules to optimize the victim's protection.
5. When appropriate and possible, arrange separate waiting areas and separate arrival and leaving times, permitting the victim to arrive last and leave first with a reasonable lag in time for safety purposes.
6. Use separate meetings throughout the mediation process when appropriate, necessary, and/or helpful.
7. Consider co-mediation with a male/female mediation team, as an option.
8. Maintain a balance of power between the couple, and, if this is not possible, terminate the mediation process and refer the couple to an appropriate alternative process. Such alternatives might include shelters, therapists, abuse prevention groups, and attorneys.
9. Allow a support person to be present in the waiting room and/or mediation session.
10. Terminate the mediation if either of the participants is unable to mediate safely, competently, and without fear of coercion. Precautions should be taken in terminating in order to assure the safety of the parties. For example, the mediator should not reveal information to one party or to the court that could create a risk for the other party.
11. Consider offering a follow-up session to assess the need for a modification of the agreement.
12. Work with diverse cultural and ethnic groups serving violent families to develop appropriate and culturally sensitive options for resolving issues related to separation and divorce when domestic violence is an issue.

Revised February 1995

Resource E:
Professional Organizations

ABA Standing Committee on Dispute Resolution
1800 M Street, NW
Suite 290-N
Washington, DC 20036
(202) 331-2258

Academy of Family Mediators
1500 South Highway 100, Suite 355
Golden Valley, MN 55416–1593
(612) 525-8670

The American Arbitration Association
140 West 51st Street
New York, NY 10020–1203
(212) 484-4000

The Association of Family and Conciliation Courts
329 West Wilson Street
Madison, WI 53703
(608) 251-4001

Center for Public Resources
366 Madison Avenue
New York, NY 10017–2311
(212) 949-6490

National Institute for Dispute Resolution
1726 M Street, NW
Suite 500
Washington, DC 20036–4502
(202) 466-4764

The Ombudsman Association
5521 Greenville Avenue
Dallas, TX 75206
(214) 553-0043

Society of Professionals in Dispute Resolution
815 Fifteenth Street, NW
Suite 530
Washington, DC 20005
(202) 783-7281

Resource F: Cases

This resource includes several role plays that can be used for the chapter exercises that call for mediation situations, or as models for creating additional role plays for training purposes.[1]

Consider the following guidelines in structuring role plays:

- Choose roles as follows: mediator, each party, and observer.
- Allow all participants to read the general instructions, but restrict the reading of confidential information to the respective parties to whom it applies.
- Instruct the parties to stay in their roles, offering confidential information only insofar as the mediator skillfully asks the right questions and creates an atmosphere for information exchange.
- Remember that the mediator's task is to use the model presented in this volume as a guide for whatever phase is under consideration, for example, first contact, opening meeting, caucuses, shuttle/joint meetings, or closing.
- After each round of role play, debrief, with the observer leading discussion (from notes) as follows: strengths, weaknesses, and suggestions for improving performance. Debriefing should include data-based feedback to the mediator from the perspectives of the parties and also the observer.

SouthCo

General Instructions

David Chang, a 32-year-old Asian-American male, works in the Benefits Department of a large environmental consulting firm. Six months ago David and a white female co-worker, Shelly Martin, were invited by the director of the department to apply for a managerial position. Shelly was awarded the job. Shelly now supervises ten people, including David. She requires David to keep a log of his calls and of his activities during the day. None of the other employees under her supervision are required to keep such a log. Recently Shelly contacted David to schedule his annual performance review, which is due in final form in three months. Shelly has suggested that the review might not be positive.

Confidential Instructions for David Chang

You have two complaints: first of all, you believe that the failure of SouthCo to promote you was discriminatory. Your past performance reviews have been excellent. You were the only minority candidate eligible for the position, your supervisor invited you to apply, and it is hard for you to understand why it was not awarded to you. Second, Shelly's treatment of you as her employee has been humiliating. You are the only employee required to keep a phone log of your calls and a record of your other work. You have written her many memos asking her why you are required to keep track of your hours and your phone calls. Shelly's responses have been unsatisfactory—she says that she doesn't know what you do, and that she is responsible for your work. Beyond that she is evasive. Worst of all, in scheduling your annual performance review she has suggested that it might not be positive.

You cannot tolerate the treatment you have received at the hands of Shelly. Unfortunately, the department director who invited you to apply for the job has been replaced. Shelly now reports to a new vice president who is unfamiliar with your work and with the situation in the department. You also have been warned by a friend who has been with the company a long time that if you do not handle your complaint well, you could develop a reputation as a real troublemaker. You are aware that others in your department have come to view you as a difficult person over the last six months. This whole series of events has been very hard on your morale and your attitude.

It would be hard for you to find another job, and you would like to stay with SouthCo. You need an explanation as to why Shelly was given the promotion instead of you. You would also like an explanation from Shelly as to why she requires only you to keep a log of your phone calls and your activities. You would like to have someone else do your performance review, or at least establish the criteria by which Shelly will do it. You think Shelly ought to have some management training. She was promoted without any background in supervision, and you believe it's showing in her approach to you. She certainly needs training in how to evaluate performance if she is to do your evaluation.

Another possibility would be for you to transfer from Benefits to General Accounting. If you transferred, however, you would want assurances that you would be a candidate for managerial positions in Accounting. You wonder if Shelly's actions to date would be approved by Employee Relations—you think that if you raised the issue she might be replaced or placed on probation. If all else fails, you are prepared to go to the EEOC and your state's human rights commission with your complaint.

Confidential Instructions for Shelly Martin

You were delighted and surprised six months ago when the department director invited you as well as David to apply for the job you now hold. You were doubly surprised when you actually received the promotion—everyone saw David as the director's favorite. It has been extremely difficult to be the supervisor of people who were only recently your co-workers. You are still struggling to establish your status both with your employees and with management. It has been particularly difficult for you to establish yourself since the shake-up leading to the transfer of the former department director. You are under extreme pressure from the new boss to increase the department's productivity.

David has presented an especially difficult problem. While the quality of his work is first-rate, he is slow in producing it, and he has a difficult time balancing multiple projects.

He has been moody and uncooperative ever since he was passed over for the promotion. If someone were to ask you to describe what you mean by the terms "moody" and "uncooperative" you might give the following examples:

- David never greets anyone in the department when he arrives in the morning or returns from lunch or other appointments and he *never* smiles.
- When his co-workers ask for assistance, he always asks them to wait or to come back in a week, before they can even describe what they need.
- His approach to new procedures or new ideas is to ask, in a defensive tone, "What's wrong with our current approach?" or to criticize ideas before a person finishes explaining them. Others on the team, by comparison, ask, "How can I help?" when approached for assistance. They ask questions or offer alternatives when faced with questionable ideas in team meetings, instead of criticizing first.

David's performance has definitely declined over time. His first two reviews were excellent, and you are quite anxious about being the one to deliver a negative evaluation. You have required him to log his calls and activities for two reasons: (1) you want to be able to document his work product in the event of a complaint by him after his annual performance review; and (2) you wanted to find a way to keep track of what he was doing without directly accusing him of poor performance. You thought you might be able to come up with a more constructive approach if you had a detailed record of his work. It is true that you require no one else to keep such a log. You know no other way, however, to protect yourself or to bring David's deficiencies to his attention.

Given David's attitude and his work record over the last six months, you do not see how his performance review can be very positive. You want to be sure that you can justify your review to your boss, who is himself a difficult man. He seems particularly distrustful of you, his newest supervisor. If this situation blows up, it could hurt you as well as David. Why doesn't David just leave the company?

The Procurement Process Improvement Team

General Instructions

Four months ago, the company's Quality Council authorized the creation of a Process Improvement Team for procurement. The goals of the team were to streamline procurement procedures, improve input mechanisms for internal customers, develop more sophisticated screening procedures with respect to the quality of purchased goods and services, and improve relationships with vendors.

After a series of meetings, a dispute has erupted between the members of the Process Improvement Team, on the one hand, and the team leader, Mr. Dan Green, on the other. Mr. Green has been editing the minutes of the meetings, eliminating some suggestions with which he disagrees. He has limited feedback to the Quality Council in accordance with his editing. He has also been limiting the frequency of meetings as the group has begun to approach consensus on several key issues. The last team meeting ended when the team angrily confronted Mr. Green concerning his editorial approach, and Mr. Green stormed out of the room. One of the team members said, "This is when we need mediation!"

Confidential Instructions for Dan Green

You have found this whole project upsetting. You do not believe that team members have taken their responsibility seriously: some are repeatedly late to meetings; others seem cynical about the organization's quality initiative; still others, whom you know to be intimidated by the more vocal group members, never voice their opinions in public, instead raising them with you privately. The team facilitator is not strong enough to control these little circuses that pass for meetings. In desperation, you have tried to control the meetings, albeit in a heavy-handed fashion. You have done what you can to increase meeting efficiency, and you have edited out of your minutes those suggestions where consensus is more apparent than real, as well as some ideas you personally view as the product of manipulation.

You personally disagree with some of the team's alleged recommendations. You are certain that if some silent members would only speak up, the team's recommendations would be quite different. This whole affair has only strengthened your belief that Apex Corporation should never have fooled around with the chain of command. Things worked better in the old days!

Confidential Instructions for Team Members

Mr. Green has been holding this team up from day one. His conduct in editing the reports and limiting the feedback to the Quality Council must stop! The group may not be functioning as well as it should—perhaps various team members are not fulfilling their responsibilities and some may be a little dominating, but that is no excuse for Mr. Green's tactics.

Particularly irritating is Mr. Green's habit of interfering with brainstorming when it goes in a direction he doesn't like—he either cuts off discussion entirely or humiliates those with whom he disagrees. He badgers silent team members if he thinks he can push them to support his point of view. Others in the organization who know Mr. Green best suspect that he is trying to sabotage the work of this team in protest of the new quality initiative. The reputations of all team members are at stake—if this conflict continues everyone could be hurt!

Mr. Jones and the Nursing Staff

General Instructions

Mr. Jones is the husband of a terminally ill cancer patient. He has been spending the majority of his time with his wife in her hospital room. Last night, Mrs. Jones was transferred to a critical care unit where families are permitted to visit for fifteen to thirty minutes every two hours. Last evening, due to the patient's anxiety over being placed on a ventilator, the staff made an exception to the rules and allowed Mr. Jones to remain by her side most of the night.

Mr. Jones's complaint today is that the staff is now asking him to visit only at the scheduled times. He feels he has encountered a rigid nurse who enforces rules without regard to patient or family needs.

The nursing staff does not think Mrs. Jones's death is imminent. The staff states that Mr. Jones's continual presence is interfering with being able to provide the very best care for Mrs. Jones.

Confidential Instructions for Mr. Jones

One of the things most irritating to you has been the manner in which the nursing staff has approached you. You have heard comments like, "I know how difficult this must be for you, but you're interfering with our ability to help your wife." This morning, the nurse manager had a conversation with a passing security guard, one you believe was intentionally staged within your earshot. Though you could not hear what they said, the nurse manager pointed into your wife's room.

You promised Mrs. Jones when she became ill that you would be with her whenever she needed you, and you feel certain that she needs you now. You want to just sit quietly beside her so that you won't feel like you have broken your promise to her.

Confidential Instructions for Nursing Staff

Your frustration level with Mr. Jones has risen rapidly. He has become increasingly unwilling to discuss visitation rules with the passage of time—at this point, he barely responds when the subject is raised, and he glares at any nurse who approaches him. Only two days ago, he was recognizing the importance of staying out of the nurses' way. He also refuses to accept nursing's assessment of Mrs. Jones's condition—that death is not at hand. Family members of other patients in the unit are noticing that Mr. Jones is getting special privileges and they are beginning to complain.

Margaret and Ashley

General Instructions

Margaret and Ashley are senior administrative assistants in a highly successful toy company.

Margaret is the administrative assistant to Alexandra, the chief financial officer, and Ashley is the administrative assistant to Max, the chief operating officer. Margaret, fifty-five, is a lifetime employee who worked her way up from the mail room. She is a reserved woman, distant some might say, not given to idle chatter. While her only managerial duty is to oversee the receptionist who serves Ashley and her, Margaret's opinion carries great weight. Alexandra seeks Margaret's opinion on a variety of topics, and she is consulted on most administrative and clerical hirings, as she was in Ashley's case.

Ashley, twenty-six, has a college degree in business administration from an Ivy League school. She joined the company only two years ago, starting immediately in her current position. Outgoing and athletic, she participates in many company social events and is well liked by all.

Margaret and Ashley are clearly the two highest ranking administrative assistants in the organization. Their bosses work together closely. Margaret and Ashley have never gotten along, and their relationship has deteriorated sharply in the last six months. For the last two months, they have communicated only by written memo or through the receptionist they share. Their bosses have been unable to resolve the problem.

In accordance with a long-standing administrative arrangement, Margaret delivered an overflow project to Ashley, just as Ashley was preparing to leave under her flex-time arrangement. Ashley returned the assignment, a supplemental report for the board of directors, to Margaret at noon the next day, untouched. Margaret could not finish the report in time for the board meeting, and both Alexandra and Max were severely castigated by the chair of the board. Alexandra and Max are at their wits' end!

Confidential Instructions for Ashley

Everyone is afraid of Margaret. She is a very formidable figure, with her perfect posture and her taciturn nature. Margaret expects to be consulted about everything, and she seems to resent your independence and your college degree. Given her judgmental attitude and her hints about your ignorance of the company history and customs, you have decided to solve any problems you encounter all on your own. Though you certainly could have benefited from her assistance at various points, you have made it this far, and now you're in pretty good shape. Margaret's fastidious recording of your comings and goings has been infuriating enough. Once Margaret went to Max to suggest that he replace you; that was it! You gave up even the necessary conversations you used to have with Margaret.

You will admit, if pressed, that you have not been a team player with Margaret. When she has come to you for assistance, you have done only what you absolutely had to under existing protocols. If really pressed, you'll admit that you made a big mistake in the way you handled the supplemental report for the board meeting. On the other hand, Margaret brought it to you in a way calculated to interfere with your schedule!

Note: Margaret does not know that you will be returning to school on a full-time basis in a year or that you have already struck a deal to come back as a manager once you have received your M.B.A. If she thinks things are bad now, wait until you're in a real management position!

You do not know if this problem can be resolved. Does anyone think that Margaret can change? How can the two of you keep your current positions given her personality?

If the mediator does a good job of moving you away from your opening position, you will disclose the following key interests:

- *To protect your reputation.* You do want to protect your reputation in the organization—you have a career to think about! You want to come back as a manager!
- *To recover from your mistake.* You feel bad about your handling of the overflow report—you want to make up for it.
- *To be treated with respect.* The monitoring must stop! Margaret needs to treat you as a peer, not a subordinate.
- *To receive an acknowledgment of wrongdoing.* Margaret should admit that she had *no business* suggesting your termination to Max.

- *To have a better working environment.* You're sick of working in an office where no one speaks and the tension is so high—you're used to getting along with everyone.

Confidential Instructions for Margaret

Ashley waltzed right in and started out with an office and a salary almost as large as yours. Ashley has never been respectful of your experience. Unlike her predecessor and virtually everyone else, she never asks your advice regarding anything. She would rather figure it all out herself, even if it means making mistakes embarrassing to her boss. Particularly irksome is the fact that she has negotiated a work schedule different from almost everyone else's, albeit with the blessing of Max and Alexandra.

It is true that you closely track Ashley's comings and goings. Given her unusual schedule, you want to make sure that she is meeting her professional obligations. Secretly, you suspect that Ashley is after your job. You think she is setting herself up to consolidate the two positions and force you out. She has gone to great lengths to become friendly with everyone in the organization. Quite vindictively, Ashley has more than once refused even to cover for you when you had personal matters scheduled out of the office. Ashley's response is always the same: "You keep such close track of my schedule, you should know I'm not available."

You are a restrained person, and the mediator will have to work to make you talk. This last assignment Ashley returned late was only one of many she has handled in a way calculated to embarrass you. You would like to see her fired. If confronted, you might have to admit that you may not have handled every aspect of this relationship well. Perhaps it was a mistake to approach Max and suggest that Ashley should be replaced, but you felt it was your duty to offer your candid assessment. The situation would really have to change for the two of you to both remain in your current positions. You will never let Ashley have your job!

At least initially, your attitude in caucus will be that Ashley should be fired! If the mediator does a good job of moving you away from your opening position, you will disclose the following key interests:

- *To protect your job.* You've worked long and hard to get where you are—you want to stay there.
- *To protect your reputation.* Your opinion has always been valued in this company—it disturbs you to think that this whole affair may have lessened your standing. You want to fix that.
- *To recover from your mistakes.* You feel bad about your handling of the overflow project and your trip to Max to suggest Ashley's termination. You want to make up to the company for those errors.
- *To be treated with respect.* You need some recognition from Ashley for your experience and judgment—you feel you have never received such treatment from her.
- *To receive an acknowledgment of wrongdoing.* Ashley needs to admit that she handled the overflow report badly—her conduct hurt both of you.
- *To have a team approach.* It embarrasses you that the two of you have not spoken for so long. You need a co-worker who will work with you and help out when you need assistance or coverage.

Resource G: Exercise Feedback

The end-of-chapter exercises have no right or wrong answers, but the points below can provide a structure for evaluating responses and for guiding group discussion (debriefing).

Chapter One

Exercise 1

Use the content of the chapter to evaluate mediator responses. Also, in giving feedback to the mediator, evaluate performance along three dimensions: strengths, weaknesses, and suggestions for improvement. Strengths would include anything in the response that answers the questions well (based on material from this chapter), while weaknesses could include either incorrect information or a breakdown in the communication process with the questioner. The third dimension of feedback—suggestions for improvement—allows you to learn from the weaknesses and take corrective action for the future. You can use the structure of strengths, weaknesses, and suggested next steps as a framework for feedback in all subsequent exercises.

Chapter Two

Exercise 1

The points listed below are illustrative only and are based on material in the newspaper articles. In a real-life mediation of such a case, the mediator would use these points as a starting place for a caucus inquiry with each party.

Parties and Conflict Grid Data in the Article "Suits Accuse Dioceses of Hiding Sex Abuse"

1.   *Parties:* Roman Catholic Church; Porter (subject of lawsuit); adult victims (plaintiffs); attorneys for the parties (for example, Jeffrey Anderson on behalf of plaintiffs); Dioceses of Crookston, Minnesota, and Fall River, Massachusetts; treatment center, Servants of the Paraclete, Inc. Remember that each party has a constituency. Attorneys for parties can be identified with the parties or considered separately for the sake of analysis.

2.   *Conflict Grid data:* some material is obviously not available in the article but may be hypothesized to be important based on the context and the standard Conflict Grid categories (Chapter Two). For example, data for the adult victims might include:

- *Interests:* restitution, healing, getting on with their own lives (new families), corrective action in the church aimed at prevention, and punishment of the offender.
- *Other facts:* statute of limitations preventing criminal prosecution, offender's admission of guilt, history of attempts at resolution through the church, treatment history, financial needs of the families, relevant law.
- *BATNA:* continue lawsuit.
- *Possible solutions:* financial settlement, preventive action taken by the church to reduce chance of future abuse, psychotherapy, public apology.

     Conflict Grid data for Porter might include:

- *Interests:* receive treatment, personal healing, forgiveness, appropriate closure.
- *Other facts:* admission of wrongdoing, completion of treatment, new job, new family.
- *BATNA:* defend self in lawsuit.
- *Possible solutions:* acknowledgment, restitution, apology, continued treatment, monitoring of future behavior, punishment (incarceration).

3.   *Elements of preliminary one-text statement, based on information from these two parties alone:*

- Acknowledgment/apology by Porter, in writing, or at some point in a structured face-to-face meeting with victims, to be determined after careful consultation with everyone
- Restitution to victims, to cover past and future medical expenses as well as pain and suffering
- Commitments by Porter regarding future behavior
- Steps by church for change in selection procedures and to improve preventive counseling options available to seminarians, priests, and church leaders
- Statement to the membership of the church regarding how the matter has been handled, and steps for resolution

Parties and Conflict Grid Data in the Article "Ruler's Wife Called Key in Agreement"

1. *Parties:* military leaders (General Cedras and others); Yanick Prosper, wife of Lt. Gen. Raoul Cedras; Jean-Bertrand Aristide, elected President of Haiti; Emil Jonassaint, President of Haiti under military regime; U.S. government (Clinton administration); the Haitian people; the American people; the world community; the United Nations.

2. *Conflict Grid data:* As I did for the previous article, I will extract and extrapolate Conflict Grid data for two of the main parties, starting with General Cedras.

- *Interests:* saving face, getting himself and his family out alive, maintaining power.
- *Other facts:* Planned American military intervention; offer of mediation by U.S. government (Carter, Nunn, Powell), Aristide's stated interest in returning, split political alignments in Haiti (support for Aristide and for military rulers).
- *BATNA:* stand and fight (and possibly die).
- *Possible solutions:* face-saving withdrawal of some sort, sanctuary in another country, negotiated timing based on interests of Cedras, and with cooperation of U.S. government.

Conflict Grid data for Aristide might include the following points.

- *Interests:* return to power, military support of U.S. government, prevention of General Cedras and others from returning to power, winning the next election.

- *Other facts:* currently residing in United States, unable to return without U.S. military intervention unless Cedras leaves willingly, mixed support in Haiti (Aristide versus Cedras), all public statements to world community regarding situation.
- *BATNA:* return through force via U.S. government intervention.
- *Possible solutions:* negotiate a withdrawal of General Cedras, with military backup according to timetable.

3. *One-text solution.* As a guide in formulating a one-text solution, consider the agreement eventually reached by the parties, as reported in the same article by the Associated Press, September 20, 1994:

> *Haiti Agreement.* The White House text of the agreement reached Sunday in Port-au-Prince, Haiti, that averted an invasion of Haiti.
>
> - The purpose of this agreement is to foster peace in Haiti, to avoid violence and bloodshed, to promote freedom and democracy, and to forge a sustained and mutually beneficial relationship between the governments, people and institutions of Haiti and the United States.
>
> - To implement this agreement, the Haitian military and police forces will work in close cooperation with the U.S. Military Mission. This cooperation, conducted with mutual respect, will last during the transitional period required for insuring vital institutions of the country.
>
> - In order to personally contribute to the success of this agreement, certain military officers of the Haitian armed forces are willing to consent to an early honorable retirement in accordance with U.N. Resolutions 917 and 940 when a general amnesty will be voted into law by the Haitian Parliament, or October 15, 1994, whichever is earlier. The parties to this agreement pledge to work with the Haitian Parliament to expedite this action. Their successors will be named according to the Haitian Constitution and existing military law.
>
> - The military activities of the U.S. Military Mission will be coordinated with the Haitian military high command.
>
> - The economic embargo and the economic sanctions will be lifted without delay in accordance with relevant U.N. Resolu-

tions and the needs of the Haitian people will be met as quickly as possible.

- The forthcoming legislative elections will be held in a free and democratic manner.

- It is understood that the above agreement is conditioned on the approval of the civilian governments of the United States and Haiti.

Exercise 2

Possible questions to the victims in diocese lawsuit article:

- Based on the information we have thus far, we can imagine what a number of your key interests might be. Which are most important to you now?
- What form might restitution take?
- Incarceration is a possibility. How do you feel about this as one form of resolution? What else would you want to be included?

  Possible questions to ask in meeting with Cedras:
- What conditions would need to be met in order for you to withdraw, instead of remaining to defend your position with force?
- Assuming you might withdraw to sanctuary in another country, what assurances could you provide to Aristide that you would not seek to overthrow his government militarily?
- What do you believe Aristide would need to hear from you in order to accept any commitments you might make?

Of course, the preceding material offers only a sketch of possible responses to this exercise. Much of what is included here is speculation, since these are questions/hypotheses/conclusions that grow from one newspaper article about each situation. This approach, however, fits very closely with the reality of any mediation, since the first documents provided, or the first telephone or face-to-face conversation with one party, are clearly not the definitive word on the parties' interests, facts, BATNAs, and solutions— but they do provide a starting point for asking questions and continually refining the mediator's understanding of Conflict Grid data.

Chapter Three

Exercise 1

Be sure to list not only mediation experience at work but also in your home and community, for example, with Little League sports or religious organizations.

Exercise 2

Regarding strengths, consider how people view you. Do they see you as an objective and fair person, one who listens well, one who cares about people? Also, include your communication skills (Resource A). Common weaknesses might include a tendency to take sides quickly, an inability to listen objectively, or a desire to take over the dispute, find an answer, and impose it on the parties. In addition, most professions have some aspect of day-to-day training and experience that is both a strength and a liability. For example, an attorney with many years experience in litigation may well have a solid grasp of the legal and human dimensions of problems, but the communication model of litigation (questions aimed at building a case for a judge or jury to decide as a win/lose event) may backfire in mediation. Also, a litigator experienced in advocating for one party may need to learn new approaches for facilitating communication among two or more parties (in the room at the same time) that allows for exploration and the creation of mutually agreeable solutions.

Translate any weakness into a learning goal. For example, in the situation described above, one learning goal might be to develop a language of mediation that (1) communicates respect and (2) elicits information in terms of Conflict Grid data from all parties. Another goal might be to learn how to confront parties about inconsistencies and weaknesses in their stated positions without alienating them.

Chapter Four

Exercise 1

As you did for the exercises in Chapter One, debrief regarding strengths, weaknesses, and suggestions for change.

Exercise 2

Test your written materials by asking someone to read and critique them. Ask the person to imagine deciding whether or not to sign an agreement to mediate after reading your materials. What points might raise questions? How can these points be addressed or changed in the materials?

Chapter Five

Exercise 1

One person's to-do list for improvements to mediation rooms included the following:

- Check the height on the chairs, since some are lower than others. Perhaps switch some chairs to give greater balance.
- Buy a flip chart.
- Clear some of the files out of the study so we can use it as a caucus room.
- Buy white noise machines as an additional aid for sound-proofing.

Exercise 2

One person's worst experience was participating in a caucus in a room that had a two-inch gap under the door and was placed three feet away from the receptionist's desk. Everyone had to whisper to avoid being overheard.

Exercise 3

One person's best caucus involved taking a walk with the mediator around the outside of the building. This provided an opportunity to get some fresh air and loosened the process, as both parties were able to stroll and talk at the same time.

Chapter Six

Exercise 1

As the mediator completes the opening statement role play, compare the content to the sample offered in this chapter.

Exercise 2

Check especially for two outcomes:

- Is the interruption dealt with in such a way that all parties stay on board with the process?
- Does the mediator eventually get to finish the opening remarks, with an orderly transfer to the opening statements by the parties?

Chapters Seven and Eight

Exercise 1

Conflict Grid data for Jack:

- *Interests:* a more smoothly functioning team, better-run team meetings, no name-calling from Dan, fairness in editing, assurance that Dan supports the quality philosophy, having interests of other team members honored as well.
- *Other facts:* reports of Dan's name-calling, Dan's rewriting of the minutes.
- *BATNA:* leave the situation as it is or go over Dan's head to have him replaced.
- *Possible solutions:* Dan changes behavior along lines identified (for example, he stops name-calling and changes his editing procedures on the minutes); team members also make changes.

   Conflict Grid data for Dan:

- *Interests:* support by team members, evidenced in attending on time, not interrupting, and contributing to meetings; better contribution from facilitator (or new person in that role); constructive outlet for frustrations (direct talks?).
- *Other facts:* team members' behavior (late, not contributing, interrupting), Dan's editing of the minutes.
- *BATNA:* continue the situation as is or make political contact to have team members replaced.
- *Possible solutions:* team members change their behavior (tardiness, contributions); Dan changes his behavior in meetings and changes his approach to editing or shares the task with someone else; a new facilitator comes in or changes in the way current facilitator conducts meetings are made.

Exercise 2

Questions for Jack:

- Could you tell me more about what you might do if Dan doesn't change? (This tracks Jack's own BATNA.)
- How about Dan—what will he do if you and the team don't change? (A reality check on how well Jack perceives the other side's BATNA.)
- How does upper management view the quality program?
- What else could be we do in this mediation to improve the overall team members' situation at work?

Questions for Dan:

- How did you end up chairing this group in the first place?
- Do you want to be in this role?
- Where does this responsibility fit in the overall scheme of things for you?
- What else could we focus on in this mediation to improve the situation for you and the team?
- What will you do if the team doesn't change? And, What do you think the team members will do if they don't see a change in your behavior? (These are the BATNA questions.)

Chapter Nine

Exercise 1

Possible one-text agreement items include:

- Team members acknowledge their past behavior and take responsibility for disruptiveness in being tardy, interrupting, and for some, not contributing.
- Dan acknowledges behavior regarding editing of minutes, name-calling, and the way he runs meetings, and makes commitment to change this behavior.
- New facilitator, or coaching to improve performance of current facilitator.
- Training for all on how to work effectively as a team.
- Honest encounter of team members with one another and with Dan regarding how they feel about the team and its role in the organization.
- Clarity from the higher-ups regarding the role this team plays in the overall functioning of the organization.

Chapter Ten

Exercise 1

Who should attend the round of talks?

Who Should Attend	*One-Text Item (Agenda)*
Jack	Team members' behavior
Dan	His behavior
Facilitator	Facilitator's behavior
Dan and Jack together	Entire list
Entire team	Entire list

Exercise 2

With the permission of Jack and Dan, consider meeting with the person responsible for all quality teams to get that person's perspective on the situation and advice about possible interests that need to be honored in the agreement involving this group.

Chapter Eleven

Exercise 1a

In providing feedback to the mediator for this exercise, pay particular attention to his or her opening summary. Does it lay the groundwork for the parties to begin communicating effectively with one another? From the beginning of the joint meeting on through to the end, there should be a transfer of responsibility from the mediator to the parties themselves. For example, the mediator may begin by summarizing information from the caucuses (with permission to disclose it), which the parties then have an opportunity to discuss, taking responsibility for their own awareness of interests (focus on self) and understanding/recognition (focus on the other side). In evaluating the process, ask this question: Do the parties eventually demonstrate these two foci (awareness/empowerment and understanding/recognition) in their interaction?

Exercise 1b

In the shuttle version, pay attention to whether or not the mediator uses the sessions for constructive coaching in preparation for the joint meeting.

Exercise 2

In debriefing this exercise, pay particular attention also to the real-life experiences that you have had with joint and shuttle approaches, comparing what you are learning in this exercise with these other situations.

Chapter Twelve

Exercises 1 and 2

As you notice the mediator attempting various strategies for impasse resolution (from this chapter or using other ideas), evaluate each in terms of its strengths (things that seem to go especially well) and weaknesses (things that did not work), and then write out your own suggestions for ways to either improve that strategy or substitute another in its place (next steps). Use these notes as a guide to offering feedback to the mediator.

Chapter Thirteen

Exercise 1

Sample questions for the case of Jack and Dan:

- *Are the most critical interests of the key parties honored?* For example, does the agreement have a chance of providing the team members with the changes they desire in Dan's behavior?
- *Does the agreement square with other facts?* Some members have in fact demonstrated lack of cooperation. How does the agreement reckon with the fact of the past behavior? Does it provide any sort of closure?
- *How will other parties perceive the agreement?* This mediation involves Jack and Dan. Does the agreement include a next step of review by team members, as well as other interested parties in the organization?
- *Imagine the deal going forward—where will it lead?* Is there a provision for follow-up built into this agreement? What if things begin to unravel? What will the team members do?
- *What do the parties think of the agreement?* What is missing? What needs to be included? What will each party do if the other side seems to forget the agreement and go back to old behavior?

Exercise 2

In observing this interaction, pay particular attention to both nonverbal and verbal responses of the parties as they listen to the proposed one-text items. In feedback to the mediator, consider changes in both the order in which items are presented, and the way particular items are framed. For example, if one approach generates opposition or derailment of some sort, practice another role play immediately, varying the way the item is framed, as well as the order of presentation. For example, can the mediator create a hearing for a proposal with an inclusive comment such as the following: "In listening to the two of you describe this, I hear very clearly that there are steps *each side* [emphasize these words] can take to help the situation. In no particular order, let me identify two or three from each list."

Another approach that gets the parties working immediately might be: "In listening to the two of you in our private meetings, I see steps that each of you might take to improve the situation. Let's think about this together right now. Start with your own behavior. What do you think you could contribute to help the other side? And then, what might the other side do to help you? Who wants to start?"

Chapter Fourteen

Exercise 1

Here is one way to draft a possible agreement between Jack and Dan:

MEMORANDUM

TO: Dan G.
        Jack D.

FROM: Sue G. (Mediator)

RE: Mediation Agreement

As we discussed in our last meeting, I am writing to summarize agreements that the two of you reached in mediation, including steps for review with other members of the Procurement Process Improvement Team. Once you have had a chance to read this draft, we can make corrections together and then schedule a joint session with other members of your group.

Background. The Procurement Process Improvement Team has been meeting since last fall, with a goal of defining and implementing steps to streamline procedures, improving input mechanisms for internal customers, and developing more sophisticated screening procedures for dealing with vendors. In response to several problems that occurred recently, the group asked two representatives of the team, Dan G. and Jack D., to meet with a mediator from Organization Development to define possible steps for improving the effectiveness of the team, including the use of meetings and other joint activities.

Following several hours of individual and joint meetings with the mediator, Dan and Jack agreed to the following steps, which are summarized here prior to being presented to the Team for discussion and review.

1.   All acknowledge that the task of the group provides an important function in achieving the mission of both the Quality Council and the organization as a whole, and reaffirm their commitment to the team approach.

2.   All agree that the best approach to past difficulties is to analyze events and learn from them, thereby strengthening the team and improving efficiency in the future.

3.   Jack and Dan will meet with team members for discussion of behaviors in meetings that have been a problem in the past, as well as areas of strength, and agree on suggestions for improvement. Based on preliminary discussions in mediation, it appears that the following commitments might be adopted by the group:

   a.   The team members and Dan agree to arrive on time for meetings, contribute to the process (instead of remaining silent or discussing issues outside the regular meetings), cooperate with the facilitator in allowing everyone to have an opportunity to speak, and work together to create an atmosphere of mutual respect and support.

   b.   The facilitator will publish a draft of the agenda two days prior to the biweekly team meeting, inviting input on any new items, so that the agenda at the time of the meeting is one that covers the needs of all members.

   c.   Dan will provide a draft of the minutes to Jack (or another member delegated by the team) for review prior to submitting reports to the Quality Council.

4.   Since the stakes regarding the contribution of this team to the overall function of the organization are high, the members of the team have agreed to seek training in collaboration skills from the Training Department. The course will be included in the budget for next year, with the possibility of the team meeting offsite for this training.

5.   Regarding future behavior, the team members agree to

take any differences or problems regarding implementation of this agreement directly to one another as a first recourse, using mediation as a second avenue should direct negotiations not accomplish the objectives (as defined by the person who raises the concern).

6.   Following review of this agreement with team members, the parties will ask the mediator to discuss the proposed agreement with the chair of the Quality Council, inviting support of the commitments reached by this group.

7.   The parties have asked the mediator to convene a meeting with Jack and Dan in six months to review progress on this agreement, and make whatever adjustments may be required.

Please call within the next two days with any questions or suggestions for change in this draft. I look forward to talking with you at your earliest convenience.

Note that there are clearly many ways to draft a one-text agreement for the hypothetical case involved in this exercise. In this particular draft, the mediator (1) aims for a positive statement that protects each of the parties (while still alluding to the concrete problems that created the conflict), (2) includes the behavioral steps that all agree to carry forward, and (3) addresses the issue of future conflict, follow-up, and review by outside parties.

Exercise 2

In the role play for the one-text review, evaluate the mediator's effectiveness in translating objections or problems with the agreement into an edit of the one-text draft. For example, does the mediator respond with statements such as, "I'm glad you mentioned that. How might we change this draft to reflect your interest [or that fact, or that reality]?"

Chapter Fifteen

Exercise 1

Look for specific behaviors in reviewing closing ceremony experiences. What might you hypothesize about the dynamics of the dispute from looking at the various features included in the closing ceremony? For example, consider things like the role of a handshake in recognizing the other side and in making a commitment for future cooperation. What cultural variables determine the selection of the closing ceremony activities?

Exercise 2

Possible closing ceremony points for Jack and Dan:

- A chance for each to briefly summarize the problems *and* the commitments for change, in such a way that the other side can hear and believe that there has been both a realistic assessment of past wrong and a realistic commitment to future change.
- A handshake to signify change.
- Some opportunity for humor or distraction to ease a transfer of focus from the rather burdensome task of discussing problems to now going forward under new covenants.
- Once the team approves, how about a social event to mark the start of a new relationship?

Exercise 3

In the role play, evaluate the mediator's performance along the lines suggested above. If one of the parties throws in a monkey wrench or introduces a verbal barb of some sort, evaluate the mediator's ability to distinguish between comments that should be (1) ignored, (2) finessed with humor, (3) confronted as points for discussion at that time (perhaps clarifying the agreement or the plans for the future), or (4) sent to caucus to further clarify the meaning.

Chapter Sixteen

Exercise 1

Create an observation checklist using the eight items identified in this chapter. Keep notes as each point is covered, identifying strengths, weaknesses, and suggestions for improvement as the mediator covers each.

Exercise 2

In evaluating the caucuses, examine the mediator's ability to ask questions of the parties regarding their inability to go forward with the joint meeting, and to generate possible remedies or changes in the process to encourage communication between the parties. To what extent does the mediator use both Level I (active listening, self-disclosing, questioning) and Level II (reframing, brainstorming, and confronting) communication skills (Resource A) to help the parties move forward?

Chapter Seventeen

Exercise 1

After you identify situations where you might skip the opening meeting, it might be useful to ask what additional requirements this situation places on you for covering the ground rules as you begin the caucus. Also ask how you explain to the parties the rationale for this change in the process.

Exercise 2

Other possible adjustments might include:

- Skipping the first contact phase. This might be reasonable when some other convening party has already taken care of the first contact requirements, and you first meet the parties in the opening meeting.
- Treating the first contact as a screening meeting on issues such as the potential for violence, and then shortening the caucus phase.

Exercise 3

In providing feedback to the mediator, evaluate the extent to which dimensions that need to be covered in the opening meeting are in fact addressed in the opening phase of the caucus (for example, ground rules).

Chapter Eighteen

Exercise 1

This exercise has significant potential for broadening your appreciation of mediation dynamics in everyday life. In most literary or dramatized accounts of informal mediation, you will see one part of the model demonstrated (for example, using confronting to address one side's intransigence or using shuttle meetings to create a one-text integrative solution), while you are left in the dark about the rest of the process. It might be interesting to speculate, therefore, about what might have happened in the part not reported in the play, movie, or book. Politicians and statesmen, for example, often report on deals struck to pass domestic legislation or to reach an international accord. In the cases you select, consider this question: What might have been the key ingredients for building rapport with the parties, analyzing the problem, and eventually creating the solution(s) to which all eventually gave their support?

Exercise 2

In reflecting on your own experience, pay particular attention to strengths that you have developed in other areas of your life (for example, communication skills or background knowledge for analyzing particular substantive issues).

Exercise 3

In identifying situations where you anticipate serving as an informal mediator, note that each opportunity to practice the model will increase your skills. As with any learned activity (sports, music, cooking), the more opportunities you have to practice each skill, the more quickly you will learn.

Epilogue

Exercise 1

Sample to-do list of skill-enhancing activities:

- Join local, regional, and national associations (for example, the Society for Professionals in Dispute Resolution).
- Set up lunch with mediators in my community to discuss ways we can support one another.
- Subscribe to professional journals.
- Sponsor continuing education training for mediators in my community.

Exercise 2

Be sure to consider all areas, including family life, neighborhood and community, government structures (local, state, national, international), private business and industry, religious and non-profit organizations.

Exercise 3

Remember that each contribution counts and that what might seem like a small step from you, added to the steps of others, has the potential for significant impact. Steps to consider are the following:

- Write a letter to the editor of a newspaper regarding a mediation perspective on a particular problem.
- Initiate a study or task force to set up systems for mediation of school, neighborhood, nonprofit, or business disputes.
- Participate in research and the creation of written materials on mediation.
- Take on committee responsibilities for local, regional, and national dispute resolution organizations.

Quick Reference Checklist

Summary of Mediation Model

I. Step One: First Contact (Chapters Four and Five)

A. Make telephone contact.
1. Ask for a summary of the problem and the events leading to the inquiry.
2. Define the mediation process, your role, and how you would use the process for this case.
3. Arrange for delivery of information packets and other written materials.
4. Secure a commitment to attend the opening meeting.
5. Schedule first meeting.

B. Arrange the meeting space.
1. Use neutral ground if possible.
2. Have enough room to allow for both joint meetings and private caucuses.
3. Ensure privacy.
4. Arrange furniture to allow for "side-by-side" problem solving.

II. Step Two: Opening Meeting (Chapter Six).

A. Explain the mediation process.
1. Cover all the essentials in your statement.
2. Describe steps (for example, opening meeting, caucuses, joint meetings, and so on).

B. Invite opening statements from each side.

C. Invite questions of clarification and answers (only after everyone has had an opportunity to talk).

D. Sign the agreement to mediate.

E. Adjourn the meeting and begin caucuses.

III. Step Three: Caucuses (Chapters Seven through Nine).

A. Begin with a review of confidentiality and then ask an open-ended question to start the conversation.

B. As the person begins to "tell the story," use active listening and questions to clarify and summarize data for the Conflict Grid.

C. Take notes.

D. Test perceptions by asking questions about how this party views the other party's interests and positions.

E. Use confrontation, evaluation of strengths and weaknesses of proposals, and focus on competing interests to loosen fixed positions and encourage movement.

F. Summarize frequently, and if necessary, float test balloons for possible integrative solutions.

G. Close with a reminder of confidentiality, an open-ended inquiry about other topics, and a request for instructions or any messages to be communicated to the other side.

H. Continue caucuses with the other party or parties.

IV. Step Four: Shuttle/Joint Meetings (Chapters Ten through Twelve)

A. Plan the next round.
   1. Ask yourself: How might we best explore, refine, and eventually reach agreement on the one-text list?
   2. In answering this question, consider:
      a. Are the parties equipped and prepared to meet with one another face-to-face?
      b. Which approach will take the least amount of time?
      c. Are there physical constraints to having joint meetings?
      d. Would telephone conference calls help the parties, or a combination of telephone conference calls and individual caucuses?

3. List the meetings in order:
   a.
   b.
   c. . . . and so on.

B. Conduct the next round of meetings, one by one.

C. In each meeting, use the SOS (summaries—offers—summaries) Model.
   1. Summaries: state Conflict Grid data using language that elevates the dispute and the parties to the higher problem-solving plane.
   2. Offers: invite offers, relay offers (if you have permission), brainstorm other solutions and ways to respond to offers, and do whatever else is necessary to cover the points on the one-text worksheet.
   3. Summaries: close with another summary of what the parties have accomplished so far, are accomplishing even as you speak, and have yet to accomplish.

D. Resolve impasses.
   1. Ask yourself: Why is the impasse occurring at this particular time? What function does it play for each party?
   2. Use one or more impasse resolution strategies in an attempt to create movement and resolve the impasse.
      a. Go back to basics by asking:
         • Are there other parties sabotaging the mediation?
         • What interests might we have missed?
         • Are there some other facts or parameters of this dispute that we have not yet identified?
         • How about the alternatives to a negotiated agreement?
         • Are there any standard solutions missing in the deal now on the table?
      b. Change the negotiation mix:
         • Invite humor.
         • Take a break.
         • Take a walk.
         • Stand up and walk or pace.
         • Suggest caucuses with key outside parties.
         • Flip a coin.

- Separate the parties.
- Buy time by adjourning the process for a while.
- Bring outside standards to the negotiation table.
- Include outside parties, such as attorney advocates, in the process.
- Isolate one or more parties for a time.

c. Challenge the party or parties:
  - "Aren't you ignoring the downside to your proposal?"
  - "How sure are you that you will win in court? At what cost?"
  - "Unless you change the way you negotiate with the other side, I predict that this whole deal will end up in a ditch."

d. Support the party or parties:
  - Coach on negotiation strategy and communication skills.
  - Offer new concepts.
  - Validate feelings.
  - Interpret the other side's behavior.
  - Give a pep talk.

e. Change the deal on the table:
  - Create a partial solution to a complex problem.
  - Separate procedural solutions from substantive solutions.
  - Organize a trade.
  - Suggest a compromise.

f. Confront regarding the consequences of impasse.
  - Are you prepared for the consequences?
  - Is impasse truly a better option for you than the deal on the table?

V. Step Five: Closing (Chapters Thirteen through Fifteen)

A. Test the agreement by asking:
  1. Are the most critical interests of the key parties and their constituencies honored by this agreement, or at least not violated by the agreement?
  2. Does the agreement square with other facts?
  3. How will the agreement be received by other key parties and their constituencies?

4. Picture the agreement being implemented and see where it leads—any unanticipated problems?
5. Ask the parties for a critique.
6. What do the parties think of the agreement?

B. Put the agreement in writing.
1. The one-text agreement will be public—make sure the agreement saves face for the parties.
2. Since the agreement needs to pass muster with each of the parties, tilt toward their words in drafting the mediation agreement.
3. Strive for simplicity in choice of words and grammatical construction whenever possible.
4. Check the document to make sure that it is positive, behavioral, and includes timetables.
5. Until the one-text agreement is finally signed, use only a single copy of it for shuttle talks and revisions.

C. If necessary, declare impasse. If you declare an impasse and end the mediation process, leave the door open for future negotiations and the opportunity to reconvene the parties if circumstances change.
1. Offer face-saving statement as to why the impasse has occurred.
2. Tell the parties how they can initiate mediation again.
3. Remind them of confidentiality.

D. Wrap up the process.
1. Include a statement that praises the parties for their efforts and their success in creating integrative solutions.
2. Close with a handshake, signing, or some other ceremony to mark the act of agreement and the beginning of living in a new world under a new deal.

VI. Interpersonal Peacemaking (Chapter Sixteen)

A. Confront the past. For many disputes, there will be a heavy focus on "sins of the past" that need to be addressed in a face-to-face meeting before the parties can move forward. You can privately coach the parties and then bring them together.

B. Use this outline for discussion:
   1. Create an agenda together.
   2. Identify past damage and current regrets as well as the stake each has in a better relationship now, that is, the motivation for reconciliation.
   3. Clarify (1) what happened and (2) the intent behind the actions (separating the two) for each problem from the past.
   4. Discuss what each side wishes had happened instead.
   5. Discuss options (the standard solutions) for what might bring about healing and reconciliation now: restitution, plan for the future, apology, forgiveness, and so on.
   6. Invite offers and exchanges from one person to another: for example, apologies, commitments to engage in a certain behavior in the future, forgiveness.
   7. Confront regarding apologies and forgiveness.
   8. Summarize and plan for the future—or declare impasse.

C. Look beyond impasse. Consider other options, such as living with the situation as it is or seeking a higher authority resolution such as nonbinding or binding arbitration, or litigation.

D. Look beyond reconciliation. Plan declarations to others who are involved in the conflict or who have a stake in the outcome.

Notes

Preface

1. A. Cuneo, M. Galen, and D. Greising, "Guilty! Too Many Lawyers, Too Much Litigation, Too Much Waste. Business is Starting to Find a Better Way," *Business Week,* Apr. 13, 1992, p. 60–66.

Chapter One

1. R. Fisher and W. Ury, *Getting to Yes: Negotiating Agreement Without Giving In* (Boston: Houghton Mifflin, 1981).

2. In *The Promise of Mediation: Responding to Conflict Through Empowerment and Recognition* (San Francisco: Jossey-Bass, 1994), Robert A. Baruch Bush and Joseph P. Folger present empowerment and recognition as the primary transformative foci for mediation, as compared to a problem-solving approach that focuses primarily on whether or not the parties reach agreement. The assumption of the present volume is that the primary focus of integrative mediation must be to determine how and why the parties differ and what conditions must be met in order for them to achieve agreement or reconciliation of some kind. The foci of awareness/empowerment and recognition/understanding are viewed as necessary building blocks for this effort. This assumption stems from the definition of mediation as a process through which a third party assists two or more other individuals or groups in dealing with their differences. Integrative mediation is therefore to be distinguished from other processes such as counseling, psychotherapy, family therapy, and spiritual direction that have as their primary focus awareness/empowerment and understanding/recognition.

3. From C. Moore, "Mediating Across Cultures," Presentation to the annual conference of the Texas Association of Mediators, Houston, Tex., Feb. 25, 1995.

Chapter Two

1. For a more complete discussion of personality variables that may underlie interpersonal and intragroup conflict, see K. A. Slaikeu,

Crisis Intervention: A Handbook for Practice and Research (2nd ed.) (Needham Heights, Mass.: Allyn and Bacon, 1990).

2.   Special thanks to Ralph Hasson for drafting this list.

3.   Fisher and Ury, 1981.

4.   Fisher and Ury, 1981.

5.   Throughout this book, I will refer to *honoring* interests as a test of one-text agreements. This is not to suggest that all interests must be honored. One party may clearly view the other side's interests as evil (Nazi extermination of Jewish people in the early twentieth century) or immoral (providing street drugs to children). In these cases, the one-text test exposes the conflicting values between the parties (and, in many cases, the mediator). An impasse results, and the parties eventually choose another avenue such as the courts or unilateral power plays for resolution. In some cases, however, it is possible for parties with seemingly irreconcilable religious and value conflicts to reach a one-text agreement on the means by which they will oppose one another (use of force or not).

Chapter Four

1.   For a discussion of the procedures, see J. M. Brett, S. B. Goldberg, and W. L. Ury, "Managing Conflict: The Strategy of Dispute Systems Design," *Business Week Executive Briefing Service,* 1994, *6,* 1–30; and the Bureau of National Affairs, Inc., "Case Study: Brown & Root's Options," *Workforce Strategies,* 1993, *4*(10), 57, 60–61.

Chapter Five

1.   JCPenney sells an inexpensive "Sleep Mate" that makes white noise; it can be placed in corridors to add privacy to caucus and consultation rooms.

2.   C. J. Holahan and K. A. Slaikeu, "Effects of Contrasting Degrees of Privacy on Client Self-Disclosure in a Counseling Setting," *Journal of Counseling Psychology,* 1976, *24,* 55–59.

Chapter Six

1.   This opening statement was written by Ralph Hasson, Diane Weimer Slaikeu, and Karl A. Slaikeu and is reprinted from *Chorda Collaboration Skills* (Austin, Texas: Chorda Conflict Management, 1994).

Chapter Eight

1.   The scripts were written by Ralph Hasson, Diane Weimer Slaikeu, and Karl A. Slaikeu and are reprinted from *Chorda Collaboration Skills,* 1994.

Chapter Twelve

1. Special thanks to P. Michael Hebert for suggesting this perspective on impasse.

Chapter Fourteen

1. R. H. Weiss, "The ADR Program at Motorola," *Negotiation Journal,* 1989, *5*(4), 381–394.
2. K. A. Slaikeu and R. H. Hasson, "Not Necessarily Mediation: The Use of Convening Clauses in Dispute Systems Design," *Negotiation Journal,* 1992, *8*(4), 331–338.

Chapter Fifteen

1. Episcopal Church, *The Book of Common Prayer,* New York: Church Hymnal Corporation, 1979, p. 447.

Epilogue

1. P. E. Salem, "A Critique of Western Conflict Resolution from a Non-Western Perspective," *Negotiation Journal,* 1993, *9*(4), 361–369.

Resource B

1. These rules have been drawn in part from: Family Law Section, American Bar Association, "Standards of Practice for Lawyer Mediators in Family Disputes"; Austin Family Mediation Association, "Rules of Mediation"; R. Coulson, *Fighting Fair* (New York: Macmillan, 1983); and J. J. Coogler, *Structured Mediation in Divorce Settlement* (Lexington, Mass.: Lexington Books, 1978).

Resource C

1. Reprinted from A. B. Thomas (ed.), *Making the Tough Calls* (Washington, D.C.: Society of Professionals in Dispute Resolution (SPIDR), 1991), pp. 3–5.

Resource D

1. Reprinted from *Mediation of Family Disputes Involving Domestic Violence,* Report of the Academy of Family Mediators Task Force on Spousal and Child Abuse (Golden Valley, Minn.: Academy of Family Mediators, 1995).

Resource F

1. These role plays were written by Ralph Hasson and Karl A. Slaikeu and are reprinted from *Chorda Collaboration Skills* (Austin, Tex.: Chorda Conflict Management, 1994).

Index